Nothing
But
Voice

To Velicia,
Keep leading the way!,

Jan Touring Mvek

Nothing But Voice

My Career Directing A Cappella

♪

Jan Touring Muck

Malva Press • Philadelphia • 2021

Nothing But Voice: My Career Directing A Cappella

by Jan Touring Muck

Published by
Malva Press
PO box 44
Devault, Pennsylvania 19432
www.MalvaPress.com

The publisher has made good faith efforts to credit all photographs
to their rightful owners and will gladly emend future printings
to add and correct such attributions as warranted.
Please contact the publisher in writing at the address above or by email at
info@malvapress.com.

For information on bulk sales, write to sales@malvapress.com.

Contact the author to schedule a speaking engagement at
JLMuck@verizon.net.

ISBN: 978-1-7378982-0-7 trade paperback
978-1-7378982-1-4 electronic book

Third printing

Design and composition: www.dmargulis.com

MANUFACTURED IN THE UNITED STATES OF AMERICA

To the members of my choruses,
for the friendships, adventures, and risks,
but most of all for the memories that make this book

Contents

Prelude

Winning the Gold Medal—
The Big Honker

THEY CHEERED FOR SEVEN minutes. It was October 3, 1983, at the Detroit Convention Center. We had just won the international chorus competition. We ran from the very top of the Center, down the narrow staircases, and across the main floor. And still they clapped, cheered, and stomped their feet. We didn't hear any of it over our own excitement. People reached out to touch us as we approached the stage. Friends tried to stop us with hugs as we ran through the crowds. Ninety-two women stormed the stage, unable to do or say anything but squeal and hug anyone close enough to grab. The stage became a sea of squiggly, shiny blue dresses with chartreuse trim.

1983 International Champions

We were no strangers to the international stage. Our friends, family, and competitors watched us bounce around the top five positions for the past ten years. All in all, it had taken us eighteen years and fifteen contests to win this Super Bowl of our singing organization, the Sweet Adelines International. And eight thousand people witnessed it. This was a magical moment in our lives—a moment to relive and dream about for the rest of our days.

I was their musical director. I am the kid who took piano lessons for eight years, sang in high school choral groups, and played the drums in the band. My formal education is in mathematics, not music. What was I doing directing the great Valley Forge Chorus on the international stage?

And winning the contest!

Nothing But Voice

Intro

It's Only One Evening a Week

AN OLD COLLEGE FRIEND of mine moves into our town and joins a women's chorus. She invites me to come with her to attend a rehearsal. We sang together in a quartet in college. I was a math major and the other three studied music. My friend thinks I will enjoy singing in this chorus. And maybe I'll join a quartet, she thinks.

This is the early 1960s. I am living the life that was planned for us. Men could start to build a business or choose to climb the corporate ladder. We women were supposed to go to school and then find employment as a secretary, nurse, or schoolteacher. We worked until we married, and then we retired to raise a family and take care of the house. I've only been married a year. I have a husband and a new baby girl. It's my time to raise that little girl.

"Oh, it's only one evening a week," my friend says.

I haven't sung since college, and I miss it. Only one evening a week? I go. What is this sound I'm hearing? It's barbershop harmony. I don't understand how to sing it. Frankly, I don't like it. But my joy that I could be singing again overshadows my hesitancy to break away from the norm. The women I meet are friendly and fun. The strange new format of the music is challenging.

My husband is following his version of the normal plan: working days and finishing his college education at night. There is no way I can be gone for an evening just to sing. Babysitters are out of the question—money is tight, and we have no family close by.

How can I join the chorus? My friend suggests I bring my daughter to her home. She has a new baby, too, and an extra crib. Her husband is willing to watch both little ones for a few hours once a week.

"After rehearsal you can pick up your sleeping baby and take her home to her own little bed—before your husband even returns from school."

I join. By joining my friend's women's chorus, the Del-Mont Chorus, I have also joined the Sweet Adelines. I learn everything I can about this unique singing format and organization.

♮

Barbershop harmony is an American art form, started in the early 1900s. In 1938 it became popular when a group of men organized what would eventually become the Barbershop Harmony Society. Women soon started singing barbershop harmony, and in 1945 the Sweet Adelines International was formed. Each organization sponsors its own quartet and chorus competitions. Contestants are decided by placement (usually first place) or a high numerical score (wildcard).

Anyone who can carry a tune can sing barbershop harmony. It doesn't matter how old you are, where you were born, or what your job is. As long as you pass your audition, you are part of the team. Once you are part of the team, a whole world of training options opens up. Members of the international singing organizations offer seminars, small coaching sessions, and weekend training sessions. Classes include how to improve your voice, how to sing in a quartet, and how to direct a chorus. In addition, you can learn how to be a leader, a good section leader, or even a competition judge.

Barbershop is an art form that allows you to express your emotions—to laugh or to cry on stage. Your audience loves to see this and often they laugh and cry with you. We do this on purpose—we want to move our audiences to tears. We celebrate! Barbershop singers (men and women) often wear sparkly costumes and dance on stage. And receive applause, standing ovations, and *bravos*! You don't get that in the workplace. And you certainly don't get that after cooking a Thanksgiving dinner and having everything come out hot and on time.

It didn't take long for me to embrace this art form. I love standing ovations!

I thought I just joined a singing organization. I found out that I would create a whole new way of life for myself and my family. I learned that if you become involved with this wonderful hobby, your life will soon be organized around performances and contests, parties and music. You will immediately have fifty thousand best friends all over the world. You will travel to places you never dreamed of visiting. You will remember that a trip to New York City was after you wore the blue costume and before you put sparkles on it and performed the "Stars and Stripes Forever" march. Never mind what year it was.

Family outings in the late spring will be scheduled for Ocean City, Maryland. Plenty of time to vacation in the sand before you compete on the contest stage. Lots of time to party in the hospitality room at the end of the day. New babies will be started so that they will be born during the years you are not competing. Grandmothers will be invited to join in the "family" vacations to help with the little one while you compete. The Men's International Contest is always during the week of the Fourth of July. You'll watch fireworks in that city. If you are married to a member of the Barbershop Harmony Society and your birthday is during the first week of July, plan on spending it—every year—listening to barbershop music. It's their annual contest time.

But the rewards are great. Hundreds of men and women sing "Happy Birthday" to you in four-part harmony. While you travel, you get to meet so many new people. You quickly get used to answering, "How many members are in your quartet?"

Little did I dream that joining this small group of women who just liked to sing would eventually take me to Las Vegas, Orlando, San Antonio, Detroit, Toronto, Seattle, New York City (Carnegie Hall), England (Royal Albert Hall), Hawaii, Sweden, four cities in New Zealand, five in Australia, and four in Russia.

But I'm jumping ahead of myself. First, I had to learn to sing in the barbershop style—four-part harmony sung without musical accompaniment (a cappella)—and sing it well.

1

Go Where the Music Is

1960–1962

AFTER A FEW CHORUS rehearsals I was asked to be the bass in a newly forming quartet. We called ourselves the Weavers. We were all stay-at-home moms, so we scheduled our meetings for the daytime. Once a week I drove my child (and her diaper bag) to one of our homes for a two-hour rehearsal. My child slept most of the time, but there were two other kids who played together in a playpen—stocked with toys, cereal, and sippy cups. Those playpens were invaluable as baby corrals.

It took me a while to remember the strange words used in the barbershop world. Singers recognize that SATB signifies soprano, alto, tenor, and bass. But the music that was handed to me was labeled tenor, lead, baritone, and bass.

I sing bass. Was the SATB bass the same as the barbershop bass? I didn't know where to find my part. I learned that it didn't matter if you were male or female: if you sang the very highest part, you were now called a tenor. Tenors usually sing notes written above the melody. Well, that wasn't me. The lead part is usually the melody line. The baritone part has the same vocal range as the lead. Both men and women are called baritones. Their notes float above and below the lead voice. The baritones will tell you that they have the most important notes in the chord because

The Weavers (© Jim Evans Studio)

it makes the chorus's unique sound. It is wise not to disagree with them. The bass is the lowest part and is usually reserved for the low altos and basses. Now I knew to look for the lowest note in the chord and to sing that. This was my first simple explanation of our four-part harmony. Over time, I learned singing barber-shop harmony well is extremely difficult.

My new vocabulary included *start at the edge*, meaning the very beginning of the song, and *sing the tag*, a few measures added to the end.

I was introduced to *overtones* and *undertones*. These are audible musical notes that no one sings. They occur when the voices of the quartet or chorus reinforce each other so strongly that a new tone is perceived by the listener. They can be heard above (overtones) and below (undertones) the notes that are actually sung. Overtones are easy to produce. In fact, sometimes it takes only one person to produce an overtone—you just have to know where to listen for it. Undertones are much harder to produce. I have no idea why. (It will be fifteen years before my chorus produces an audible undertone. We hear it on a recording of one of our contests. Yay!)

The other members of the Weavers wanted to compete in the next regional quartet contest. In my innocence I said, "Sure." No one told me I would spend my days making costumes, learning to wear false eyelashes, attending quartet-coaching sessions, and then rehearsing an hour a day the week before contest. Our entrance onto the competition stage was nerve-racking. We didn't trip or forget the words to our songs, but we were nervous and insecure enough to worry we might. I don't know where we placed, but it was not memorable.

Two years later the Weavers were no longer a quartet, but I was still with the Del-Mont Chorus. My friend who had invited me to join the chorus was our director. When her husband was transferred to another town, she recommended to the governing board that I take over the director's position. Why not? In college, I directed my sorority choir for their annual Greek Sing. I had no doubts that I could direct a chorus. It seemed like the next logical step for me to take for this chorus I had joined. My husband had finished school by then, and I thought he would be an excellent babysitter for our two-year-old little girl. It never occurred to me that the fact that there was another baby on the way would make any difference in my family life. This was a new and challenging opportunity for me—and it was music! So I said, "Yes, I'll do it."

Directing the Del-Mont Chorus gave me a chance to learn and then to teach and perfect the basics of good singing. We were now a chorus of twenty singers. All choruses over fifteen members were eligible to compete every year.

1963

I guess now is a good time to tell you about the first time I directed a chorus in the annual contest. We were to sing two songs in the barbershop style. Most competing choruses chose a ballad and a fast-rhythm number (called an *uptune*). The seventeen members of our chorus were instructed to stand behind the stage and wait to enter. I was nestled into the side curtain and watched as my chorus walked onto the darkened stage. They took their places on the risers.

I was supposed to follow them, cue the emcee that we were ready to sing, and then begin our songs. From where I stood, I saw a red exit sign high on the wall at the back of the stage. I realized that if I went on stage and walked behind the chorus, I could go out the exit door and escape this awful experience called *the competition*. I froze. Time stood still. I didn't even breathe. My feet wouldn't move. Fortunately, I came to my senses and stepped onto the stage. Had I not, the ramifications of my actions would have been worse than actually stepping on the competition stage.

There was a time, with only nineteen singers on stage, the Del-Mont Chorus placed tenth among thirty-five competing choruses. We were so proud of our placement that we promptly called ourselves the Mighty Mites. We were learning the basics of good barbershop harmony singing, and that learning was paying off.

1964–1965

During this time, a new Sweet Adelines chorus called Valley Forge formed—it was just a half-hour drive from my home to their rehearsal location. Valley Forge was looking for the best they could find as their director. Jim O'Toole, a member of the Barbershop Harmony Society and well known as an excellent singer was suggested. He became Valley Forge's first director and in 1965 he took the chorus to their first contest.

When contestant number 28 was announced, the curtain opened, but all twenty-three singers had their backs to the audience. They were dressed as hobos with brightly colored patches sewn all over their black shirts and pants. Before they even sang, you could hear the rustle of the audience trying to see what was happening on stage. From backstage, a police whistle sounded, and the last hobo ran onto the stage, chased by a costumed policeman—the director, Jim. He blew his police whistle again, and the little hobo ran up onto the risers to join the chorus. Then all the singers turned to face the audience, completely surrounding and protecting the little tramp. There were dirt smudges on their faces. The pitch pipe blew, and the contest began. The hobos sang "Laugh, Clown, Laugh" and "When I Leave the World Behind."

Putting a little drama like this into the contest was something new. That flair became Valley Forge's personality—gutsy, entertaining, unique, and fun. They loved the way the audience reacted to their pre-contest antics. They placed thirtieth out of thirty-nine choruses that year—not very high, but everyone was talking about what Valley Forge had done on the stage.

1966–1967

In 1966, Jim decided to resign. About this time, Ann Gooch moved from Florida to Millville, New Jersey—an hour-and-a-half drive from Valley Forge's rehearsal hall.

Ann Gooch's résumé was impressive: international music school faculty, candidate music judge, tenor of the Troubadour quartet, twice an international quartet finalist.

Valley Forge again reached for the stars and offered Ann the director's position. To win her over, they agreed to pick her up and return her home for every rehearsal and performance—a three-hour round trip twice a night. Chorus members signed up and took turns fetching Ann. Those who drove her home often did not return until two in the morning.

Ann directed them at their next contest—they placed eighteenth. (They didn't like thirtieth very much.) The following contest, they placed sixth. The chorus sang and danced and marched all over the stage. They were challenging the status quo for staging. Other choruses followed Ann's lead and started thinking outside the box. Ann developed a staging team to add pizzazz to Valley Forge's performances. Valley Forge singers were having so much fun that the word spread—new director, new chorus, new moves. Good music and excitement. Valley Forge's membership grew to about forty.

As director of Del-Mont, I couldn't help but be fascinated with what Valley Forge was doing. Del-Mont had stopped growing—the excitement was gone. But there was still much more for me to learn, especially under the direction of someone like Ann Gooch. Valley Forge was enticing. I knew it was time to leave the Del-Mont Chorus. My husband had earned his degree and was home at night to stay with the kids—all three of them by this time—while I made the round trip to Valley Forge. It was OK for me to move on. I wanted to go "where the music is." Valley Forge was

The Valley Forge logo.

creative, new, and unique. Ann was an excellent director. So, I transferred. It was in December 1967.

1968

In early January, twelve other members of Del-Mont decided to join me. This included the assistant director, the four section leaders, and the president. We increased Valley Forge's membership to fifty-four. I found out later that Del-Mont considered us the troublemakers in that small chorus, and they were quite glad to see us go (or to get rid of us). We all wanted more—we wanted to sing well and do staging and have fun. Valley Forge already had an assistant director, but they wanted to take advantage of another director in their chorus, so I became their second assistant director.

We loved singing for Ann. She was the ultimate performer. This group was crazy with new and exciting things to do. They put staging into their songs. They moved and marched and sang, all at the same time. They worked hard. They wanted to sing and

Valley Forge loved to dance.

entertain to the best of their ability. We "troublemakers" willingly volunteered for the Ann Gooch Taxi Service.

♮

The regional contest was in four months and we newbies wanted to compete. Learning the music in time was not a problem, but we had to make our own costumes. One day, the troublemakers came to my home armed with material, scissors, sewing machines, and glitter. We cut, pinned, stitched, and sprinkled for an entire day. We made fourteen costumes. It was an assembly line. Late in the afternoon, we put everything away, cleaned and vacuumed all the glitter, and the house looked like nothing had happened. We competed and placed second. We were thrilled. (The winners were the Ramapo Valley Chorus under the direction of Renee Craig.)

At the previous year's competition, Ann's quartet, the Parfaits, won first place and became eligible to compete at the international level. They were rehearsing during the day and choosing their competition outfits to match their name. Parfaits! Four pastel colors—blue, green, pink, and yellow. Six months into all this fun, Ann learned that her husband had been transferred back to Florida. Jeez! Suddenly, the Parfaits needed a quartet replacement. The chorus needed a new director.

Ann, a tenor, recommended that I audition for her tenor part in the Parfaits quartet. That was fine, except I was a bass. (Ann has this ability to encourage people to leave their comfort zone and try something they have no business trying.) When I auditioned, the high notes of the tenor part were easy to sing, but I sounded just like a bass singing tenor—full and rich. I had no idea. On the spot, Ann said, "Sing with me."

The new Parfaits in 1968: Nancy, Candy, Connie, and me.

Together we sang the tenor part to her song. I had to match her tone and style as we sang. I heard it. The sound she wanted. I matched it, and the Parfaits had a new tenor—me. I was wearing yellow and on my way to compete on the international stage in Hawaii.

Two things I learned during our trip to the Islands for that first competition:

♪ Be sure your family knows they will sightsee without you while your quartet is competing. You will join them when your competing time is over.

♪ Never listen to a new idea while standing in the wings ready to compete. You will think about the change throughout the entire competition instead of the music you are supposed to be singing.

We didn't score very well that year. We were too distracted.

♮

With Ann leaving, the Valley Forge board set out to find another director. By that time, I had learned enough about our craft to recognize the good from the average. I felt that each director who auditioned for us lacked the personality and style that was Valley Forge. Valley Forge was a "full of life" chorus.

Finally, I volunteered to be the interim director until a more competent person could be found to lead this energetic and organized group. With the help of Ann Gooch's recommendation (she felt that although I didn't have the experience, my potential was great) the board agreed to my request to become the interim director. My confidence in becoming the permanent director of a fifty-four-voice bunch of dynamos was at a low ebb. I didn't even know how to start a big chorus rehearsal. Someone else had to do it for me. I decided to take a crash course in directing a thriving barbershop chorus.

My leadership training began. And I learned that I really knew nothing.

I attended every concert given by other choruses. I sat close to the front and over to one side so that I could watch the director's hands. With my eyes on the director and my ears on the chorus, I watched and listened, learning how the director's moves affected the chorus's sound. I listened to what worked, what didn't. I watched how the singers moved on the stage.

The two directors whom I decided to emulate were Renee Craig, with Ramapo Valley Chorus, and George Avener, with Island Hills Chorus. They were winning contests every year, first one and then the other, back and forth for eight years. I wanted to find out how they did that!

When I first became the interim director of Valley Forge, directing a large chorus was physically challenging. After each three-hour rehearsal I came home exhausted and with tired arms. It was obvious to me that if I wanted to continue, I would have to do something about my arm waving. The chorus couldn't watch all the extra movement and were learning to ignore it and just look for the timing. They didn't need to see all the extra gyrations. They wanted to watch my hands. When my hands went below my waist, I lost them. They wanted to watch my face, too. And when my hands went above my head, I lost them again. Worse, when my arms flew all over the front of my body, the audience became distracted by my direction. I decided to eliminate all the extra motion—just stop it. Every rehearsal I planned to eliminate one extra motion. At home, I sang and directed one of our songs while facing a mirror. That made it obvious to me which motions were unnecessary. I changed my directing. Don't flop my wrists, keep my hands as part of my arms. It really wasn't long before I had the stamina to last three hours. Directing an a cappella chorus has very little to do with keeping time and everything to do with

A rehearsal. I was on my way.

directing the sound. The more efficient my motions, the better they sang. It was an awesome responsibility.

One of my fondest memories of this time was attending a seminar taught by Freddie King. Fred was a music teacher, quartet member, and chorus director in both the Sweet Adelines and the Barbershop Harmony Society. He was known throughout the barbershop world for his music and his sense of humor. He was often called to emcee chorus performances. At the end of the seminar he said to our class, "Someday, one of you will be on the competition stage winning the contest. It's available to any of you. Reach for it."

I didn't think he was talking to me.

2

One Giant Leap

LEARNING HOW TO MOVE my hands did not make me a good director. It was much more than that. So much more than that. So much to learn. For instance, as a singer I was trained to watch the tempo notifications on the written page. Barbershoppers sing with a more flowing sound, often mimicking American diction. We are aware of *stress words* (words we give emphasis to when speaking, like *love*, *run*, *sweet*). And we know other words are less important (like *and*, *the*, *to*), so we quickly move past them. I learned that we sing as we speak.

Directing this free-flowing sound is one of the most important talents to develop. The chorus sings with such emotion that you feel as though you are a soloist, and the chorus is your voice. There is no *t* sound in the middle of the word *little*. *Little* is sung *lih-dul* with the accent (stress) on the *lih* and not on the *dul*. Not all American English is acceptable. The words *could you* (from "how could you believe me," for example) are never pronounced *could chew*. When I hear *could chew* and *won't chew*, it's like hearing someone scraping their fingernails on a blackboard.

It took weeks for the chorus to remember this. And after they did, every time a new member joined the chorus, we'd hear it all over again. It wasn't long before a gentle reminder from one of the members made it magically disappear. I called it the osmosis syndrome. It worked many times when I heard a sound that I knew was from someone new. I never had to mention it. It would just suddenly disappear.

♮

The Sweet Adelines hired a new education director to conduct a seminar in our area. This was Floyd Connett. Floyd was an accomplished barbershop singer, arranger, judge, and coach. Valley Forge wanted me to attend his classes. He introduced us to vowel matching, and I heard a whole new way to sing good barbershop. "How do you do that?" I wanted to know. I found out it was easy to explain, but not easy to hear and not easy to teach.

For instance:

Love is *luh-ve*, not *lah-ve*. In order to tune a chord, *every member* must sing the word the same way. Any variation will upset the ring of the chord. Ring? Ever sing in the shower and hear your voice reverberate around the walls? That's a quick way of explaining *ring*.

To demonstrate vowel matching, Floyd brought with him, all the way from Seattle, the 1962 Women's International Champion Quartet, the Sea-Adelines. I sat in that class almost the entire day and tried to hear what he taught. I struggled. I listened and listened and still could not differentiate the good from the bad. The quartet sang a vowel correctly and then one member distorted the sound. Finally, almost at the end of the day, I heard it. An epiphany! A flash of a light bulb. I understood. I heard the ring of a matched-vowel sound.

Thank you, Sea-Adelines.

Now I just had to figure out how to transfer that knowledge to my chorus members. I was supposed to hear, all the time, this matched-vowel sound when directing my chorus.

I decided to introduce one vowel a month. That would give us four rehearsals on each vowel. Every time we sang a word with the monthly target vowel, I stopped the chorus and corrected it immediately. It didn't matter how many times I heard the vowel or if the vowel was in the same song or in any of the other songs we rehearsed, I stopped us again and again. When it was the month for the *oo* vowel, I found out that it could be improved by just keeping the shape of your mouth in the form of a soft kiss— like when you gently blow out a candle and try not to spray the wax all over the room.

As we worked on each vowel, to keep us focused I ignored all the other vowels that weren't matched. The hardest one to ignore was the *ow* vowel. Nothing like a *now, clown, ground, bound, mountain* to put the shivers down your back while you worked to make something else pretty. Ouch! *Ow* is a diphthong: ah-oo. (A diphthong is a single syllable with two vowel sounds.) I always knew what a diphthong was, but I sure didn't know that everyone in the chorus had to turn the diphthong at the same time and that I was the one who had to direct it. I learned how to do this by watching Jim Clancy direct his Vocal Majority men's chorus. He used a slight inward bending of the wrist to move the target vowel (T*ah*) to the diphthong (*eem*). Time. Jim's direction was so gentle you could hardly see it. But it worked.

Occasionally, a song included a triphthong like *wow*: oo-ah-oo.

And then there were *mm*s and *nn*s that needed to be directed along with the diphthong. I used the same Jim Clancy movement to make sure the turns were all sung at the same time. The chorus learned to watch me closely.

Some adjacent words use the same sound. You don't need to change your mouth to produce both words smoothly—sometimes you just need a flip of the tip of the tongue. Example: *you look* as in "just the way you look tonight." yooo loooo ktoo (and don't forget to direct the *nn* in *too-nnnah-eet*). Then drop your jaw just a smidgen to sing the *ah* of night. We brought mirrors to the rehearsal so that we could see what our mouths looked like as we sang each vowel. We wanted to look similar but sound the same. Every day, as I prepared for my rehearsal time with the chorus, I had to reach inside my mind, decide what I wanted to hear, and then figure out how to teach it. It was new and different every time.

Valley Forge sent me to every class, every concert, and every competition that was available. For me, keeping my ears and eyes open and my mouth closed was the best way to learn. I found out that if the chorus was having trouble producing what I was asking them to sing, I had to see what my hands were doing. I would go back to my bathroom mirror, sing what I wanted to hear, and try to make my hands and arms produce that same tempo and sound.

Teaching the chorus all that I learned was a fun exercise. When they didn't respond to what I wanted and stumbled, I changed what I was doing with my hands. Then I asked them if the change worked and if they understood what I wanted. If they didn't understand, they were quick to tell me. Then I would try something else and ask for their reaction. We worked together until I was pleased with the way they sang and they were pleased with the way I directed. That was the fun. The challenge was to remember it for the next rehearsal. Together we learned how to phrase a song, how to drive the tempo of the uptune, and how to sing a ballad with love and emotion. Sometimes it took several rehearsals for the chorus to produce the sound that I wanted to hear them sing. When it happened, when they were able to sing this way, sound and excitement filled the room. We laughed and cheered and jumped up and down. Our relationships became stronger and our music more beautiful.

Over time, we developed a special sign language for me to talk to the chorus during a performance. With my back to the audience, I was free to do anything I wanted. If I wanted them to listen to each other to sing more in tune, I pulled at my right ear. A difficult passage that was executed well got an immediate thumbs-up. At the end of a well sung song, I waited a nanosecond before I turned around to accept the applause. Just time enough to mouth the word *wow*. The chorus knew they had done a good job and that I was pleased with what they did—and they smiled.

There was so much to learn, so little time. This chorus was on a mission.

While I learned to be a director, the spirit of the chorus blossomed. I was swept up in their fun. Always after a rehearsal there was a food-and-drink stop before going home. Chorus members had parties and corn roasts with their menfolk. They went places and did things together other than at rehearsals, and at the same time, they maintained strong chorus management. I learned to have fun with them.

Looking back over this time in our lives it was clear that Valley Forge was chorus driven. It wasn't "Jan's chorus." It was "the Valley Forge Chorus." As I taught them music, they taught me what it was like to be a member of their chorus. They made it clear to me what they wanted to be, and they did their best to give me what I wanted and what they thought I needed. This feeling went beyond just music. It included friendships, moral support, caring, and people management. This drive to be the best was evident in all their activities.

♮

By 1969, I had directed Valley Forge for about eight months. It was March and soon it would be contest time—the first contest with me as their interim director. I had taken the job as interim director after Ann left the chorus. I wasn't confident I could do the job as well as she did. Ann had been a firm leader when she first came to Valley Forge. She knew all about the barbershop

craft and the international organization. We relied on her judgment. We had risen to second place in competition when she left
us. But competing as the Valley Forge *interim director* just didn't
feel right. It was time to make a decision. I asked for the permanent director position. The chorus vote was forty *yes* and ten *no*.
Not unanimous, but good enough. Neither I nor the chorus knew
exactly what to do to become a top competitor, the way Ann had
known. It became my job to learn how to lead them musically to
wherever they (and I) wanted to go.

This first regional chorus competition as the new director
was exciting. They loved to compete. They guided me through
the process. At our breakfast on contest day, I was encouraged to
eat and then get up and talk to each member at each table. The
chorus members needed to know that I was in control of myself.
If anything unusual happened on stage, it would be me who had
to handle it. No one else. Trust was paramount.

I think sometimes it's easier on the nerves to direct than
to sing in a competition. As a director, you can see neither the
audience nor the judges. The audience is usually other contestants who know everything about what you are doing on stage
and, although they are supporting you, they still have a critical ear. This contest was the big league. Not at all like directing
the small chorus from my earlier days. Almost like a different
world.

We placed second. Again. This was a big thrill. I had felt pressure to maintain the contest placement established by Ann. The
success felt good.

It must have been obvious that I was uptight while we were
competing. The chorus wanted a relaxed director to lead them.
For the next year's contest—in 1970—just before we left the
hotel for the contest site, dressed in our contest clothes with full
makeup and hair coifed and sprayed, someone emptied a full bot-

tle of cold duck into a huge wine glass. They handed it to me to take the first sip, insisting I take a big one. I'm sure it wasn't the wine but the laughter that calmed my nerves. This became a ritual for our competition years. It was a good luck charm.

♮

Valley Forge maintained their high scores at competition. We gained new members. New performance opportunities came our way. I had been their leader now for three years, and that's just how long it takes to meld together a new director and her chorus. We all became more focused on winning the regional contest. It was the music team's decision to have every member bring a tape recorder to rehearsal and record their part. These tapes were turned over to our section leaders for evaluations. We looked for correct notes and tonal accuracy and maybe a timing problem. The tapes were then returned to the member along with comments. Sometimes they were asked to repeat the recording and resubmit it.

A final deadline for the tape program was established—three weeks before contest. Those members who didn't pass or didn't turn in their tape were not permitted to compete with us. Because of these requirements we lost two singers: one for wrong notes and the other (one of our very good baritones) because she just didn't feel like turning in a tape. The chorus turned to me for a decision. There is always "director's discretion" built in to everything having to do with what goes on the stage.

It is never wise to sacrifice the chorus for one individual. If a singer didn't know the notes for a performance, I was the one to ask her not to attend. She may not have liked it, but those standing near her on the risers sang better if they didn't hear her wrong notes. Following the rules, I said no. Our baritone didn't sing. She was sure we wouldn't win competition without her. She left the chorus shortly after we competed.

Despite this new program, we had a whole lot of fun and we knew we were singing well. People began to look forward to hearing and seeing Valley Forge perform.

In 1969, we placed second. The Island Hills Chorus, directed by George Avener, placed first.

In 1970, we placed second. Renee Craig and the Ramapo Valley Chorus won first place. Ramapo Valley had a 120-point time penalty—and still they won.

In 1971, we placed third. George Avener and the Island Hills Chorus won the gold that year.

In 1972, Valley Forge was frustrated. We had come in second and third for too many years. That year we decided that our two contest songs would be ones we loved. We would sing the bejeebers out of them and let the chips fall where they may. What did we have to lose? It was surely Ramapo Valley's turn to win this year.

First we searched for two pieces of music that were fun to sing and would please the audience—a ballad and an uptune. Ann Gooch continued to be a part of the growth of Valley Forge, so I sent her my two suggestions. Without saying a word, by return mail, she sent me a different ballad. It was obvious that this was a better ballad than the one I had chosen to use for our competition. Ann had not said a word about my suggestions—she just sent a better song. And so we began to learn "Each Time I Fall in Love."

Choosing the music for the uptune was easy. We reached out to Freddie King for his arrangement of "Undecided." This was such a good song for Valley Forge that I never even thought it should be sent to a music judge to see if it qualified as contest material. So what if it ended on a jazzy sixth chord? Who knew *do-wah* wasn't a word?

The choreography team, with Ida Bilodeau as the chair, went to work. Ann Gooch had chosen Ida to design a choreography team for Valley Forge. This was a new challenge for Ida and a good one. The following years brought Ida recognition as a coach for her staging and performance skills and eventually as a show-manship judge for the Sweet Adelines International. Ida and the team invited me to attend as the guardian of the music: can we sing and move without losing our sound? We decided to sing our ballad first. No more motion was added other than the natural movement of a singing chorus. The uptune would be their chal-lenge. Many hours were spent creating and redesigning the stag-ing. Many more hours were spent creating and teaching us the movements. We did fancy footwork with strong hands and arms to go along with the very strong music.

When we were about finished creating the choreography, Mary Ellen David, our costume chair, asked to see what we had done. Mary Ellen was creative. She worked part-time in the cos-tume department for off-Broadway stage shows. She also was an extra for films. She laughed as she told us one of her roles was as a homeless person lying on the street, covered with a blanket. One arm was all that showed. Mary Ellen took notes as the team performed our choreography for her. Then she designed our cos-tume. One costume. Duplicated fifty-four times. This is what she came up with: a beautiful royal blue gown made of a soft corduroy material, which, under the stage lights, looked like velvet. On the long-sleeved bodice, she put a sparkling starburst made of shiny, silver pipe cleaners. The side seams of the skirt were toward the back of the dress and were open from the waist to the floor. Under this skirt were silver hot pants and, for the front row only, real silver boots. Everyone else wore silver material over their shoes to make them look like boots.

To make the hot pants, Mary Ellen asked each member to purchase a pair of white men's boxer shorts. They put their name on the shorts and gave them to the costume committee. The costume committee sewed the front of the shorts shut and attached pieces of shiny silver material to each side of the shorts. Voila! Silver hot pants!

My costume was the same style dress, including the open seam and hot pants, but I had silver sparkles sewn all over the blue material.

Knowing we were going to sing the ballad first, Mary Ellen designed a two-for-one costume. As we sang our ballad, the skirt hung straight and did not show our silver hot pants. At the first sound of the uptune, we all turned quickly toward the center of the chorus and thrust our outside leg through the slit, to expose to the audience boots, bare legs, and hot pants. Yes!

Every member wore the hot pants—short, tall, skinny, and all other sizes. What a thrill it was for some of our members to be dressed in high fashion! Not one person objected.

Hot pants and boots for all.

♮

Two years before the contest, as Valley Forge Chorus prepared to compete, we were named the hostess chapter for the 1972 competition convention. Lennie Brown was our convention chair. This was not the first time Lennie had been in charge of a convention. She was a seasoned administrator (thank goodness). We scheduled the Traymore Hotel in Atlantic City, New Jersey. Friday evening was the quartet contest and Saturday, all day, were the choruses. Six months before the date of the competition, the hotel informed us that it had closed. Gambling was coming to Atlantic City and the hotel was going to be torn down and rebuilt into a hotel casino. All the beautiful marble floors were trashed.

We couldn't find anyone else to take us. Now we had no venue.

The husband of one of our members was the general manager of the Marriott Hotel on City Line Avenue in Bala Cynwyd, Pennsylvania—a forty-minute drive from our rehearsal hall. Lennie met with him, told him what had happened, and asked if he had any suggestions. Her first words to him were "We are desperate."

"Well, we can do it here," he answered.

"Can you build a stage?"

"We can build a stage. Ask for anything you need, and we'll do it."

Done. We had our convention venue.

The contest took place in the hotel ballroom. Lennie worked closely with the management of the Marriott, who helped us move the convention from Atlantic City. We borrowed a quartet shell from the Freedoms Foundation, headquartered in Valley Forge, and we used our own risers to put on the stage for the chorus contest. Six months later, and one day early, we were to arrive at the Marriott to set up the risers and position the quartet shell for the next evening's quartet contest.

Once again, our menfolk from the Valley Forge Chorus helped us. At 6:30 on Thursday evening, Ken and Lennie met George Johnson and Tom Brooks (and Tom's truck) at the Freedoms Foundation and picked up the quartet shell. Next stop was our rehearsal hall, where they loaded our risers onto the truck and headed to the Marriott. Their route took them under a railroad overpass that was too low for the truck. Our driver didn't know that. Now the truck was stuck. And it was pouring down rain. Lennie and George were standing in the rain trying to direct traffic around the truck when the police arrived.

With a smile, an officer suggested "Try letting the air out of your tires."

Yes, sir! That worked. They freed the truck and continued to the Marriott—arriving at 10:30 that night.

The stage was there, but it was facing in the wrong direction.

When Lennie saw it, she said to the hotel workers, "The stage isn't right."

"Whaddya mean it ain't right?"

"All these people over here will not be able to see the stage." The ballroom was L-shaped. "You've got to turn the stage."

"Does that mean we have to tear it down and start all over?"

"Yes. You gotta do it. You can't have all these people not being able to see the competing choruses. It would be a disaster. The hotel's name would be mud, my name would be mud, and the chorus's name would be mud. You can't do this to yourselves—or us."

And they tore down the stage, turned it, and set it up again.

♮

The next day the convention began. The hotel swarmed with suitcases and women in fancy costumes. Each of us had our jobs to do. We had spreadsheets that listed all our names and where we were supposed to be at all times. We were so busy taking care of all the choruses, quartets, and judges that we hardly saw each other during the entire day. As the hostess chapter, we were scheduled to compete last.

The backstage crew had their own spreadsheets, timed to the minute. There were no walkie-talkies. The men relied on their watches to make the traffic pattern work.

In the ballroom, the stage was perfect. But when the crew tried to open and close the curtain, it dragged on the floor and took forever to move.

We were all in our hospitality room getting ready to host the competitors when Lennie ran to the room and put out the SOS. "Valley Forge, I need help!"

The response was immediate. "OK, what do you need?"

"Anyone who doesn't have a job, you've got to come to the stage and help pin up the curtain."

The hotel sent out for safety pins and there we were, sitting on the floor, pinning the curtain up six inches.

We had more than 1,000 people facing the straightened-out stage and the pinned-up curtain—the largest convention to date.

♮

During the contest there was some free time for me. When it was time for Ramapo to compete, I sneaked down to the ballroom to hear them. They sang well, but I thought they might be taking a chance with the music they chose. I felt they had left room at the top for someone to score more points than they. I was charged, but never said a word to the chorus. On the way back to my room I ran into someone who had apparently attended one of our pre-contest rehearsals. "You don't have enough softs in your ballad."

Jeez! Just what I wanted to hear. Everyone is an expert!

In the solitude of my room, I sang through our ballad several times, found a few measures that would be quick and easy to sing very, very softly. It would make the presentation of the ballad even better. I decided to present it to the chorus.

It was time for us to get ready to compete. We went to our rooms to dress and do our makeup and hair. There was no time for us to warm up in the schedule. We knew that in the traffic pattern we would have fifteen minutes in the warm-up room—and none before that. But we *had* to warm up and I *had* to go over our new soft spot.

We found a place in the hotel where four hallways came together. The chorus divided themselves into four groups and stood facing the intersection. We found two chairs and put them in the center. I put one foot on each chair and stood up so everyone could see me. This was quite a sight—fifty-four women in full makeup and costume singing in the middle of a hotel hallway!

We did some vocal warm-ups and then I introduced the volume change. We sang very, very softly. The chorus loved it, and I think they immediately sensed the power in the change. We practiced it several times and then I said, "Now don't worry about this. Do not think about it while you are singing. When we get to this part, just watch me and I will warn you it's coming. Just follow me, and it will be OK." I wanted to reassure my chorus because I was remembering the Hawaii quartet contest where I had spent the whole song worrying whether I would remember the change.

Oops! I just broke Contest Rule #1. *Never* make a change with music, staging, or position on the risers for two months before any contest.

We sipped our cold duck and began the traffic pattern to the stage. Our performance was flawless. The audience whooped and hollered. It was thrilling.

Ken Brown was one of the stagehands for this contest. He was backstage during the announcement of the top five choruses. Fifth place was announced, then fourth. After the emcee announced third, there were only two choruses left—Ramapo and Valley Forge.

George Avener, who was also standing backstage, heard Ken say, "Valley Forge has a real chance."

George answered, "No, they don't. I've never beaten Renee Craig. I don't think anyone can."

♮

In the ballroom, Valley Forge waited for the final announcement. They were grabbing any hand they could find and squeezing hard.

♮

The chorus knew not to cheer until the first-place winner was announced. We might have had a time penalty and placed sixth! We might have come in second again.

Then the announcement came, "And in second place, the Ramapo Valley Chorus."

It was like an explosion ready to happen, a volcano ready to erupt. No one moved.

"And in first place..."

WE WON!

With Jeanne, Maureen and Lennie. Our first regional gold medal.

One of our score sheets had one word on it, "Wow!" To justify the one-word critique, the judge later said, "You had to be there."

After so many years being second and even third, we were now regional champions. Back home, at our rehearsal hall, we had our celebration party with our menfolk. After so many years we had won the contest. But there was no time to rest. Now we had to maintain and even become better. There was another contest in our future. This was the first year that the Sweet Adelines organization sponsored an international chorus contest. The winner of each regional contest was eligible to compete—and that was us. The first contest was in Washington, D.C., in eighteen months.

Winning the regional contest had become something we did every other year. Once you've learned how to win, you always remember what it takes to get there. We felt we *owned* the regional stage, and in reality, we did. This qualified us to compete at the international level. We had reset our goals.

3

Day by Day

Between Thee and Me

THE CALENDAR FOR AN internationally competing chorus is as follows:

1 Spring: Win regional. Compete in the international contest in eighteen months.
2 Skip the next spring regional contest. Compete internationally that fall.
3 Spring: Win regional. Compete in the international contest in eighteen months.

Repeat 2 and 3 as many times as desired.

We had many strong-minded members who took over the administration duties of the chorus. There were committees for costumes, staging, financial, marketing, and social, as well as a governing board. That was fine with me. I didn't want anything to do with those things. I had enough with choosing the music and figuring out how to sing it. We all had our part in making this chorus a fast-moving group! And it worked. (One year, when it was time for the election of officers, we actually had two members argue who would be the better president for the upcoming year. With most groups, the one who loses the draw gets to be president.)

Maybe this is why we didn't think of us as a director-run chorus. The music and onstage activities were my responsibility. The chorus had a chair for everything else. I was told that there was a director's discretion or *final say* clause attached to everything that had to do with performances. All else was their responsibility. I really didn't care about the administration of the chorus. I didn't want to know every little thing that went on. I just wanted folks to sing smart. Here's why: After any performance you may hear the public say, "Wasn't the chorus wonderful?" "How clever!" "Weren't the costumes great?" The chorus was the star. Anything that didn't sound or look right quickly became the director's fault. "Why didn't the director see (or change) that?" This is why final say is the unwritten rule during most discussions involving the performance. I needed buddies to be able to discuss decisions that required that final say. Here's where Lennie and Ida came into my life.

Lennie Brown was a get-things-done person, a strong organizer and leader. She was often chair of a project and sometimes the president. Our international organization in Tulsa, Oklahoma, had heard how she was able to have a well-managed convention and sent the executive secretary to our contest to observe her methods. Lennie was that good.

Ida Bilodeau was a teacher and chair of the performance and choreography team. She led the way as we became known for our stage presence and pizzazz. She was always concerned about the way we presented ourselves to the public. The Sweet Adelines appointed her to the international teaching faculty. She traveled all over the world as a judge, coach, and teacher.

We developed a strong business relationship: Ida for performance, Lennie for administration, and me for music. We also became friends. It was bound to happen. Our respective responsibilities and interests in the Valley Forge Chorus forced us to make contact with each other almost every day. Is it any wonder we became glued together for so many years? Lennie and Ida supported me while I learned to lead. They helped me to navigate through all the non-musical responsibilities that a director must fulfill. My buddies helped me as I worked with the members of the chorus. They reminded me to be sure to speak to those who had stepped outside their comfort zone to do the job of chorus emcee, to sing a solo, or to do anything that put them in the spotlight. "Be sure to compliment them on their performance." They reminded me to encourage and support chorus members. "As a director, you must make eye contact with every member of the chorus when we perform or compete or even when we rehearse," said Ida. Ida made me do this. She told me that most directors do not know how to look at the whole chorus. Directors are prone to look at only one side of the chorus. Ida wouldn't allow it. She reminded me when I forgot. Valley Forge never stopped encouraging me to be the kind of director they wanted, and I was eager to become that person.

♮

In the beginning, making the decisions that affected the music of Valley Forge was daunting. They (my buddies) must have seen that little person sitting on my shoulder saying, "Are you sure? Are you sure?" Is there anyone in this world who doesn't know that little person sitting on their shoulder? While I never doubted my ability to direct this chorus, some of the decisions I had to make were way out of my comfort zone.

One day, my buddies took me aside and said, "Trust your instincts. What you are doing is right. Try not to second-guess yourself."

This meant I had to acknowledge my inner thoughts—my gut feelings. I had to listen to those feelings, make a choice, and then watch to see the results. I slowly began to enjoy taking the risk. I started to lose the feelings of doubt. "Go away, little man!" became my mantra.

To become a better director, I had to develop this trust in myself. I had stifled this feeling for many years, but now I was taking my finger out of the dike, and it felt good! A thought would pop into my head—something new, different, and always fun—and I didn't question it anymore. Most of the time it was with the music, but often it was just something fun to do when we were together. It was just me. The response of the chorus to these moments made it fun for the chorus and helped me develop a freedom of leadership. This forever changed my life.

♮

It was natural for the three of us—Lennie and Ida and me—to meet often, planning and implementing the everyday happenings of our chorus. Is it any wonder that we were called the triumvirate? Although I'm not sure it was a nickname.

Ida and Lennie.

Our Rehearsals

The music was the glue. It was also a place for each singer to develop her own special talents. There were costumes to design, posters to paint, scenery to build, sound equipment to buy, newsletters to write, forms to fill out, and a million other tasks that help an organization run smoothly. We had to work together to get it all done. We wanted our chorus to be the best in everything we did. There was no time for any of us, including me, to be queen for a day.

My job was to make sure that everything we put on the stage was the very best it could be—that included music, costumes, staging, lights, sound—the works. Finances, travel arrangements, scheduling performances, organizing or planning any trips were all handled by others. And all our various responsibilities were equal. We expected our members to give their one hundred percent to the work they had chosen to do for the chorus. But everyone's one hundred percent was different. If a singer could only learn her notes and words, then that was her one hundred percent, and I expected no more or less. This do-your-best attitude permeated the chorus. Some members said that it seeped into their everyday life.

When I was very young, a professional musician (an old man) told me that you can't admire and criticize at the same time, so you have to make a choice. Two more carryovers from childhood were "Judge not, that ye be not judged" and "When you point your finger at someone, remember—there are three fingers pointing back at you." A leader has to exercise judgment, but she doesn't have to be judgmental.

As the chorus worked together, it became clear that each of our members had her own strengths, and I learned something from every one of them. For instance, Mildred, a baritone, couldn't stand poor diction. Woe to the member who stood next to her and sang an improper vowel. She corrected the errant singer on the spot. Often when we had trouble making a phrase sound more musical, Mildred couldn't stand to be silent any longer and spoke out about our poor diction. She asked to suggest a way to fix it. We'd try it, and it made our music sound even more beautiful. Done! Many members knew more than I did about bits and pieces of our chorus, but I realized that I needed to see the whole picture. Many strong trees make a forest, and the forest was my forte. To get to where we wanted to go, it was the governing board's job to take what the chorus members knew, put it together with what I knew, and make it all work.

♮

The Valley Forge Chorus was an organization made up entirely of volunteers. Volunteer singers, volunteer scene painters, volunteer newsletter writers. Working with a volunteer group is different from working with employees. Employees may be stuck in a bad job, but employees can't leave; they need the job. The same is not true with a volunteer group. If the director is nasty or the rules of the chorus are overly strict, volunteers vote with their feet. What happens at every rehearsal can affect the membership of your chorus. If volunteers don't like the rehearsals or they don't like your attitude, they leave. Employees can't do that. Sometimes I think that the director is totally responsible for the attendance at rehearsals.

In my early days as director, Valley Forge was thought to be a bit unfriendly. As the director, I wondered if that feeling of unfriendliness might be coming from me. I didn't pay much attention to guests. I had my rehearsal plan to follow and I didn't deviate from that plan. Soon, it was easy to look at the rehearsal as a guest might see it and not as an existing member. And then it became easy to actively welcome those guests. I would just change the rehearsal plan on the spot when guests visited. Add some fun vocal exercises or make a quick mini performance by singing at least three of our favorite repertoire songs, just for the guests. Take a few minutes from rehearsal to introduce the visitors and ask them to tell the chorus about themselves. It worked. We didn't hear the word *unfriendly* anymore.

Many of our volunteer members came long distances every week, so it was important to me to have a well-planned and productive rehearsal. I never considered that someone would leave the chorus. But I did know they could leave if they thought they were wasting their time. I learned early that it was not good to dismiss one or two groups early on a rehearsal night so that other sections could work alone with me. As a director I had to respect the time volunteer groups donated.

♮

One goal of mine was always to teach one new thing and have one big laugh at each rehearsal. Teaching something new each time was necessary to keep the chorus challenged, but making the opportunity for a big laugh was not something I could plan. It had to come from them. To teach that one new thing, it had to be repeated three times. With a volunteer group, there will be absences, and most members will be away for only two weeks, mostly due to sickness and vacations. When introducing something new, in order to reach every member, it must be repeated at three *consecutive* rehearsals. By the third rehearsal, it will have been heard by everyone.

The atmosphere around the rehearsal hall encouraged that big laugh. Sometimes it would happen in the middle of a song when we made a huge mistake. Sometimes a one-liner could be heard from the chorus. We found fun in everything we did. I loved hearing them laugh.

Sure, we made mistakes. You can't learn if you don't make mistakes, and the chorus knew it was OK to tease me when I made mine. Fixing mistakes is fun. How else can you feel the joy of success? I don't like the word *fail*. Trying something is the only way to learn. A "failure" is just a wrong path. I'm proud of my chorus because they were constantly willing to try new things.

♮

Rehearsal night, for most of us, was an evening away from life. It was like a cocoon where we could recharge our batteries. I asked that members forget about everything but the music when they came to rehearsal. We reminded each other how good it was to be together doing something we loved. Coming into the rehearsal was a warm, loving, and exciting feeling. We learned to leave the world behind. The chorus rehearsal became a place where we could relax and just be ourselves. Chorus members knew that it was OK to make a funny comment in the middle of the evening to break the tension or just have fun.

At some point, the chorus decided that during the occasional ten-minute break, we would call one of our members to sit in front of us in our hot seat (a folding chair that faced the chorus). With their permission, of course, we asked them any questions we wanted. We learned where they were from, what they did before joining the Valley Forge Chorus, how many kids they had, where they wanted to retire, or anything else that we found interesting. We also asked some very funny questions. The clever answers made us all laugh. The hot seat worked well for us: it helped us get to know one another.

I knew every member's name and something about each one of them, although it wasn't wise to get too emotionally involved with their personal lives. But there were times when I was told things in private. When appropriate, I would quietly put people with the same need in touch with each other. They could talk together without fear of being judged, and it helped them because they now had a friend who understood.

We loved being together. We loved the chorus rehearsals. We tried to make the time together a special time for everyone. As the director, I was not left out of the mutual support and encouragement. One rehearsal night, it had been very difficult for me to leave my home. As I walked from my car to the hall to join the chorus, Ida came down the sidewalk to join me. She took one look at my face and said simply, "How are you?" I burst out crying, hard, and with her arm around my waist she walked me away from the door. We found a place to sit and stayed a few moments. Then together, we went to the rehearsal. It was showtime. I left the world behind, with Ida's help. I felt better, and the chorus never knew.

The chorus was made up of strong-willed women, and there were strong factions among them. We had constant turmoil. But it was exciting and challenging. It made us a vibrant chorus, and we kept gaining new members.

♮

One time, when our schedule was light, it seemed to me that it would be fun to teach my chorus how to direct our music. Would they want to know? I asked them. Ten members signed up to come to rehearsal one hour early for a ten-week director's clinic.

It's hard to teach people everything you know in ten weeks, but we all learned quite a bit about directing—including me. We started out with the basic hand movements, depending on the tempo of the music. We learned waltz, foxtrot, and march tempos. We worked on quick tempos and clean and precise cutoffs. Then we added more difficult moves.

Teaching the art of directing the diphthong was quite challenging. I found out that some of my budding directors still didn't know what a diphthong was. They had been in the chorus ten years, and the diphthong was still unfamiliar to them. This made me realize they weren't singing our music correctly, so there was still work to be done at the chorus rehearsal.

One attendee stood out from all the others. There was something about the way she moved her hands and body that was graceful and fluid. She was eager to learn, although she didn't know how to read music, nor did she play the piano. Years later, Claire became the leader of a large chorus whose director had just resigned. Every time I see her, I tell her what a good director she is. She tells me that she is just doing what I taught her. She says she watched me all the time and now, when she's stuck with how to make something happen, she says to herself, "Now what would Jan do?" That's nice to hear, but we both know it's much more than that. I remember that I learned what I needed to know by watching the best directors I could find and mimicking what they did—and then making it my own. That was hard work. It takes analysis and drive to incorporate someone else's ideas into your own style. My prize student and her chorus are now winning blue ribbons and competing internationally. We have fifteen directors in the Sweet Adelines world who were once singers in our Valley Forge Chorus. We are very proud of them. Every year, at every contest we attend—regional or international—we point them out and say with pride, "She was in Valley Forge." They will always be a part of us.

4

A Busy Two Years

So now we had eighteen months to prepare for the contest in Washington, D.C. There was music to learn and choreography to design and teach. There were costumes to design and make. To help with our annual finances, we often hired out to organizations to entertain at their events. We had local performances to organize and execute. And, in addition, every two or three years we produced our own show.

Our *performances* were the parade format—a group of songs tied together by an emcee, usually lasting forty-five minutes to an hour. Our self-produced *shows* were two hours long. Forty or forty-five minutes of music and staging built around a theme, fifteen or twenty minutes for an intermission, twenty minutes to a half hour for a guest entertainer (usually a championship quartet) and then, in our finest formal costume, a five-song parade finale of the "Best of Valley Forge."

It was time to plan our next Valley Forge show. Barb was our chair, and one of her responsibilities was to suggest ideas for our guest entertainment. She thought Renee Craig would be great—one woman and her piano—for a half hour.

What? No quartet?

Yes. Barb contacted Renee and invited her to be on our show. We knew Renee as the director of the Ramapo Valley Sweet Adelines chorus, but she was so much more than that. She was also a coach, arranger, and entertainer. Her profession was as a songwriter in New York City for a music firm that created jingles for product advertising. She lived north of New York City, about a three-hour drive from us. Renee was surprised and very pleased to be invited to entertain our audience. On stage she played and sang some of the jingles she had written. Who could forget the cigarette jingle she wrote: "Kent—with the micronite filter"? The audience enjoyed hearing these familiar tunes and laughed with her when she shared their stories. She sat at the piano and sang one of her original songs. As her finale, the chorus joined her onstage to accompany her as she stood center stage and—with a handheld mic—sang the solo of "Scarlet Ribbons."

Renee (reprinted from Pitch Pipe © *Sweet Adelines International)*

The audience gave her a standing ovation. Renee loved our show. We were thrilled that she had shared her talent with us. She thought Valley Forge should "just do shows." This was a wonderful time together.

♮

A bit of non-barbershop music slipped into our lives. Ken Brown was part of the management team of the Hilton Hotel in our town. He and Lennie invited my husband and me, along with Ida and Dan Bilodeau, to join them in the cocktail lounge for a performance of a group called the County Line. They were good. Their three guitars, played by Mike, Curt, and Bob, made wonderful toe-tappin' folk music as they sang popular, well-known songs. At the end of the evening they came to our table to say hello. This was a regular event each time the Hilton invited the County Line back for an extended gig.

We became friends, and they soon began to attend several of our performances and contests. Bob, the leader and lead guitarist, arranged a few songs for us to sing (not barbershop). Years later we included one of them, "Long Ago and Far Away," on our very first (and only) cassette tape recording. Bob also wrote and arranged an original song for us that we used for the title of our next show, "Wasn't That a Time." His arrangements added special and unique music to our performances. The County Line were with us when we won our first regional contest.

The following year, The Bron's Tones, the international quartet champions, attended our regional contest and stayed at the home of the Browns. At the same time, the County Line was performing at the Hilton, and Bob was invited to have dinner with them. Of course, the quartet sang for him—it was the best of barbershop and folk music. They would meet again.

♮

And then, it was time to get ready for the Washington, D.C., international contest. First, we had to choose our contest songs. You can't decide on a costume or choreography until you know what you are singing. The ballad was an easy choice—the same one we sang when we won the regional contest: "Each Time I Fall in Love." We liked it and we scored well singing it. Why not use it again?

Now for the uptune! "Undecided?" I don't think so! It was a good idea to choose a better barbershop arrangement, especially since the Sweet Adelines Judging Committee had just rewritten some of the rules of the music arrangement category. "Goodbye, My Lady Love" was the choice. The choreography committee gave its stamp of approval. (It was smart to check with Ida and her team before all competition music was chosen. Wouldn't it be terrible if they weren't excited with the music and still had to design smashing choreography for the contest stage?) When designing choreography, it is always good to have a surprise somewhere. In the middle of this fast-moving uptune were sixteen measures of pure energy. The team designed a move that we called the accordion. And the costume team designed costumes to show it off. Our outfits were red slacks and red vests. We had a white blouse with long sleeves, ruffles at the wrist, and a white jabot. And white boots.

The choreography for the accordion was this: We stood on five-riser rows. As we began to sing these sixteen measures, we all turned quickly to face the middle of the chorus with our outside hand resting on the outside shoulder of the singer next to us. Keeping the rhythm moving, the center of each row marked time but did not move. All others took eight quick steps backward (on the risers!). The farther away you were from the center, the longer the steps you had to take. You had to move far enough away from the center so that each arm stretched out as we marched backward. The arms of both sides of the chorus formed one white, straight line across the entire row. Then, for the next eight beats, we marched forward to the center position—making the accordion collapse. The white line was broken. Then we did it all again. We finished with a snappy step that brought us back to our original riser position—all members facing forward. The audience saw five very straight lines appear and then disappear on the stage. This was extremely difficult and quite nerve-racking for the members at the ends of the rows. They had to walk backwards on the risers.

Through the years Valley Forge would often see our choreography moves appear onstage many times as other choruses adapted what we did to their songs. The accordion move was never one of them.

♮

And there we were, ready to compete at our first international contest held at the Washington, D.C., Hilton Hotel. One evening, while strolling through the hotel lobby, we heard some familiar folk music. Yep, it was the County Line playing their gig at the Hilton Hotel.

Lennie: "Hey, Bob, the Bron's Tones are here at the hotel!"

Bob: "Can you find them? Would they sing during our final set tonight?"

She found them—and at 11:30 p.m. we were in the Hilton lounge listening to the Bron's Tones barbershop quartet singing to people who had just heard an evening of country-folk music. By the applause of the audience, we knew they liked it!

♮

At the end of this contest the top five chorus placements were announced. We weren't one of them. International had decided to withhold the names of those choruses who placed below fifth. This decision was not well received. Shortly after we returned home, we received a letter from one of the competing choruses. They had decided to find out where all of us placed and they asked us to respond with our total points score. When they were tabulated, we received our answer. We were sixth. The next year the scores were published.

Several weeks later, International sent us a video of our performance. When we watched it, we remembered that the stage had been made with wood placed over hydraulic lifts. We sang our two songs with our choreography and the entire stage lowered about a foot. We hadn't felt this, but the video showed that the stage sank below the lens of the stationary camera. No one told us!!

♮

In October of 1973, we had just returned from Washington. We were preparing our repertoire for the holiday season. It was close to Christmastime when a phone call came from *The Mike Douglas Show*. This TV show was filmed in Philadelphia, and they wanted a local group to sing Christmas carols in front of a backdrop of stained-glass windows. It would open and close their Christmas shows. Taping was Monday. We got the call Thursday.

The discussion whether or not to do this was typical of our leadership's decisions:

No! What will we sing?

Yes! We already know six Christmas songs.

No! We'll never get enough singers.

Yes! We'll send out a poll.

No! We haven't rehearsed.

Yes! We'll have a Saturday morning rehearsal.

No!

Yes! It's *The Mike Douglas Show*!

Yes!

Email messaging was nonexistent. The phone-chain chair was notified. She called five people, who in turn called five people, who called five more people, until all members of the chorus were notified.

We scheduled a rehearsal for Saturday morning, refreshed three Christmas carols, added three fun Christmas songs from

With Lennie and Mike Douglas.

our repertoire ("Jingle Bells!"), and put in a little staging. We were ready. On Monday morning we met the producer, who listened to our songs. Of the six songs we had prepared, he chose the three carols. Our red-and-white outfits were perfect for the camera and looked great in front of the stained-glass windows. We taped the show and then had time to stay and talk to Mike and the stage crew. It was a happy time, and many pictures were taken.

Mike Douglas.

Johnny Mann.

And for the next three years, we saw ourselves on TV, opening and closing the Christmas Season for *The Mike Douglas Show*.

And still it didn't end. When Johnny Mann was a guest on *The Mike Douglas Show*, he needed a chorus to direct. We were invited back to the show just so Johnny Mann could direct us. The song was "Jingle Bells." That was easy because everyone knows "Jingle Bells." But it was still our arrangement, and Johnny was not familiar with it. This is the way the show solved the problem. Johnny stood ten feet from the chorus. I stood closer to the chorus but out of range of the camera and directed the song. Johnny could see me and when the arrangement became unfamiliar, he would glance over to me and mimic my directions. The camera covered just the chorus and Johnny. Problem solved. The television audience never knew the difference. Brilliant!

We were asked to sing a second song, and we chose our favorite winning song, "Undecided." This was such a great showstopper and a good finale for us. We loved being in show business. Every member of the chorus began to feel like a star.

5

Building the Sound

WINNING OUR FIRST REGIONAL competition was not a given. We hadn't expected to win. But we did, and now our mantra was "never lose again." Getting to the top was hard work. Competing at the international level would be even harder. We set our sights on winning regional again and qualifying for the next international competition, which was in Seattle, Washington.

We did win and then we had eighteen months to prepare. Our toughest challenge at this time was for all of us to learn to sing with better vocal production. This was no small challenge, for we were now about seventy members. I learned how difficult it is to sing good a cappella harmony.

A cappella singers cannot tune to the piano—nor can they use Pythagorean tuning. Just (or pure) tuning is the tuning that must be sung for a cappella chords. Notes must be sung on the high side in order to make the chord "lock and ring." If you are working with a chorus, this means that every member of each section must sing each note accurately. Ideally, it will sound like one voice singing the same note. Each of the other parts tunes to the lead (melody) line. Depending on the chord you are singing, what was once sung on the high side now must be sung on the low side just to make the chord tune.

Does this make sense? To some chorus members it does, and they can analyze each chord and tune it properly and analytically.

To the rest of us, we just use our ears to tune the chord. Most chorus members use the listening method to learn how to tune to each other. This helps to eliminate one of the biggest challenges of a cappella singing: Each singer must be able to blend her voice with the singers standing around her. The vowels must match, and the vocal production must blend. If one cannot hear those who stand nearby, there is a good chance the chord will be out of tune. This is not because wrong notes are being sung; it is because the voices haven't tuned to each other.

The opposite of "ensemble singing" is "gang singing." This is when a bunch of friends get together to sing all the songs they used to know. Lots of fun. Not much tuning.

One of the special talents of a director is to place the singers next to—or near—another voice that will amplify the sound. This is where listening skills come into play. We want to hear a stereo sound, where no individual voices predominate. This allows each voice to be fully used. Singers don't want to be shushed because they are placed in the front row and told that they are singing too loudly. Proper placing of the voices will produce a full, rich stereo sound that can then be used to interpret any style of singing.

Once you have the voices in the best spot for the sound, it is important that you leave them there for at least two months until they have learned to blend and support the voices around them. If you continually move your chorus members around the stage, you will lose a good bit of the lock and ring that creates the wonderful a cappella sound. Voices learn to enhance each other as they sing together. I learned this from one of my chorus members who approached me during this time. And I quote, "When you moved me from the front row to the second row, it took me three months to blend my voice with those around me. Then you took away the voice that was behind me and substituted a different part. It took me another two months to blend my voice with hers."

By your students you shall be taught.

♮

One year Sweet Adelines International focused on proper vocal production. They wanted us to sing correctly. Throughout the country vocal classes were taught at every music school. We learned how to breathe and how to raise our soft palate. We learned to stand with our arms correctly hanging at our sides and the correct position of our mouths and tongues. We learned how to stand by putting our weight forward on our toes and then settling back until our heels just touched the floor, knees slightly bent. Sore thigh muscles followed every lesson.

We lay flat on the floor to feel the effect of deep breathing. We leaned over a chair to feel what it was like to use our head resonators.

Ann Gooch was our special friend and came to Valley Forge as our coach to help us sing well. She was the first to introduce us to good vocal production. She knew we were not interested in words like *larynx* and *trachea*, so she taught us with methods we could understand. For me, she recommended a book called *How to Train Singers*, by Larra Browning Henderson. It became a well-used training manual.

As Ann walked back and forth listening to us sing, she stopped in front of one of our members, Carol, and said simply, "You have a nice voice." Carol will never forget the compliment. This was our Ann.

She placed all of us on the risers in order to produce a bigger sound. The basses stood in a V formation, starting at the center-front and fanning out as they were positioned up the higher risers. Then she placed other voice parts around the basses. We kept these riser positions for many months. Later, as a finale for one of our performances, we sang "Battle Hymn of the Republic." Center-front on the first row was Sue, our clarion bass voice. As she sang her bass part, she felt that it wasn't her sound that she heard. It was the sound of the entire bass section. It was a huge rolling bass sound. She wanted to take a breath, but she was afraid the bass sound that was coming out of her mouth would stop. All these people singing around her were making her voice come out like the entire bass section. She felt "an ungodly feeling. A little frightening." Ann's training was paying off.

One evening I was performing with a quartet, singing the tenor part. I heard the sound of my quartet coming straight at me from the back of the room. My tenor part was loud and clear, but I didn't think it was me who was singing—it felt as though someone else was singing my part. I wanted to listen, but I was afraid that the tenor part would stop. It's a good thing I didn't because it *was* my voice that I heard. It was an incredible experience.

These are some of the feelings—almost out of body experiences—that keep a cappella singers coming back for more. We had lots of them.

♮

The future months brought others to our chorus to teach us to sing better. Each had their own tricks to help us understand what we were supposed to do to improve our sound. We finally had so many tricks that we had our own rap song. Stand up straight, suck in your stomach, lift your eyebrows, raise your soft palate, bend your knees, keep your head level, sternums up, tuck in your derriere, squeeze the dime, shoulders back, sing through your eyes, and so on and so on. (Some of these were good, some were not...but we were learning.)

It was time to get a little organized with all this education coming our way. One day, in the local newspaper, I read the story of Janellen Farmer. She was a local gal who had just graduated from Curtis Institute of Music in Philadelphia with a major in voice. The paper said she was starting a children's choir. I had to find her. I wanted to know if she could help my chorus learn to sing. This was no small task; there were now seventy-five of us. Janellen invited me to her home. I could not believe that I was on my way to interview a vocal teacher from Curtis Institute to see if she was the right one to teach my chorus. It was easy for me to describe to her the sound I wanted to hear: stress free, open, supported with lots of resonance and no (or minimum) vibrato. Janellen knew exactly what I was asking for, and so we began working a plan. She was about to become a very big influence in our lives.

Janellen would come to our rehearsal every Wednesday evening for two hours. We would schedule four members (one from each section), to leave the chorus rehearsal and go to a separate room for an hour of coaching. At the end of the hour, they would come back to rehearsal and four more members would go in for the second hour. We did this for almost two years. Members could choose to come back for another session if there was an opening. Each paid one quarter of the cost of the hour. Some members continued with private lessons. Six months into the project, the sound of the chorus matured. I was awestruck. We created a unique and beautiful sound that stayed with us for many more years. We were recognized by our sound. Other Sweet Adelines would say, "Listen to that chorus. It sounds like Valley Forge." We were very proud.

We never lost the love we had for our sound. New members learned our sound by listening and matching the sound around them. It just happened. It was osmosis again. And now that we could sing, it was time to turn our attention to our choreography. Let's dance!

6

What? Dance, Too?

WHEN ANN GOOCH BECAME our director, she introduced us to the skill of doing choreography while we sang. We thought she was crazy when she asked us to sing and move at the same time. But she insisted and we obliged.

"Ya-da Da-da Da-duh." Feet moved and hands beat out the rhythm. Not all of us loved it.

"I joined the chorus to sing, not to dance."

Ann persevered. It was worth it. Incorporating this type of physical performance into our music was a little different for our organization, and we were among the first few choruses to add staging to enhance the music. Ann chose two of our members to start the choreography team. To their surprise, she chose Gail to head the design stage and Ida to be the teacher and organizer. (Ann had the knack of developing a person's potential.) Under Ida's guidance the choreography team grew immediately. A year later, when I became the director, Ida asked me to join the team. I thought I was asked to protect the integrity of the music. Soon I was totally into the team's creativity. I forgot about being a director and just enjoyed putting motion into the music. It was comfortable being just a team member. Ideas flew around the room. Some were shot down and some were cheered. I was not always the one to protect the music from too much staging. It was others who would stop me when I became too "creative."

With Ida at the helm, we were a team of equal value. Everyone's ideas were valid. I knew that I had become just a member of the team when they announced that one of my ideas was stupid. I agreed. In the earlier years, we were able to meet during the day—as long as there was a playpen for the little ones. The kids loved playing together and learned how to be friends. They had their own little den. (Did the disappearance of the playpen give rise to the man cave?) We worked from nine in the morning until three in the afternoon. Then the next day we would come back and review our work. Sometimes we threw everything out and started again. Some days we would still be working when our older kids came home from school. This was the perfect time to see how a choreography move looked when the whole chorus was

on the risers. We asked the kids to put down their schoolbooks and stand on four steps of a staircase. We taught them to do a motion so that we could see how it might look with a full chorus. We heard "Oh, Mom!" many times.

We wanted the choreography for our contest songs to be near perfect. Not all of the team attended every session, and just when we thought we had it right, another member joined us and recommended some changes. We started again from the beginning and made the adjustments. Seeing the project from their eyes created a fresh look at our design. This was hard work, but we did it. We also learned that having too many members on the team making decisions was time consuming. When we were all satisfied with our work, Ida had a small team do the final editing. That worked well.

Sometimes, when we presented choreography to the chorus, not all of them were pleased. We came up with a plan. We invited two or three of the naysayers to come for a choreography session. They arrived with an attitude—we don't need to dance. We wanted them to realize that we had made sure any choreography we designed enhanced the music and made the singing easier. When they came, they couldn't believe how much we guarded the music. It took only one session. They never asked to come a second time. They trusted us.

We knew we were blazing a new trail for the chorus. We decided not to be bound by any laws, people's criticisms, or lack of support. We were safe with each other and thrived on our relationship. As our confidence grew, so did our reputation. Valley Forge became more successful. We gained chorus members. People began to take notice of the Valley Forge Chorus.

We continued to compete and win on the regional stage, but we always came in second in the showmanship (maybe that should be *show-ma'am-ship*) category. This upset some of us, because we were known for our creative choreography and staging. Yet we never came in first in the category of showmanship. We asked, "Why are we winning contests and only coming in second in showmanship?" And then Lee, a twenty-one-year-old member, came up to me and said, not all that sweetly, "It's you!"

I swallowed hard, said to myself, "Hang in there. Breathe slowly. Don't punch her in the nose."

And she said it again, "It's you! We are dancing and singing and having a great time and all this stuff that we're doing goes through you because you are in front of us—but it stops there because you are not a part of it."

From then on, I tried to do better by being a part of the staging—to move with the music, maybe dance a little. Lee kept pushing me to be a performer on the stage—to look like I was having the time of my life and that I just loved directing this chorus (which I did). At the end of a performance, I would quietly

say to Lee, "Is that what you mean?" And she would quietly say, "It's better." Jeez!

Finally she said, "OK. It's good. That's what I want you to do." And that's when we started coming in first in the showmanship category. What she was saying was that we had not been a unit. The chorus was performing together, but I was just somebody out there waving my arms. I don't think the chorus had any idea what (or who) was responsible for this change in our stage presence scoring, but I felt it. I loved being a part of the show. I loved that now we were coming in first in the showmanship category. I loved becoming a ham. Many of us were naturals with being a ham—with smiling and the freedom to move your body with the natural movement that suits the words. If our members were uncomfortable with this, we encouraged them to let their feelings show on their faces.

We were always challenging ourselves. True to the tradition of Valley Forge, we were constantly discussing different options— and rarely agreeing—with all our strong-willed women. We were all risk takers with unique ideas and the desire to try something new. The tigers were straining at their leashes but still pulling in the same direction.

Ya Gotta Have Heart

As Valley Forge's reputation grew, so did Ida's. She was asked to coach other choruses, help them design a choreography team. (She knew that it was better to have a team than only one choreographer who did all your choreography.) Quartets asked to have her coach them. She was invited to be on the international teaching faculty. She taught and coached throughout the Sweet Adelines world. The new chorus in Sweden was her favorite destination. With her permission I will paraphrase the notes from one of her class handouts:

Showmanship: The creation and communication of magic that enables the performer to visually reinforce the musical spell that has been established and to more effectively transport the audience into the realm of a story told to music.

This magic is not an accident. We must be musical actors communicating the story to the audience with more than just our voices and our musical product. It is said that a cer-

tain percentage of your audience hear with their eyes. We need to let our faces show the emotion that we are singing. We need to act. We need to sell. We need to rehearse the acting until we become the character in the story we are telling through song.

Expressing emotions and acting is very difficult. It takes much work and rehearsing. However, when your entire chorus is acting the role visually and with sincerity, the musical performance is uplifted into the intangible something—the magic for which we are all striving.

The Uptune

We had a certain method to creating our choreography:

1 The director must tell you what kind of interpretation she will use. The choreography can be made cute, dynamic, sexy, or any other adjective. For instance, the song "Rock-a-Bye Your Baby with a Dixie Melody" can be sung cute and flirty or like a red-hot mama. This is the decision for the director to make. It affects the style of choreography you use.

2 Choose a word that you will use for all the choreography. An example would be words like dynamic, simple, flirty, powerful, classy, and loving. Does all the choreography fit your chosen word?

3 Search for a well-known person who exemplifies your adjective. For example, Marilyn Monroe exemplifies flirty; Ethel Merman, powerful; and Prince, dynamic.

4 Design the choreography following these guidelines.

Designing the choreography for "Nobody's Sweetheart Now" (our winning contest uptune) is the perfect example of the strug-

gle to do it right. Our team was having a difficult time coming up with the theme for our competition song. We were looking for perfection. It was important this year. We felt we had to design something outstanding that fit the song, and we were running out of time. We tried different ideas, but none of them satisfied us. Then we tried again. Nothing was right.

"Painted Lips" was our working title, but the real name of the song was "Nobody's Sweetheart Now." We thought of Michael Jackson's style, but we decided that wasn't right either. Finally, we popped a video of Liza Minnelli into the VCR. There it was. The jazz hands. Liza had energy in her hands, in her arms, and in her legs.

"That's it! That's it!"

We put Liza Minnelli into our staging. It was so like Valley Forge. When we got to the part of the song that says, "When you walk down the avenue," we used the TV staging of a car commercial. This time it was jazz legs. We felt that we had a choreography plan that the chorus would love, that allowed us to sing our best, and that presented the Valley Forge Chorus at its finest. Done! Now it's time to put it out there.

7

Internationals Two and Three

1975–1977

SWEET ADELINES CHORUSES WERE popping up all over the country. The international organization must have felt it was time to redistribute the regional boundaries. Some regions had fifty choruses eligible to compete, while others had only nine. Regional competitions were also lopsided with quartets. Region 15 included Eastern Pennsylvania, New Jersey, and Long Island. Ramapo Valley, Valley Forge, and Island Hills, all big choruses (over seventy members), were in Region 15. Just south of us, in the Baltimore–Washington, D.C., area, was Region 14, with two more big choruses, Dundalk and Elkridge.

With the redistribution, Valley Forge and the southern Pennsylvania and New Jersey choruses were put together with the northern Maryland choruses to create Region 19. This meant we no longer competed with Ramapo or Island Hills, but we gained Dundalk and Elkridge. At that time, Dundalk's director was Freddie King (see chapter 1). In 1975, the Dundalk Chorus and the Valley Forge Chorus would go to Seattle, representing Region 14 and Region 15 (even though both choruses were in Region 19).

That's a lot of plane tickets.

Seattle is almost 3,000 miles away. At the time, it cost $153 for a round-trip ticket. (In 2019 dollars, that trip would cost $739.)

Lennie talked to Doug and Suzanne, the Atlas Travel agents that she hired to book business travel for her company. Suzanne asked, "Why don't you charter a plane? It would be cheaper."

That's all the incentive Lennie needed. A quick call to the contact for the Dundalk Chorus and the answer came back, "Check it out. We're in." So the planning began.

To pay for the trip, we all saved money. And we raised a bunch of it. Valley Forge had two big fundraisers. We put together a

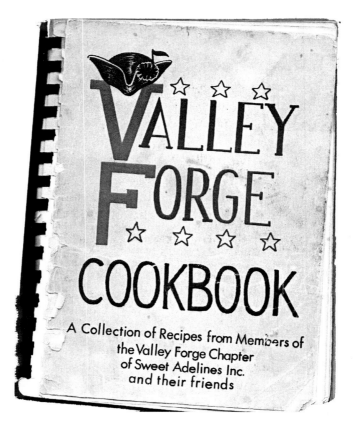

My welll-used copy of the Valley Forge Cookbook.

Valley Forge Cookbook. Almost every member, past and present, shared at least one of her favorite recipes. To personalize the book, Barb drew crazy stick figures on each page. The cover was red, white, and blue. When it was done, late one night a couple of members, with a few of our menfolk, went to the newspaper office where they worked. They made five hundred copies of the book, then collated and bound them. No one at the newspaper ever knew.

Most of us still use this cookbook, because it is the very best. Every time I am asked to bring something to a potluck supper, I whip out the *Valley Forge Cookbook* and make a triple-batch of Baked Bean Surprise. My cookbook has lost its cover and has notes and food smudges all over the pages. I wish I had a clean copy.

The men of Valley Forge put on a Monte Carlo night for us. They did it all without our help. (We were busy rehearsing.) They promoted it, charged an admission fee, located and manned the gambling tables, and ordered and served the drinks. This was a fun, successful evening, and it greatly added to our finances.

At the same time, we were going back to contest for a second shot at the international competition, and we were determined to sing well. It was time to bring in a top coach to help us. Sylvia Alsbury, from Arizona, was our choice. Sylvia was an international arranger, judge, teacher, and our friend. Sylvia, who knew what the judges wanted, listened and watched us rehearse our two contest songs. Then she asked, "What are you doing?"

We had stopped moving with the music. We were concentrating only on the singing part of the contest. "Well, we're supposed to sing well," we said. Then Sylvia took several of us aside and said, "You look like you are afraid, clinging to the risers. You've got to risk it." Then she turned to the chorus and repeated her comment. She wanted us to move more, but we had people within

Baked Bean Surprise
from the *Valley Forge Cookbook*

Submitted by Muff Allen

This is the recipe from the *Valley Forge Cookbook* that I use most often. Every time I am asked to bring something to a potluck supper, this is what I bring. If I triple the recipe it will feed thirty people with leftovers. I freeze the leftovers in two-serving containers—perfect as sides for a quick meal. Sometime during the gathering, someone always asks me, "What makes them so good?"

I confess, "It's the crushed pineapple."

Ingredients
- 1 can (28 oz.) baked beans
- 2 Tbsp. Worcestershire sauce
- ½ cup brown sugar
- 1 small onion, chopped
- 1 green pepper, chopped
- ½ lb. bacon, diced
- 1small can crushed pineapple
- ½ lg. bottle ketchup (probably around 10 oz.—use your judgment)

Preparation
Brown bacon; remove to casserole. Throw away fat. Add brown sugar, onion, and green pepper in same pan used for cooking bacon, and brown. Add all ingredients to bacon in casserole and mix. Bake at 300 for about 2 hours.

I accidentally baked it 3 hours uncovered. It was crispy but delicious.

Extra good when made the day before.

the chorus who were arguing that the choreography was keeping us from singing well (all those tigers, straining at their leashes).

The old comment "I joined the chorus to sing, not to dance" was changing the way we were preparing for contest. We didn't know any better. We were known for our staging and reaching out to the audience, but now we had members who only wanted to sing well. Now we had something to lose. Some thought that if we danced and moved about the stage, as we usually did, it would detract from the overall scoring of the contest. We were new to the international world. But Sylvia wasn't. She told us to risk it. We put ourselves back together and became a "risk it" chorus once again. After that, we never forgot that performing was more than just the music.

The time was getting near for our trip to Seattle. Our plan was to spend the preceding night at the airport. We'd leave Philadelphia at 4:00 a.m., then fly to Baltimore and pick up the Dundalk Chorus. The plane was a United DC-8, and the cost to charter it was $34,000 (over $180,000 today). Doug, from the travel agency, was there in Philly to make sure we all were boarded. Lennie and the chair for Dundalk didn't want members of each chorus all sitting together, so when they assigned the seats, they alternated the rows—one Valley Forge row, one Dundalk row.

The trip to Baltimore was short and uneventful. Boarding the Dundalk Chorus was not. It was taking forever, one person every five minutes and we had seventy to board. "I'm-in-charge-Lennie" stormed off the plane and found out the agents were checking the social security numbers of every Dundalk member—something that had already been done. She stopped that. Problem solved. The plane was finally loaded. All was well. We took off. Lennie later received an apology letter from United Airlines.

On board, Valley Forge had a stack of red, white, and blue "Support Valley Forge" ribbons with them. As soon as the fasten seat belt sign was turned off, every Valley Forge member got up, turned around in her seat, and pinned one of these ribbons on the shirt of the Dundalk member seated behind her. That started it. When the flight attendants wheeled the drink cart to the center of the plane, it was bedlam. No one stayed seated. Everyone visited each other around the drink cart. They served us for a while and then left the cart in the aisle and hid at their station. The pilots talked to us on the intercom. "Would you people please disperse yourselves from the middle of the plane instead of all standing around the bar? This will make handling the plane much easier." We complied—almost. Suzanne, from Atlas Travel, met us in Seattle. She took us to our hotel. It was a good thing. By then we needed all the help we could get.

Being together with Dundalk made the transition to Region 19 an easy chore. They were such a fun bunch. We heard that four of their members (a quartet) were shopping in Seattle before the contest began. They bought four wild hair wigs, each in a different hair color. Since they stood center-front for the contest, what better time to wear their wigs than at their first contest rehearsal? Freddie King was speechless. Dundalk was laughing so hard he didn't know what to do or say—maybe because one of the quartet members was Freddie's wife, wig and all.

Seattle was foggy. We saw Mount Rainer one day, visited the Space Needle the next, and that was it. One comment from the emcee on stage was this: "Seattle women have wonderful complexions because they have so little sunshine." And "Please don't love our city too much. We like it just the way it is." It was all in good fun. Maybe?

When it was time to compete, we were in the traffic pattern, and moved to the backstage area, ready to enter the stage. The preceding chorus had just left the stage and the stagehands motioned for us to enter—just as the emcee announced the intermission. We stood on the risers behind the curtains for a good half hour while the audience went to get something to eat, and the judges retired to their private room for refreshments and rest.

We survived. "This is the year," we said. "If we are champions, we will handle this." We were—we handled the waiting well. We placed fifth, moving up one place from the D.C. contest. We were beginning to congeal as a chorus. Four of my chorus members gave me a wooden plaque they had found in a shop in Seattle. They signed it on the back. It read:

Roses are red.
Violets are blue
You are our leader
And we love you.

I loved it.

Chorus members Linda, Ellen, Carolyn, and Pat found a plaque in Seattle that showed two little teddy bears with balloons in their hands, running away from a large alligator who had one foot on a scooter and was pushing as fast as he could with the other foot, trying to catch up to the bears. The alligator was saying, "I must hurry, for there they go, and I am their leader." This put into words exactly how I felt about the chorus. Before we competed on the stage, I read the words to the chorus. They told me later that it had made them feel strong and confident on the stage. They knew how I felt about them and that I loved them, just the crazy way they were. And I did.

After the contest, we were given a cassette tape recording of our performance. One of the chords we sang had a very low note, which we did not think our basses could sing. They couldn't. It was an undertone—our first—and now we had a recording of it. Yay!

♮

During this competition week, while everyone else was out on the town having dinner together, Millie found one of our Valley Forge Chorus members alone in her room with a loaf of bread and a jar of peanut butter. She had brought it from home so she could make herself a sandwich for her dinner. She had barely scraped together plane fare. When we came home from Seattle, we realized that we were going to be traveling to international competitions, hopefully often, and there were some members who would not be able to attend without some financial help.

Millie went to work on it. She created the Angel Fund for each of our next Internationals. Millie discreetly discovered who needed financial help to cover the hotel room and cost of the plane ticket. When our members heard about the Angel Fund, the donations poured in. No amounts were specified, it was completely volunteer. The people who used these funds varied from year to year. No one was ever left behind for financial reasons. Each year, when it was time to go to International, one of the husbands from the group asked Millie to collect as much money as she could, tell him how much more she needed, and he'd make up the difference. He then gave that amount to the Angel Fund. This was all done very quietly—so quietly, in fact, that the fund had three names: the Angel Fund, the Dream Fund, and the Sunshine Fund.

♮

As a P.S. to this story, there was one member who was on the receiving end of the fund most of the time. Then one year she approached Millie with an envelope and said, "Now it's my turn to give." And she did. She reimbursed the Angel Fund the entire amount given to her through the years.

♮

The next International was held in London, England. Valley Forge placed first in the new Region 19's contest and qualified.

Immediately after we won the contest and returned to our hospitality room, we found posters of London pinned to all the walls. There was a red rose on the table for each of us. The men had planned our celebration. And celebrate we did. At three in the morning, there was a knock on the door. You can imagine our surprise when we opened the door and saw two big police dogs held on leashes by two very big security men. Politely, they said, "Quiet down a little." We did. End of party.

I had no idea what songs to choose for the contest in London, eighteen months away. I couldn't find any song that would excite the chorus. One day, I was talking to my friend Gene Cokeroft, a musical icon from Miami. He mentioned that he had thought a song from 1909 would make a good arrangement and would I be interested? It was "Cubanola Glide," composed by Terry Von Tilzer. Gene suggested changing the words to "Pennsylvania Glide." That was easy. This song was something different. No one had ever heard it before, it would be fun to sing, and I knew the arrangement would be terrific. Valley Forge learned it and then developed the choreography for it. It sounded great.

London was magnificent. We were so honored to perform in Royal Albert Hall. We visited as much of London as we had time for.

We placed fourth that year and moved up one more step toward number one. We did end up retiring "Pennsylvania Glide." It turned out that it just wasn't our kind of song. It was a good contest song and choreographed well, but it was too old, too different, and too unfamiliar. We never sang it again. But we still smile when someone mentions it.

♮

After the London contest, we had one free day before the plane left to take us home. Barb and I were sitting in the hotel wondering what to do with our time. She said to me, "Let's go to Paris." I thought she was crazy, but she repeated the idea. I hesitated again but she didn't listen to any of my negative reasoning. Suddenly we were on our way to spend one day in Paris.

We ran. We ran to the train station that takes you to Paris. It was a two-hour-and-fifteen-minute ride.

How We Did Paris in a Half Hour

When we arrived, we grabbed a taxi and said, "The Louvre." We ran to the lady at the front desk and asked, "Où est la *Mona Lisa*?" (I used the smattering of French I had left over from my school days.) She just pointed in the direction and we took off. We were surprised to see the Winged Victory as we scurried along the corridor. Ida always told us to stand like the Winged Victory.

The *Mona Lisa* was so small.

You can't go to Paris and not see the Eiffel Tower. We wanted to go all the way up. They told us it would be an extra fee to go to the top. We said OK. The two attendants did not look happy with our answer, but we didn't know why. The first part of the ride was magnificent. It was so high we saw all of Paris from the large windows. The attendants took us up the final distance to the top. This elevator was smaller and traveled much slower—and made loud, funny noises. Unless we stood by the window, we saw only sky. The view included the beams of metal holding the cables of the elevator—very close to the windows. Our attendants looked at each other and we thought we could see perspiration on their foreheads. Were they nervous? I was.

We were famished when we landed back on firm ground. Here we were, two Americans who didn't speak the language, looking for a restaurant. We saw a small café that served wine and light fare. We had no idea what we ate, but whatever it was, it was delicious. So was the wine. The owner of the café was not there and the young men who waited on us (garçons?) made us laugh all the time.

I have a wine glass collection at home. I try to buy one glass each place I visit. "Would I be able to buy the wine glass I used?" The young waiter said no. Then, realizing that his manager was not in the café, he wrapped up the glass and motioned for me to hide it. I put it in my pocket.

We wanted to visit the artists in Montmartre, but we couldn't leave the café without getting hugs and a kiss on both cheeks from the waiters. I was enveloped in the biggest bear hug. I thought I heard a snap, but there was so much laughter I wasn't sure. It was getting late, but we managed to spend some time in the artist colony at Montmartre. There was no time left to see Notre Dame. We took a taxi to Paris Gare du Nord and made the last train to London. As the train whizzed through the streets of Paris, Barb tapped me on the shoulder to look out the window. There was Notre Dame. We smiled.

The next day we were on our way back home. My wine glass was in three pieces, but some good glue and steady hands made it like new. Today it stands, glued together, in my curio cabinet along with my wine glass collection of memories.

Once home, we went right back to work. We had so many more shows to produce and performances scheduled. These were the best of times.

8

Gospel Train—Happy Birthday to Me

HOW DO SEVENTY WOMEN keep a secret from their director? I've always loved gospel music. (In my next life I'm going to direct a mixed-voice gospel a cappella choir). I had heard Renee Craig's chorus sing her arrangement of a medley she called "Gospel Train." It had the songs "Joshua Fought the Battle of Jericho" and "Ezekiel Saw the Wheel" together in one song. Wow! It was no secret that I would love to have it in Valley Forge's repertoire.

Without my knowledge, Ginny, the birthday gift ringleader, asked Renee if we could sing her song. She answered, "Of course." When it arrived, the chorus realized that the two gospel songs had five key changes in the music. But they learned the whole song during special rehearsals. I knew nothing about it.

It was my birthday, and the chorus was ready to give me my birthday present. When I walked into the rehearsal room, they were all bunched up on the risers with a great big ribbon wrapped around them. A large bow was attached to the front row. They sang "Gospel Train" for me. I was so happy. I loved the chorus for their gift of music.

Our team immediately created choreography for the medley. We made tambourines out of ten-inch red paper plates by cutting out the centers. Then we pasted red streamers down one half of the round plate, which gave us room to grab the plates and shake them. For performances, we gave a real tambourine to Ginny. She stood on the third row, slightly left of center—perfect

Big birthday present.

for hiding the real tambourine. No one could see it, but it made enough noise to sound like each member of the chorus had their own tambourine. For performances, we divided up the red paper plates, and as we entered the stage we placed the correct number of them on the ends of each riser step.

"Gospel Train" became our finale. While the emcee said our farewells, we passed the plates down the rows, one to each member. On cue, close to the end of the song, the red tambourines would appear. We shook them and tapped them and swung them up over our heads. Ginny's tambourine made the sound. It was a wild and crazy finish. "How'd you get them?" we were asked. "Where did they come from?" It made the perfect finale.

The first time we performed "Gospel Train" for a large crowd was on the Saturday night championship show after we had won the regional contest. We warmed up in a room far from the stage. The choreography was quite new, and we really didn't know it very well, but we all wanted to sing this new song for the region. We were singing last on the show, so we spent our warm-up time refreshing our minds with the new movements. And naturally, with our thoughts on our feet, our singing wasn't wonderful. The stage crew and other performers waiting to sing would pass through the warm-up room. Those who heard us "practicing" were questioning the contest results. "Did they really just win the contest?" They must have been thinking that we were never going to make it.

It was almost time for us to sing and we were still rehearsing the new choreography. We came on stage like gangbusters and started our allotted three-song package. It was the last song at the end of the show. I felt the responsibility to make sure the chorus remembered all the new movements. I knew the choreography well and was prepared to remind them as they sang so they would know what was coming up next. Little did I know!

"Gospel train's a-comin'. Children git on board!" And then it started. The chorus's singing developed a life of its own and took off. They were ahead of me with the choreography, and I realized that I had better get out of their way because they were totally in control. They were just driving that music right out to the audience. I stopped trying to direct them and just enjoyed being in front of them. All I could do was watch them laugh and tap their tambourines. I was laughing the whole time because they were having so much fun. They knew what they were doing to me. They were ahead of me, and it was making me step aside to let them go. I honestly felt they might run me down. And they knew that I knew what they were doing.

I loved the standing ovation.

9

Twangs and Dolphins and Elephants

As a director, I've learned that conducting with visualization tools helps all singers remember the basics of good singing. Consider "Take me out to the ball game / Take me out with the crowd." If you want the chorus to maintain a smooth sound between the two phrases, without taking a breath, you might say, "Picture yourself on a smooth road coming to a bridge over a river. *Game* is the end of the road and *take* is the landing on the other side of the river. Picture your car (your voice) going onto the bridge at *game* and landing on the other side at *take*." A little help with some support from your hands will make going over the bridge smoother, and the chorus won't drop the sound between the phrases. This makes it easier in the future when you find the chorus is getting tired and dropping the sound between words. Just lift your hand over the bridge—the chorus will follow. And at rehearsal, for a little fun you might yell, "Don't get wet!!" as you approach the bridge. You can obviously use this motion for many other songs, and I'm sure you can find a better example than *game* and *take*.

Music that has a chromatic scale going down will sometimes sound as though each note is labored. I asked my chorus to picture a beautiful, wooded, spring creek flowing over a waterfall until it joins the holding pool at the bottom—soft and cool and peaceful. Try it. Use your hands. You will quickly get the "rocks" out of the passage.

Sometimes, you have to improvise. During one performance, we sang a country and western song. The chorus was having so much fun—they were totally into the song. But we came to a couple of measures that I felt should be sung with a twang. We had never talked about doing it that way at rehearsal, and here we were in the middle of a performance.

I wrinkled my nose, twisted my mouth, and maybe even pretended there was a banjo in my hand. The chorus must have understood what I was doing, or they felt the song needed something, too, because the sound of a western twang filled the auditorium. They were in tune with each other and with me. We laughed and sang our way to the end of the song. Yes, the audience loved it. These moments are magic at a performance—something you just can't explain. Or plan.

♮

When teaching a new song, the effort to direct the correct phrasing and tempo can be maddening. Your arms flail and your fingers snap. Your hands clap and your foot taps. You try all sorts of devices to get the chorus to sing it right. It doesn't work. Most of the time it's because the chorus hasn't yet learned the notes and words, and they can't begin to do what you want until they have learned the music. Hint: teach well the notes, phrasing, and correct vowels *first*. *Then* add the pizzazz. It's harder to relearn the notes and vowels than it is to relearn the correct phrasing.

Be open to learning new tools from strange sources. The trainer of the dolphins at SeaWorld says that he makes big motions at the beginning of the new lesson for the dolphins. When they have learned the new trick, he then starts reducing his motions until the dolphins respond to bare finger twitches. I found that it works with large choruses, too. The coach of a professional baseball team makes the pitcher who has a fastball practice improving his fastball. He doesn't try to make his curveball perfect and forget the fastball. This isolation is hard to practice when taking a chorus into a contest. Maybe the best way to explain it is this: don't waste time correcting small mistakes; make sure the best part of your chorus is as perfect as you can make it.

♮

When you have seventy members of an active chorus and you want to make a slight change in the interpretation of a phrase in your music, you must have all seventy members understand where you are heading and then follow you. In other words, you must tell them.

We were working on a rhythm change in one of our songs. It was taking a long, long time for the chorus to get it. I was getting just a tad frustrated—trying all different kinds of words and directions to make it work. In desperation and with a smile on my face I said to the chorus, "Getting you to make this change is like trying to move a herd of elephants." Be careful what you say. The following rehearsal, we tried again to learn the rhythm change. At a given signal, I heard the sound of an elephant coming from a chorus member, and I saw her raise her arm like an elephant's trunk and snort. Then I saw seventy women throw peanuts at me. But we learned the change.

♮

Sometimes you need more than visual cues. Sometimes you need to be able to say something to help guide your chorus. 1n 1984, Mary Lou Retton won the gold medal for individual all-around gymnastics. That year, it was written that her coach said to her, as she walked out on the floor to compete, "Remember, Mary Lou. Never better." Brilliant, short, easy to remember. A comment like that will stay in your brain during your performance, not a long, profound, motivational speech that you try to remember but ends up distracting you. That's great coaching.

10

PVIs

THE REGENT FOR THE newly formed Region 19 was Jo, better known as Big Red. She was tall and had red hair. It was her job to put together our new governing board. Big Red added me to the group, along with my buddies Ida and Lennie. When we started to work together, we were loud, we laughed, and we made decisions. One decision was to choose me as the region's new director of musical activities (DMA). My job was to make sure, at each regional meeting, that there was some kind of musical education for the directors, assistant directors, section leaders, arrangers, and choreographers.

As DMA, I traveled around Region 19 to visit and coach choruses and quartets. The first quartet I coached was an unknown foursome from the Elkridge, Maryland, chapter called Signature Sound, which won the international quartet contest many years later. Thus began my coaching career. My reputation was growing. I was invited to fly to Florida and Canada and, by invitation of International, to fly to England to coach a new chorus. My style of coaching is low key. I'm sure this is one reason they chose me to visit a brand new chapter in a brand new country: I wouldn't scare them.

Valley Forge was busy singing for our audiences and preparing for contests and shows. We thought about following Renee's suggestion to "just do shows," but what would we give up? Contests? We didn't think so. We continued on this busy path, trying to do everything. And for four years, while I was DMA, I wondered why I believed them when they said, "Oh, it's only one night a week."

Why do you always remember things you'd like to forget? There were two important lessons I learned about coaching during this time.

Number 1. My first-ever teaching weekend was at a retreat in Jacksonville, Florida. The scripts were written by Sally Eggleston, who was the premiere faculty for this international event. I was in training and would team-teach with her. She had sent me a copy of all the scripts so that I would be prepared. Friday night came, but Sally didn't. Her plane was late. I think they call this "baptism by fire." When she arrived later that evening (after the class was over), she didn't seem at all worried that I wouldn't be able to handle her class by myself. Maybe she didn't know I was new? Her confidence in me was awesome. The rest of the weekend ran smoothly, without a hitch. This was not true for all my early assignments.

Number 2. A chorus hired me for a weekend coaching session. Friday night I was asked to get to know the chorus by listening to them sing several of their songs and then to party with them afterwards. Some members of the chorus had asked for private vocal instruction (PVI), so they invited a local vocal teacher to visit with them on Friday night. She was to take a few chorus members into a special quiet room and give them, one at a time, a PVI. When their vocal coach was late—really late—they asked me if I would do the PVIs for the group. Inside I screamed, "No! I don't do PVIs! Never have! Never wanted to! Never will!" Outwardly I said, "Oh, please, no. We can wait for the vocal teacher." Then I realized that their suggestion was not a polite request. This was an outright order for me to start work.

I was stuck. I knew I had no formal schooling in the world of vocal arts. I was sure this was the end of my coaching career.

They were going to see that I was totally incompetent when it came to vocal production. But, with a smile on my face, I walked into the room, closed the door, and turned to the group with confidence. One by one we started down the line of eager and excited chorus members. The first person began to sing. I heard her tight voice trying to come out. I took her head and gently moved it while she was singing. It relaxed her enough to make a major change in her sound. Good. The second singer had a nice voice, but she was singing with her chin tilted up in the air, completely tightening her vocal cords. "Put your chin level with the ground," I said. Yay! It worked. She sounded much better. The third singer began. "Come on, stand up straight. Don't crunch your windpipe so that the air doesn't come out smoothly." Bingo! Another success.

We were bonding and enjoying working with each other. It started to be fun because I was having some success and feeling good about my musical worth. Then the door opened. The real vocal teacher had arrived. "Well, let's start all over again with person number 1, shall we?" She nodded to me with a sweet smile. I wanted to hide and then run out of the room. I was sure she would be upset with what I had done to her students. I moved to the side of the room as she took over the class.

Starting with the first student, she listened to her sing for a while. Then she took the student's head in her hands and moved it around—exactly as I had done. Inwardly, I was thrilled, but I remained silent. She continued down the line. "Put your chin level with the ground," she said. Yep! And the next singer? "Stand up straight." Hooray! I breathed a sigh of relief. The official voice teacher had validated my suggestions. With a start like that, the rest of the weekend went beautifully.

But I still won't do PVIs.

11

Showtime

OUR CHORUS LIFE NOW revolved around contests, singing entertaining performances, and producing our own shows. To have a show of our own meant choosing a theme and finding music to fit that theme. Then we added staging, dialogue, and costumes. To help our shows reach perfection, we learned lighting and sound management. We auditioned and hired other performing groups to add variety (and time) to our shows. We secured a venue that was affordable and big enough to seat our expected audience. We created our stage manager position for one of our chorus members. Her job was to coordinate all aspects of the show during the dress rehearsal and the final performance. She cued the lighting, sound, and chorus movement on the stage. She wore a headset with mic.

Our shows were more theater than concert. Whatever we dreamed of doing, someone in the chorus stepped up to play the part. This included tap dancers, soloists, and actors with speaking parts. If we needed a male actor, we found a volunteer. The shows became so intricate that we picked the next show chair before the current show was even presented. Each chair served for a three-year rotation. Our show chair was usually a member who volunteered because she had an idea for the show and wanted to see it through to completion. Our first meeting was open to anyone who wanted to attend. This was a wild and creative idea fest. The show title and theme were discussed. Music availability was explored. (You can't have a theme show if no suitable music is available.) The director was always there.

After the open meeting, the entire event was turned over to the show chair. She chose two assistants—one to manage the performance and one to manage the venue. The show chair worked closely with the director. (Remember the "final approval" for all performances?) Our rehearsals, music, and staging were planned in three-month intervals. We continually reevaluated because we were often invited for unexpected performances and had to rehearse the lineup, or we needed more or less time to learn new music or staging. This was done together by three people: the show chair, director, and staging chair. Our goal was to have all the music and staging learned a month before show night. This gave us the last four rehearsals to put the show together.

Rehearsal number 1 was the first act—the theme of the show—complete with staging and emcees. (The second act was right after the intermission, and that belonged to the guest performers.)

Rehearsal number 2 was the third act—the finale—and a review of any places in the first act that needed work.

Rehearsal number 3 was the final work session.

Rehearsal number 4—the last rehearsal and the fourth before the big night—was the dress rehearsal with all three acts. No stops, no changes, only fixes for major goofs! We rehearsed it all. The emcees spoke, we entered and left the stage, we introduced the imaginary guest quartet, and we even practiced accepting the applause.

We made no big changes to the music the last month during these four rehearsals. They were run-throughs with a "sink or swim" attitude. It was a learning time for each individual to be aware of what she needed to do to be her one hundred percent on our stage. It was time to let the chorus be responsible for the quality of the show. Oddly enough, the chorus's sound improved as their confidence developed. The one thing we didn't want to happen was to call the chorus for a dress rehearsal at the venue and then make them stand around while we adjusted the lights and the props. Therefore, our tech rehearsal—lighting, curtain, sound, and props—was done another day, or, depending on availability, two hours before our final dress rehearsal at our venue.

The stage manager was responsible for both the tech and dress rehearsals. A take-charge person was absolutely necessary at this time—someone who knew exactly what was happening and could move many chorus members around a stage. Cooperation from the chorus was a given.

"I'm-in-charge" Lennie was often one of our stage managers. We were comfortable being in her hands. She made sure I was in the right position on the stage and that I moved at the appropriate time. I was not in charge. It was refreshing. I could enjoy the show and not be worried about anything.

We were ready. It was show time.

Stars and Stripes

Our show chair, Barb, wanted the chorus to sing the Sousa march "The Stars and Stripes Forever" and march around to the back of the risers, come up and over the top, and then march down toward the front of the stage carrying an American flag. And she wanted to end with the boom of a real cannon. John Peterson, a member of the local men's barbershop chorus, had arranged the Sousa march. He was thrilled to share it with us. It was an incredibly complicated piece of music. The tenors were the piccolos, the baritones were the trombones, the leads were the trumpets, and the basses were the sousaphones and drums. And it worked. The husband of one of our members was able to borrow an honest-to-goodness cannon that fired multicolored paper confetti.

In order to march down our risers from the top back row, we needed an additional set of steps to get up from the back. Our stage management team borrowed another set of risers from the Mainliners men's barbershop chorus and placed them against the back of our own set. This made steps up the back to the top of our risers. Ida and our choreography committee made little pieces of colored paper with numbers on them representing each member of the chorus. They were color-coded according to what part each person sang. Everyone had her own number. This made it easy to teach each person where they needed to be and when.

We didn't want one part to be predominant. We were still a four-part chorus. The staging team moved the colored slips around on a tabletop until they figured out how to have the front row go around to the back of the stage, followed by the rest of the chorus, as they marched up and then down from the top riser. We shouldn't have lost our sound just because we were moving. But we did. We solved the problem by making an audio recording of our singing. During the performance, we played our song through the sound system of the theater and sang along with the music as we marched around the stage. The audience never knew. As the front row divided itself in half, they turned to the outside of the stage and disappeared behind the risers, followed by the rest of the chorus. Stagehands (our men) gave each front-row woman an American flag as they came around to the back. The two groups met in the middle behind the stage, stepped up the extra set of risers, stopped at the top, faced the audience, raised the flag, and then proceeded down—in step—to the front of the stage, all while waving the American flag. The rest of the chorus followed the front row. We had five rows of marchers coming up and over the double set of risers. When all members had made it back to their original row, the front row marched around in a circle and lined up in front of the chorus. And then the cannon went off. Bam! Confetti spewed over the audience. End of show.

♮

During the following months word spread around the region that Valley Forge had sung the "The Stars and Stripes Forever" march. At the following convention (in New York City, before the creation of Region 19), late at night after the Saturday night show, George Avener asked us to do the march for him. We thought he was kidding. There was no way we could perform: We needed two sets of risers. Our risers were on the bottom floor of the hotel. Island Hill's risers were on the top floor in a large hospitality room.

But George wasn't kidding! So, the men of the Island Hills chapter said they would get our risers. They lugged them through the hotel and up the service elevators to the top floor. In the meantime, word had spread all over the hotel that the Valley Forge Chorus was going to do "Stars and Stripes" in the Island Hills hospitality room on the top floor. It was a midnight performance. The room was big enough to have the risers set up back-to-back. Then all the convention members that could fit crowded in to hear us. We sang for them. We marched up and down the risers and around to the back. We came up over the risers proudly waving imaginary flags. The room was full of singing, clapping, marching people. We didn't need our taped-in music. We didn't have the cannon, either. But that probably would have alerted the fire marshals and caused the hotel to be evacuated. Oh, well!

Burlesque

One year our show chair, Lennie, wanted a burlesque theme. What a resource we found in an aged couple who lived next door to one of our members. They had been in vaudeville. Lennie and I

visited the neighbors for an afternoon and listened to the memories of the wonderful acts that we could pay homage to our show:
Burns and Allen, Jimmy Durante, and Abbott and Costello—or
our versions of them anyway—all made their way to the Valley
Forge Chorus's stage. The neighbors told us about the Cherry Sisters, who sang off-key and had rotten fruits and vegetables thrown
at them from the audience. And then they told us of the men's
ballet. Ballet? With men? We looked at each other. You're kidding. "Just ask them!" the neighbors said. "All they can say is no."

The Ballet

The first act we created was the ballet. Very quickly we had eight
men volunteer to learn to dance. These were our brothers, friends,
and husbands—and they all thought this was going to be a fun,
easy task. For their ballet, we chose the song "Mighty Lak' a
Rose."

> Sweetest little fellow, everybody knows,
> Don't know what to call him but he's mighty like a rose.
> Lookin' at his mammy with eyes so shiny blue
> Makes you think that heaven is comin' close to you.

We felt that there was no need to learn the four-part harmony
because no one would be listening to us anyway, so the chorus
learned only the melody line. We recorded it so that the men could
learn to dance to the music. The men's first dance instructor was
from our chorus. Gail had a background in ballet and was trying
to teach them rudimentary ballet steps. It wasn't working. Her
comment to us was, "All they do is carry on and giggle. They're
not listening to me."

The gentleman who volunteered to play George Burns for our
Burns and Allen skit came to the rescue. His friend Seymour was

a professional ballet teacher. Aha! He agreed to use our recording of "Mighty Lak' a Rose," and he created a dance routine for the men.

At their first rehearsal together, Seymour did a couple of pirouettes. This got our men's attention, and Seymour had no trouble with giggles after that. He took no pity on them, and he taught them difficult steps. Their muscles were sore, and they moaned and groaned after each rehearsal. But soon they learned to dance and twirl their *male* partners.

For their dance outfit the men each bought a pair of long johns and gave them to our costume team to dye—*pink*. Then the team made pink netting tutus for the men out of old Valley Forge costumes. Seymour insisted they wear high-top black shoe-boots. "If you don't have them, buy them." On their heads they wore identical short, blond wigs.

On stage, the chorus sang with their hands clasped in front of them at their waists. No smiles. This was serious business. As we sang the men onto the stage, they started all in a straight line but soon they paired up—doing lovely spins and dips with their partners. As they spun around the stage, they caught the eye of the chorus members and broke into a big laugh, but that was all gone by the time they turned around to face the audience. This was serious business for them, and it was not funny—except to the audience. I have never heard a sold-out auditorium shake with so much laughter. And when the dancers clasped the thigh of their own partner, held him by the hand and spun him around, the uproar was huge. The audience was laughing so hard we could not hear ourselves sing. The men did a wonderful job, sore muscles and all.

Shortly after that show, we were asked to sing on the Saturday night show after the regional competition. We invited our male ballerinas to perform with us. They agreed. We think they

Men's ballet.

agreed because they liked the screams, laughter, and cheers that came from the audience. They were the stars. Isn't it amazing what eight men in pink tutus, blond wigs, and black shoe-boots can do to 1,500 women?

The Cherry Sisters

The biggest surprise for the chorus was our very own Cherry Sisters. Two of our quiet and unassuming members decided to rehearse singing out of tune in order to audition for the part of the Cherry Sisters. They were wonderfully awful. We didn't know they were such hams. When you've been trained to sing accurately, it is hard to sing out of tune.

Fake fruits and vegetables were provided to the audience members seated on the front row. Someone snitched on us, though, and real fruits and vegetables were sneaked into the auditorium. The culprit was the houseguest of one of our members. The house-

guest raided their host's refrigerator for all their dry vegetables—
carrots, celery, but thankfully no bananas or tomatoes. The real
stuff.

Jimmy Durante

For our Jimmy Durante scene, we looked once again to Renee
Craig for music. She had an arrangement of a medley of Jimmy
Durante songs, which included "You Gotta Start Off Each Day
with a Song," followed by "Who Will Be with You When I'm Far
Away?" and ending with "Can Broadway Do Without Me?" Two
members of the choreography team heard about a teacher at the
local high school who knew all about Jimmy. The teacher showed
the team the many movements that Jimmy made, and the team
incorporated all of them into our choreography. We really were
channeling Jimmy Durante as we sang. All of us found a floppy
hat, similar to what he wore, and as our emcee announced,

Durante in poison!

"Jimmy!" we struck the Durante pose. Hot-cha-cha-cha! We learned to throw our hats from our heads to our hands. Our own "Durante" put on a fake nose and did a solo shtick on center stage. Sue said she never would have done it without the nose.

We hadn't yet learned our choreography for the Durante medley when we were asked to put on a class for one of our regional meetings. We chose to demonstrate how the Valley Forge Chorus learned new choreography. In front of the entire region, Ida and her committee taught us the Durante choreography. Gutsy...but a very effective class.

Gypsy Rose Lee

Down the center of the risers she stepped, while the music played "Let Me Entertain You." Dressed in a black gown with long white gloves, she had a slight smile on her face. Slowly she raised her hands and carefully removed a glove—one finger at a time. When the glove was off, she threw it to the audience. With a toss of her head, and a mischievous grin, she turned her back to the audience and, as she glided off the stage, reached behind her to pull on the back zipper of her dress. Then she was gone. One of our older gentlemen, who remembered Gypsy Rose Lee, complimented Kathi on her portrayal. "You moved just like her." This comment is what Kathi remembers most.

Bugs, Trees, and Bees

Who ever heard of a whole show about bugs and animals and trees? Mary Ellen David was creating all kinds of costumes for our diverse membership. We dressed our smaller members as bumblebees and ladybugs, and our tall people as trees. Some of us were just kids wearing sneakers running all over the stage.

Bumble bees and...

We even had an outhouse that the stage crew had built on the top
riser next to some "trees." Our music was fun and happy.

Our script committee wanted six of our shorter members to
form a dance line as we sang "Jeremiah Was a Bullfrog." Mary
Ellen came to the rescue. The chorus dancers wore white flippers

...ladybugs

on their feet. The stage crew darkened the theater and showed a black light on them. The flippers and a bit of their costume were the only things visible as we sang and they danced. At show time we heard the audience laugh and applaud throughout the whole song. The bullfrog feet were such fun to watch!

I sang Phil Harris's version of the song "The Preacher and the Bear." (My one and only solo in 29 years.) I didn't get much encouragement from the chorus (perhaps they were too young to know Phil Harris) but no one said no. An arrangement was available, and so the chorus learned the music. It was show time, and at the end of my song, as the audience applauded and I took my bow, the door to the outhouse swung open, and out came a six-foot-five-inch-tall bear (performed by George Krebs, our tallest husband). He actually ran after me. I backed away from him, not expecting this nor knowing which way to run. The bear finally got close enough to whisper, "I'm supposed to pick you up." So I let him pick me up in his arms. As he carried me from the stage, I saw the chorus watching us. Darn them! They were laughing. It was bedlam on the stage. They got me.

I had no idea what came next. Intermission, I hoped.

♮

One hidden ingredient to the success of Valley Forge's performances may have been that their director—I—didn't have a solo voice. The chorus was my voice. All the music we sang was songs that I loved.

12

The Road to the Big Honker

COMPETITION WAS MY FAVORITE part of the Sweet Adelines life. It was awesome being the leader of ninety strong, focused women. It filled me with incredible love, respect, and a desire to succeed for my chorus of tigers. Being their director was a comfortable place for me to be. Knowing what was going on in the hearts and minds of my chorus members was important to me—they had a chorus personality. I kept my eyes and ears open to whatever was happening, so that I could guide them as they navigated each contest venue. As director, I felt responsible for what we put on that stage. This is true for all of our performances, but the contest magnifies these feelings—and the responsibilities. There is electricity in the air all the time.

1979: St. Louis International

We were going to St. Louis, Missouri, for our next International. A few months before the contest, one of our front-row members moved to another state. We were heartbroken that she wouldn't be with us. We all loved watching Muff on the front row. She had competed with us many times and wanted to compete with us this one last time.

Why not let her sing? She knew all the music—and the choreography. She knew how to compete. We knew that having Muff onstage would be a positive influence on our attitude. This is one

Muff, The St.Louis Hitchhiker.

time when my director's discretion was used. Muff would sing with us. She was overjoyed, and we were, too. She couldn't believe that we would really let her sing. Of course, we would! She was family.

♮

We were contestant number one on the stage in St. Louis. Stage lights were dim when we entered the stage. The lights that allowed the director to be seen by the chorus were still turned off. Our first song was a beautiful ballad that starts out very, very soft. When you are directing something soft and heart-felt, your hands are usually in front of you and your motion is soft and warm. This can be quite effective if done right. But the chorus has to see the face and the hands of the director. The stage lights were not turned on. That day, from the stage, my chorus was looking at a black silhouette. How did they pull it off? They said they watched my body. They knew me so well that I could direct them with no hands, just my head and the motion of my body. Thankfully, the lights came on very quickly once we started to sing.

We didn't score as well that year—fifth, one placement lower than the previous contest in London. The unexpected placement made for one of our biggest after-contest celebrations. We were sad and frustrated, and I was in tears, but we still had a big party. (We always had a big, raucous party after our competitions. Even when we lost. Except in 1983. When we won. I think we were all emotionally exhausted.) We learned the St. Louis audience hadn't liked the way we were scored on the contest stage. We came home, and the supporting letters started to arrive. "I loved your performance!" "You should have placed higher!"

♮

At home, we turned our thoughts to new songs for our performance repertoire. The first song we learned was "That's Life." We sang it for a short while until we stopped feeling bad about being fifth. Can you imagine feeling bad about placing fifth at the *international* contest? Go-lly!

1979–1980

After St. Louis, it was time to think about the regional competition held in the spring of 1980. The winning chorus would go on to Phoenix in the fall of 1981. Choosing the songs for any contest is one of the most difficult things a director does, because it can make the difference where you place. Directors of competing choruses always have their antennae up looking for good contest arrangements. They start choosing songs for a contest as soon as possible, even a year or more in advance.

The songs have to be "suitable for contest." Songs that are unsuitable for contest can include anything that is patriotic or religious or anything that has too many jazz chords. When you hear music you can usually tell, just by the sound, if it is church music, opera music, jazz, or folk. So, too, you can tell if a song is barbershop by the arrangement and the interpretation. You have to follow the contest rules. And, to really score well, the chorus must love singing the songs. Picking songs for a contest is no easy task. I hated it. But that year, I sensed the frustration in my chorus. They had decided that this was the year they *would* win the darn contest. Whatever it took. Jeez!

Choosing the uptune was easy. "Nobody's Sweetheart Now" was a Renee Craig arrangement. Her arrangements always scored well. For the ballad I chose "Who'll Take My Place When I'm Gone." The arrangement had lots of built-in emotion that my chorus would love to sing. And lots of chords that would sound good. It was not an easy song, but when other choruses had sung the song in contest, it scored well (when sung well).

My next job was to interpret these songs well enough to win a contest. This time I went for help. Who was the best? Renee Craig. At the time, Renee lived about a three-hour drive from me. She invited me to her home, and we sat together at her piano and experimented with the interpretation of the ballad. She changed the notes at the ending to make it easier to sing. Then we played a phrase, analyzed it, changed it until we felt it was good, and then added it to the song and reevaluated the change. This was the most creative day I spent with the most creative person I knew, and we produced an outstanding interpretation. Valley Forge would love this music.

♮

The following year (1980), Renee came to our chorus to coach us for the regional contest. When Renee coaches a chorus, she likes to direct them, too. I watched her from the side of the room. The look on my face worried my chorus. "She's not happy," they thought, but I was trying to understand what Renee was doing—and why. It was her core teaching style that interested me. There was more to her than *just do this, then do that*. I was trying to learn how she was teaching the chorus. After any coaching session you have to reinforce what was taught until the chorus is proficient with the changes. I had to be able to do that. It wasn't easy. Renee is a creative genius with her music. Sometime late in the afternoon session, the light bulb lit—dimly, but it lit. A little piece of Renee had seeped into my soul. This would forever be part of me. Don't ask me to explain it. I can't and I don't want to. It's precious and it's mine. Thank you, Renee, for sharing yourself with us.

Onstage in Phoenix

We were singing our best, and we expected to do well. Onstage our first song, "Who'll Take My Place When I'm Gone," was great! Our uptune, "Nobody's Sweetheart Now," was next. When we came to the first chorus, we lost the rhythm for a few seconds—this is better known as "got out of sync." That was OK. Those things happen and sometimes it is how you handle the mistake that affects your score. When we repeated the chorus, we were out of sync—again. Shoot! The chorus heard it. The judges heard it, too. After we competed, we came into the auditorium to hear the other contestants. I spotted Ann Gooch sitting on the front row and plopped down on the space beside her.

Ann waited for a quiet moment and then said, "You got out of sync."

"Yes, I know"

Ann said nothing in response.

I continued, "I was afraid that was going to happen."

Turning sideways in her seat and looking me straight in the eye, Annie said, "Then it's your fault."

It really was! I should have searched for it at rehearsal and made sure it didn't happen on stage. Woulda, coulda, shoulda. My chorus knew why we were out of sync, but it took forty years, and my writing this book, before they told me what happened. One member got excited and jumped the tempo. Several others followed her. She did it twice.

We came in second that year—by twelve points. That's twelve points, out of 3200. We snatched defeat out of the hands of victory. This time, the after-contest party was the best. We wore our red second-place medals with pride. It wasn't what we wanted, but second place at International was not too bad.

1982–

Then it was back to regional competition with the same two songs we competed with in Phoenix. We had to win this to be eligible for International in Detroit. Like she did before International in St. Louis, Ann Gooch came up to coach us. After the session, Ida was driving Ann back to the airport and they had some time to talk. Ann sat in the car before saying goodbye to Ida and said, "You'll never win until Jan gets rid of her fear of winning."

Shortly thereafter Ida gave me a book entitled *The Fear of Winning*. I read it. And there came a day after that when I finally acknowledged to myself that Ann was right. I was afraid of winning. Now to find out why.

I was an amateur, not a professional musician. What was I doing here anyway? Until now, every director who had won the international contest was a well-known musician in the barbershop world. Some were arrangers, vocal teachers, music teachers, coaches, judges. Some had a doctorate in music. Each of those directors had something to offer the Sweet Adelines. They were given opportunities to go places and do things and to train big choruses. Everyone wanted them to coach their chorus. But me? I felt I didn't have the background to be—or to even become—what an international championship chorus director was expected to be. I was afraid I wouldn't measure up. I felt I had no special talents to give the Sweet Adelines. I felt this even though I was on the international faculty and taught all over the world. It felt like being considered an expert in your field but not having a college degree.

The fact that the chorus was ready to win forced me to acknowledge that feeling of insecurity. It didn't matter that I was afraid; I couldn't let my chorus down. I had to do my best to get this chorus ready to win the contest, which meant I had to do my best to get myself ready to win. The chorus wanted it. It was our time. I made the decision, if we won, to accept the consequences, whatever they might be.

Ann once told me, "You are not going to win until the chorus wants to."

This time they wanted to, but was I holding them back? One of the former members of Valley Forge, who had become a judge, was heard to say, "You're never going to win with Jan as your director." Fortunately, I didn't know this until after we had won. The desire from the chorus was so strong that not trying for a gold medal was not an option.

1982

Valley Forge was formed in 1965 by women who were strong-minded, who had opinions and voiced them at any time. They were also fun-loving, supportive women who cherished their chorus and the friends that were with them. Going into this contest brought all of that strife and support to the surface.

Won Regional. On to Detroit.

We had to do something different this time. It may have started with our bass section leader, Betty Sheets (affectionately called Sheddy Beets). She gave each of us a ring, a small brass ring, with a little blue ribbon tied to it. This was to remind us of the merry-go-round we had been on for too long. It was time to grab the brass ring. Many of us wore this ring to rehearsal, including me. I kept it on my little finger, so it was visible as I directed the chorus. Some of us put it in our bathrooms where we saw it as we dressed for work. Just looking at that ring was a constant reminder that there was a chorus goal and that together we had a job to do. Each of us made a personal commitment to the chorus.

Costuming

The costume committee went to work designing our Detroit costume. It had its problems trying to please a hundred women. Many designs were thrown in the trash can. When the costume was finally decided upon and presented to the chorus, one of our women announced that she was "not going to wear that thing on stage." But by this time, the committee was settled. We made the costume.

It was a new version of an older one. Chartreuse trim on a royal blue satin dress. The top was covered with a see-through blue jacket trimmed in the chartreuse. Who ever heard of putting chartreuse and blue satin on a contest stage? Mary Ellen David did. She helped design it. And our chorus member wore it. It was one of most talked about costumes of the contest. We had T-shirts made for our illustrious costume committee. On the front of the T-shirt it said, "We dressed Valley Forge for Detroit," and the back said, "And they loved it."

The Songs

As director, it was my job to choose which songs to sing, and I decided that we should take the same two songs into contest one more time. They were strong songs, and we had performed them twice on the contest stage. The chorus had a lot of good muscle memory for these two songs, and I knew that would make for a confident chorus. But I also decided to give the songs a rest.

From the spring 1982 regional contest to March 1983, we didn't sing the two contest songs. Giving the songs a rest would make them fresh and exciting when we brought them back. Some of the chorus members were angry with me. Some understood. Some just went along. Finally, in March 1983, I brought the two songs back to rehearsal. We knew how to make these songs competition ready. We had plenty of time for good singing, good vowels, good staging, and a good confident attitude. But it was no small feat. We worked on the most difficult tasks first and then slowly added the good staging. As the weeks went by, we got better and better.

Some days directing the Valley Forge Chorus was like leading tigers; other days I could hardly keep up with them. Each one wanted to go her own way, but they also each wanted to reach the same destination. If there were five different roads all leading to the same place, there were five different right ways to get there. Typical of the Valley Forge M.O., when we were working on vocal production, there were those who thought we should be working on vowels. When we worked on vowels, the people who heard us drop the ends of phrases complained that we weren't working on the right technique. The staging people always wanted more time at rehearsals. This arguing about priorities was constant. Fortunately the chorus still worked with me, but I could feel their dissatisfaction.

Finally, the only thing left to perfect for the contest should have been the easiest for Valley Forge to do. It's called "transcend the technique." In other words, keep the good technique and sing the message. We had to put our heart into the music and reach out to the audience, pulling them into our song. Winning is so much easier when you can produce this emotion, send it to the judges, and then on to the audience. But the chorus was concentrating so hard on singing perfectly that they couldn't let go for that one last step.

Two Months to Go

The chorus couldn't let go, and in two months we were leaving for Detroit. Try as I would, I couldn't find the key to make them fly. I thought it might be me...that I was too close to them, knowing how much they wanted to win and how hard they were trying. Was my directing too structured? Was my face too stern? Was I not moving freely enough as I directed? They were almost ready, and we didn't have much time. Should another director take them into the contest with the freedom they needed to win? I wondered.

Yes, of course. Just down the street from me lived Conrad Keil, a top director from the Barbershop Harmony Society. He was a happy, loveable guy who would be able to make the chorus love and laugh with him—and I felt they would sing for him. The chorus was already well prepared. It would just be a matter of making it happen. I had found my Plan B to give this chorus their gold medal, but I didn't mention it to anyone, not even to Conrad.

Final Coaching Session

About this time, we had our final coaching session. We flew Ann Gooch up from Jacksonville. It was a weekend retreat, and the entire chorus stayed at the lodging. We started Friday night and went to Sunday noon. It was our last session—do or die. After this weekend, no more coaching before the contest. The chorus has to sing for their director, not their coach.

On Friday night, Ann stopped into my room and asked, "What do you want me to do this weekend?" And I replied, "Ann, I can't

With Annie Gooch.

loosen them up. They are singing as well as I can get them to sing, but they are so uptight that our music has no life, no love. I'm stymied. I can't figure it out." She nodded and said OK. Then she left the room. End of conversation.

The following day was an all-day coaching session. No one would believe that just two short months before we competed for our life, Ann made us sing the ballad fast, as an uptune, beating out the rhythm with our bodies. We were putting crazy choreography in a schmaltzy ballad singing, "Everything must have an end, so the poet says. Doo, doo, wah!!"

Then we sang the uptune slowly and sweetly, as a ballad. All the training we had been doing went out the window. All our well-thought-out choreography was gone, all our perfect vowels were butchered. And who remembered what parts of the songs were supposed to be soft and others loud?

But oh, did we have fun! That Saturday night was party night.

Sunday morning was a whole different program. It was back-to-work time. Ann put the songs back together for us. We rehearsed for about two hours. As I directed, Ann tweaked a couple of spots that needed to be improved. Then we began to work on singing the songs with that illusive finesse. I still couldn't release their heart. Ann stepped up before them and directed the contest ballad. It was beautiful—full of love and heart and all the things I so wanted them to have.

I burst into tears. I sobbed and cried out to them, "Why will you do that for her and not for me?"

End of rehearsal, hugs all around. I have no recollection of the rest of the day. But I do know that the rehearsal the next week was completely different. As we rehearsed the ballad, I asked them to put their voice in the palm of my hand and that was right where they needed to be. It was wonderful. We worked together to put the finesse into the songs.

We did more than just practice our music to get ready for competition. The chorus members decided to do vocal warm-ups at home—ten minutes every day—to strengthen their singing voice. And they began walking regularly to build up their physical strength, because they knew the week at the contest site would be grueling.

We also talked about the message of the ballad. We shared our feelings, what we thought about while singing "Who'll Take My Place When I'm Gone." All of us needed to be thinking along the same line in order to put our song into the hearts of the audience. So, chorus members shared their feelings. And I shared mine. My second husband and I were recently married. Second marriages are big decisions. We were learning this song while Darrel and I were making this decision. I talked with the chorus about what this song meant to me. I didn't want to be without Darrel, and this song cut through to my heart. Those chorus members who didn't have their own story sang about mine.

Practicing the Warm-up

We left nothing to chance. Not even how long we needed to prepare before the actual day of competition. How long did it take Valley Forge to be ready to sing the contest songs? How much time should we allow for that warm-up? During one regular practice session before competition, we looked at the clock and started our usual fifteen-minute warm-up.

Jan: "Ready?"

Chorus: "Nope. Sing some more."

We sang a couple of our favorite songs, making sure these were only the ones we sang well.

Jan: "Ready?"

Chorus: "Nope."

More songs. More praise. More smiles.

Jan: "Ready?"

Chorus: "Almost!"

One or two more great songs.

Jan: "Ready?"

Chorus: "Yes!"

We sang our two contest songs next...And we nailed them.

How long did we need? It took one and one half hours of warm-up before we felt ready to go onto the contest stage. We finally had produced the sound we loved. We were ecstatic.

Arriving in Detroit

When we arrived at the hotel, suitcases in hand, everything was an omen. One room number was 111. "It's an omen!" There was a double rainbow outside the hotel lobby. "It's an omen!" I now know what "being in the zone" means. There was electricity throughout the hotel, all centered around the Valley Forge Chorus. Our scheduled rehearsals were mostly to keep our focus. We sang our contest songs and refreshed our memories of the message of the songs. Our minds were focused. All talk was centered on the *now*.

The Day Before

The day before we competed, we were having our final rehearsal. In walked Muff, Linda, and Jean—all members who had moved far away. They came to see us compete. Then in came Ann Gooch and her husband, Jim. They wished us well and stayed to listen. We sang our contest songs. Our sound spun around the room. You could feel the energy. Ann cried. As she left our rehearsal room, her parting words to Jim were, "We just saw the winning performance." (She told us this story after we won.)

Contest Day

Contest day started with our scheduled breakfast in one of the hotel dining rooms. Part of the tradition was my walk around the room saying something to every chorus member—always touch-

ing them on the back or arm, sometimes giving a hug. I wanted
to make personal contact with each and every one of them. After
breakfast came makeup and hair. Five of our members' rooms
were used as makeup rooms. The chorus had ninety-two women
who needed to put on eye makeup, false eyelashes, and rouge.
One stylist helped with the hair. Our oldest member challenged
our team to fix her "droopy eyelids."

In full makeup and lacquered hair, we met for our final one-
and-a-half-hour warm-up. It was at this moment that something
extraordinary happened. Two of our members had been friends
until a sharp tongue came between them. One stood two riser
steps below the other on the competition risers. She could feel
vibes coming from above. She didn't want anything to pierce our
harmony. She didn't want to go on stage like this, didn't want
these feelings to be responsible for losing the competition. Nothing should stand in the way. In her mind she had to "get it done."
Now. She wanted to be friends again.

"I'd like to be friends again," she said, turning to face her
friend.

"OK," was the answer.

Hugs. It was done.

It didn't take as long as we thought for us to begin to produce our Valley Forge sound. We shared our cold duck from our
giant wine glass. We went back to our rooms and slipped into
our costumes. No one talked about home, husbands or boyfriends,
kids. No one let her mind drift to tomorrow's to-do list. We were
focused on the contest. We were in the zone.

We got the call from the traffic pattern guide that the competition bus was picking us up from the lobby. After making sure all
the members were out of their rooms, I hopped on the elevator to
join them. As the elevator doors opened, the sound of Valley Forge
was everywhere. In chartreuse and blue satin, chorus members

were singing their rendition of "Mood Indigo." It's soft but very energetic. The music wants to keep the tempo moving but fights to keep the soft sound. We called it "hushed intensity." There was another chorus in the lobby waiting for their bus to take them to the contest. They listened to us sing and later said they knew then that winning the contest was not theirs this year. From that moment on, "Moon Indigo" has been our fight song.

At the Detroit Convention Center

We followed the traffic pattern for the chorus and soon were lined up backstage, ready to enter and compete. Something happened to us at that moment. Our energy intensified. You could feel it. The first woman in line entered the stage, her head held high, her strides long and full of confidence. This walk was picked up by the next woman in line. It rippled over the entire ninety-two members of Valley Forge as they entered the stage. I waited by the stage entrance and smiled, sometimes gently touching them as they strode by. "The feeling" was all around us.

The emcee spoke: "We are ready for our next contestant. Please close the doors. (Pause) Contestant number 26, from Valley Forge, Pennsylvania, under the direction of Jan Muck...the Valley Forge Chorus!"

The stage crew felt it. They told us that they knew we were the winners when we walked on stage. People in the audience who had started to leave to get something to eat, came back and sat down to listen when they felt us enter the stage. They didn't know us, but they knew something really big was going to happen. It was our energy radiating from the stage.

Our ballad was first and started with these words. "Everything must have an end." It was by far the hardest part of the song to sing. The melody line is eight notes going down the scale. It is so easy to sing each note a little flat and end up out of tune and in a lower key. This is a very dangerous way to begin a contest.

"Just give me the first three notes, and then I'll be OK," I said. "That's all I ask of you." As a director, I often told the chorus that for me, the most frightening part of a contest was after the pitch and before the first sound. Your arms are raised, ready to begin. You know as they descend to start the first sound, there is no turning back. You don't really know what you are going to hear. But whatever it is, you have to go with it. I think I may have held up three fingers on stage as a reminder, and then I raised my hands and began.

They sang. It was an in-control, accurate, clear sound. I knew the rest of the contest package was going to be OK. Our uptune was next. Valley Forge was well known for fun, creative choreography and energized singing. The audience expected nothing less.

Let me try to explain this choreography. The first words of our second song were "Painted lips, painted eyes, wearing a bird of paradise." We used jazz hands and quickly brought one hand to our lips and then the other hand to our eyes. Then we performed the peacock move.

"Wearing a Bird of Pa-ra, Pa-ra-Dise."

We stood in five rows, on four steps of risers plus the floor. On each of the strong beats (the capitalized words), starting with the front row, one row at a time shot their arms straight up over their heads, then keeping their arms straight, they slowly lowered them to their sides—much like swimming the breaststroke.

The front row started on W, the second on B, the third moved on P, the fourth had the next P and the fifth (the top row) moved on D. All our arms settled at our sides at the same time. Our see-through blue sleeves made our arms look purple. With our blue and chartreuse costume, our movements looked like a peacock spreading out its blue, green, and purple colors—a symbol of paradise. We didn't know this color-effect would happen. The audience reacted with audible oohs, and some even clapped. We all heard it. I saw it. But the video missed it.

In six short minutes it was all over.

We had done our best, just what we had practiced. Because of this, we were ready to accept wherever we placed. We were actually quite calm for the remainder of the competition.

In the convention center, they made the announcement. We were *first*! We had just won the international chorus contest.

The emcee asked, "Would the Valley Forge Chorus please come to the stage to accept their medals?" The audience screamed and jumped up and down. We ran from the very top of the center, down the narrow staircases, and across the main floor. And still the audience clapped, cheered, and stomped their feet. We didn't hear any of it over our own excitement. People reached out to touch us as we approached the stage. Friends tried to stop us with hugs as we ran through the crowds. Ninety-two women stormed the stage, unable to do or say anything but squeal and hug anyone close enough to grab. The stage became a sea of squiggly, shiny blue dresses with chartreuse trim.

We had won! How do you put words to such an incredible day?

We were no strangers to the international stage. We had competed every other year for the past ten years. Our friends, our family, and even the other competitors had watched us bounce around the top five positions, but never reaching the gold. All in all, it had taken us eighteen years and fifteen contests to win this Super Bowl of our singing organization, the Sweet Adelines International. And eight thousand people were there to witness it. This was a magical moment in our lives—a moment to relive and dream about for the rest of our days.

I wore that gold medal every day for four months. Although I didn't sleep with it, I know some chorus members who did. This

(reprinted from Pitch Pipe *© Sweet Adelines International)*

With the 1983 Big Honker and the International Director's Trophy.

win had an impact on my life. My fear of not measuring up is gone. The little man on my shoulder who said, "Are you sure? You can't do that," is gone. I know that if I put my mind to something, I will be able to succeed. I've done it, and I can do it again, any time a challenge presents itself. I am no longer afraid of success. I don't think any of us are.

♮

At the time, Ann Gooch was in charge of promoting Sweet Adelines throughout the world. She went to Australia with the recording of our winning performance. It played on their national TV. For many Australians, the first barbershop chorus they ever heard was the Great Chorus of Valley Forge.

Our uptune lived on, too. In the many years since that performance, we have often heard comments about how Valley Forge "owned that song." Other choruses were hesitant to use it as a competition song. People still remember our staging and sometimes greet us by holding a jazz hand up to their face and calling out "Painted lips" as a hello.

I Believe, I Believe

Following our win in Detroit, I wrote this letter to my chorus for the *Valley Forge Voice* newsletter

---

I BELIEVE, I BELIEVE

In reflecting on the months before contest and that wonderful week in Detroit—we believed. But how did we reach that point? We worked hard, but we've been working hard for years. This year was different. It is astounding the level of personal commitment that each of us made. The challenge to reach a high level of achievement was constantly put before us at each rehearsal. We never let down. We worked alone and we worked together. We critiqued and corrected. We laughed, we cried, and we fought. We were committed. For the six months before contest, the plan began to unfold. We had the right coaching at the right time. Each component of a good performance was rehearsed at its proper and planned time. The parts began to fit together in their right order. The game plan was followed, sometimes against strong oppositions, but faith in each other glued us together toward our goal. After our performance at Hershey, Pennsylvania, we thought we might be able to do it. After our performance for our region, we knew. I knew. I knew that you knew. You couldn't describe it, you couldn't explain it, and you couldn't make it happen. It showed all over my face and you read me well. Confidence, love, joy, excitement, dedication.

Winning is not the end for us. It's just a step along the way. Singing barbershop is one of the most difficult and challenging forms of musical entertainment. I want to challenge the professional world to sing as well as any good barbershop chorus can sing. No, barbershopping is not for everyone, but neither is opera. Why should one be of higher acclaim than the other? We have audiences to entertain, new ideas to try, new directions to pursue, and we have the resources to do it. Look at us. Look at the talented members of our chorus who worked with us these past months. We have their expertise to tap. Our region is another talent bank and our International organization has given us unbelievable direction and support.

This is a beginning, an open door to finding out what really lies ahead for Valley Forge. We can now choose our direction. Let's risk it.

Jan Muck

13

The Art of Performance

The Picture

WHEN WE SANG AND people looked at us, we wanted them to like what they saw. And we didn't want them to be distracted from our performance by anything. We worked hard to make this happen. Whether we were a small chorus, all standing on the floor, or a large chorus standing on risers, we took pride in how we looked. The back row was the face of the chorus. No "deer in the headlights" look on this row. The members who stood there were at the top of the picture frame. We made sure that those who stood on both ends of that row looked like they were the same height. We wanted the picture to hang straight. We left no empty spaces on the back row that might make the audience wonder why the space was unfilled. Did she fall? Is she sick? Did she not show up at the last minute? Is she OK? Instead, the audience listened to us sing.

We made sure each member had a window to see the director. Their friends in the audience could see them, too. This was important to our members. The front-row folks were the most visible to the audience and they had to look and move together. Their faces had to be expressive, too. And, just like the back row, they had to appear similar to each other. In either row, we were careful not to put our five-foot-one dynamo next to our five-foot-ten statuesque bombshell—in spite of how well they sounded together. The front-row people had special responsibilities. They worked together as a team. Often, they had extra rehearsals to synchronize the movement of their arms, legs, feet, and hands. And faces, too. The unit look was an awesome responsibility. Each year, for those who wanted to be on the front row, we held auditions to evaluate their face and body movements. The auditions were held on a rehearsal night. I did not attend auditions, but I was made aware who the candidates were. After all, we *are* a singing organization, and there are some people, because of the sound of their voice, who should not be on the front row. The members who were the judges needed to know how I felt about the candidates. Did I think they were suitable—either visually or vocally—to be on the front row? And as a director, I was clever and discreet with my response, for I knew that I had trouble concentrating on the music if I had an inexpressive face or body in my direct line of vision. Oops!

When a singer wasn't chosen, we gave her the reasons and then suggestions for how she could improve. One woman was told that she didn't stand up straight enough. Her rib cage wasn't lifted. (This was called the monkey stance: leaning slightly forward—with a sunken chest—and with your hands hanging in front of your side seams). During the following year that singer worked hard to correct her posture. At the next audition she was approved for the front row. When her name was announced, the chorus applauded. We were proud of what she had accomplished.

The ends of the rows, on both sides of the chorus, added to the unit look. Where they stood was especially exposed to the audience. The choreography by these members was distracting if it differed from the rest of the chorus—like an arm too high, or a hand that bounced with the tempo of the song. We were extra careful of the costumes for the end people, too. We looked for wrinkled side seams, uneven hemlines, anything that just fit too tight or too big.

It was impossible to have the perfect-looking chorus. But we tried. Before every performance we made sure our placement had no empty spaces. At this time, we also checked the sound and made necessary small changes in case one voice was predominant. (Yes, it's a valid concern. Some voices just don't blend, and they must not inadvertently be standing next to each other!)

We *never* sang with all parts standing together. You can't hear the harmony and therefore you can't tune the chords. It was the "shotgun approach." Most members liked to harmonize with other parts around them. Sometimes my performance team suggested different positions to make it easier for the emcees or specialty acts to move around the stage. We bartered to adjust the positioning to both look and sound the best and provide the best mobility. Directors have a favorite sound they are trying to create, and every director forms it differently.

We kept in mind the comfort of the audience. We didn't want them to leave at the end of the performance remembering the one person whose pants were too tight (Were they going to split when she moved?) or even just the one person who kept moving side to side because she was behind a tall person and couldn't see out. Woe to the one person who stood on the end of any row and moved four feet away from everyone else so that she more clearly saw the director. She suddenly looked like she was the soloist of the chorus. It happens, and when it happens the audience will watch her throughout the entire performance, waiting for the solo. (I have been to such a performance. I wondered why the director allowed that person to do that. It could have been corrected right there on stage—and the audience might have applauded the correction.)

Most choruses used a pitch pipe to establish a starting key. We nestled our pitch pipe blower within the chorus, not on the front or back row. At a performance, the cue to sound the pitch pipe was a discreet signal from the onstage emcee or director. The audience had fun trying to find the person who was blowing the pitch. Many in the audience were not even aware that there was a pitch being sounded. My *pointing* at the pitch pipe blower as a signal was not an option.

When Was a Song Ready?

You can't take back a bad performance, and as the director, it was up to me to decide when a song was ready to be put in our lineup for performances. Some opera singers who prepare their students for a recital do not let their students perform a song until they have been singing it for a year. We didn't wait that long! When all the learning was completed, and the chorus was beginning to "own the song," it was time to get it ready for the stage.

I remembered being taught to ride a bicycle by my big brother. He held onto the seat of my bike and ran beside me. He let go but when I started to fall, he grabbed the seat and straightened my bike. If I wobbled, he held tight. Finally he made me ride and wobble without his help, and the more I rode by myself the better I became. Finally I was free. At rehearsals, you constantly stop to correct the music, give instructions—grab the seat of the bike. There comes a time when the chorus just wants to sing without interruption. They don't want to be stopped. That's the time to let go of the bicycle. When that happened, just like a child, the chorus forgot most of what they had been taught. They wobbled on the bicycle. They sang it again, without stopping. The more they sang it, the better they sounded. Soon they were on their own. Sometimes I had to pick up the pieces and put the bike back together. I had let go of the seat too soon. When I was able to put on my "admiring" ears, not my "critical" ears, we performed the song. From that time on, I only grabbed the seat when the chorus was headed for a crash. The hardest lesson I learned was not to make changes to the notes or the basic pattern of the song immediately before a performance. This is especially true before a competition. Our goal was to make no major changes during the three weeks before we performed or competed—on stage, our muscle memory won every time.

My mantra was "The day of the contest or performance, let the little things go."

The Applause

It's called command of the stage. One day I watched a TV performance of a concert with Pearl Bailey. My screen was only thirteen inches wide, but I saw and heard her magnificent performance. After her finale, in front of thousands of people, she stepped forward to within three feet of the front edge of the stage. She stopped and didn't move. Her face was radiant. She was happy, and her eyes looked over the entire audience. She knew she had given them a fine performance and, by just standing there, she encouraged them to shower her with applause. And the audience responded to her invitation. She just stood there and absorbed five minutes of a standing ovation. The longer she stood there, the more they clapped. Then she slowly walked, in turn, to each side of the stage and faced that portion of the audience. They responded to her with more applause, bravos, and complete adoration. She did not mouth the words "thank you," and she did not nod her head. She returned to center stage and looked all around the audience and smiled. She stood there. The audience exploded. And the applause was deafening. It was magical.

We adapted Pearl Bailey's response to how Valley Forge accepted applause. After each song I stood tall, turned around to the audience as they started to clap, and took two steps forward. Then I just stood there. No bowing at the waist, no "thank you, thank you, thank you." I didn't wave an arm to each side of the chorus for the audience to recognize them. The chorus turned to face the audience and gave them their biggest smiles. We made sure to include the sides of the audience and the balcony. When the applause was about to subside, it was time for me to take one tiny step forward and turn toward the chorus. This signaled to the audience that the performance was continuing, and the applause would slow down. They were ready to hear more music. The timing of this was crucial, because we wanted the audience to enjoy applauding for us. If the emcee was to talk, the little step forward signaled her to move toward the microphone. Sometimes the applause didn't stop, and I was *forced* to just stand motionless at the front of the stage and wait. Yes!

Most exciting was the applause we received after the final song of one of our shows. À la Pearl Bailey. The chorus looked out at the audience and saw them up on their feet. Big smiles came on our faces as the applause swept over us. I stepped forward until I reached the front of the stage and stood there for a while. A long while. The applause kept growing. Then I stepped off center stage and moved to the side, turning my back to the audience just enough for me to look at the chorus. The audience whistled and screamed. They wouldn't stop. As I went back to center stage, they kept standing and clapping. There was nothing to do but stay there and wait till the audience was ready to slow down. It was a long time. I heard the chorus laughing behind me. They teased me later and told me they were taking bets as to how many seconds I could hold the applause. They loved it, as I did, and I said to them, "You guys are so bad." They giggled...Glorious!

Planning Your Standing Ovation

Performances start when the audience watches you enter. Sometimes we entered from the back of the room and walked through the audience. We moved briskly to the staging area and smiled at them along the way—which said our hellos. As we positioned ourselves on the stage, the audience began to analyze what type of an evening they would have. It was at that time they looked at our faces, examined our costumes, checked out the director, and all the other non-musical parts of our presentation.

Most of our performances were an hour long. We chose our repertoire along the lines of the following graph, making sure we always had a smooth flow between our music and our presentation. Let me explain this graph.

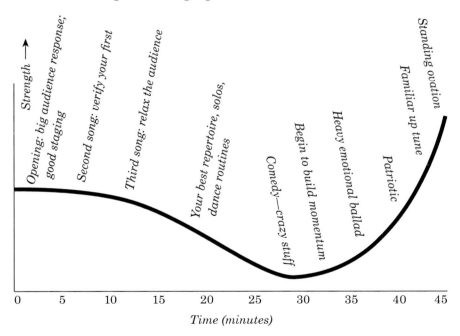

Time (minutes)

Planning Your Standing Ovation © Jan Muck

The opening song was an important part of the performance. It was our introduction to the audience. It said hello and gave them an idea of the kinds of music they would hear during the evening. Our opening song was always the best of who we were. It was a fast-rhythm number with plenty of choreography. It was like a firm handshake and eye contact when you meet someone new. The audience expected to see and listen to this kind of concert. Choosing our second song was almost as important as the first. We wanted to keep the audience interested in who we were. That was the time to present another good, easy to listen to, familiar song. It was definitely not as explosive as our opener, and we found that an uptune without choreography was a good choice.

It was now time to slow down a bit and allow the audience to relax and enjoy us. A light fun song did the trick. No heavy ballad, not yet. That came later. Experience told us how to fill the next few minutes with songs that made the audience laugh, cry, sigh with memories, or just want to sing along with us. We were careful not to put two songs that sounded alike one after the other. As our visit with the audience continued, it was time for the crazy, silly songs that we loved to sing. They didn't have to mean anything; that time just allowed the audience to relax and catch their breath with something different from what we had been singing. The spot near the bottom point of the graph was for the songs that we *never* used to open or close a show.

As our finale, we used at least three songs to build momentum to our standing ovation. Purposely, we added more and more excitement to our choice of music until our last song lifted the audience out of their seats while applauding our performance. It didn't matter which specific songs we chose for those last three songs, but it did matter what type of song and in what order we performed them: we had to ensure that we kept building the level of emotion from song to song. Sometimes we ended with a fast, loud song, sometimes with an emotional song that brought the audience to tears, like "God Bless America" or "Battle Hymn of the Republic."

Sometimes we had such a good time singing for our audience and they were so responsive to our songs that we thought of it as saying goodbye to old friends with a big bear hug. They wanted to stand and applaud, telling us that we had given them an enjoyable evening. Can anything be better?

If you take each of the songs you've chosen for your performance, put them in the order that follows the performance graph, and choose a variety of emotions to present, you will end your performance with exciting songs that literally lift the audience off their feet.

And you have your standing ovation.

14

Performance Memories

Orpheus Club

THE ORPHEUS CLUB OF Philadelphia invited us to be guests on their February 1986 show. This is one of the oldest men's singing groups in America. It was founded in 1872, and they have continued to perform three concerts a year at the prestigious Philadelphia Academy of Music. Each year, they invite well-known musicians and opera singers to perform as their guests. In 1986 they invited the Valley Forge Chorus to share the stage with them.

At that time, the director of the Orpheus Club was Dr. Clyde (Bud) Dengler. His first phone call to me was an invitation for the two of us to meet and discuss the content of this joint show. It was my feeling that this great man of music would tell me what he wanted for his show and I would say, "Yes, Dr. Dengler." Not so. He came to my home and sat across the table from me. His first words were, "What do you think would be the best way for us to make a good show? Here's some music, which ones would work best for us to sing together?" I became a partner to this show. I added the Valley Forge touch to the Orpheus Club. Bud wanted a men's cancan dance, and together we planned how to make it happen. Oh, my goodness! Can you imagine all the men in the audience wearing tuxedos, all the women wearing their most beautiful formal gowns—and on the stage, the Orpheus Club men doing the cancan? Ya gotta laugh.

Bud and I chose three dates for our joint rehearsals. We talked timing, applause, and finales. We chose several songs to sing together. Dr. Dengler wanted the men to sing the barbershop arrangement of "Lida Rose" as the women sang its duet "Dream of Now." We located the eight-part arrangement from the Barbershop Harmony Society and shared it with the Orpheus men. Bud and I shook hands and began getting ready for our joint show. The songs we were going to sing together were all arranged in four-part (SATB) harmony. That meant that the women had to sing the two high parts (soprano and alto), and the men sang the lower notes (tenor and base). Our baritones and basses rebelled. Alto was difficult for our women basses. "The music is too high!" became their battle cry. I sensed that a mutiny was brewing— they didn't want any part of this joint show. I said, "I'm going to make you do this if I have to drag you, kicking and screaming, the whole way!"

It worked and they made it fun, laughing and teasing. They just didn't sing those notes they couldn't reach. The sopranos sang them. This was new and different, and we all—men and women—had a good time as we sang together. But there was an undercurrent of sadness during our rehearsals. The mother of one of our members was very ill. Her parents had tickets for the concert. The morning of the show, Mimi's mom passed away. Mimi knew her mom would want her to sing on the performance, and she did. After the show, she told us that directly in her line of vision, there was a beautiful chandelier hanging from the ceiling of the theater. She was able to "see" her mom sitting there in that wonderful seat, and she sang to her.

Was the show successful? Fifteen years later the men were still talking about the evening as being one of the best shows the

Orpheus Club had ever presented. We were told that this was the first time the audience had ever given a standing ovation—to anyone. As successful as our show was, as much as we wanted to, we never sang with them again. The Orpheus Club never repeated a guest performer.

Harrisburg Fair

The general manager of the annual fair in Harrisburg, Pennsylvania, (the state capital), was a neighbor of one of our members. He had attended many of our shows and knew of the places we had performed. One year he hired us to sing at five locations throughout the Harrisburg Saturday Fair Day. Each location had its own stage, sound system, and lighting. And each stage had its own theme—jazz, country, gospel, and so on. We were to repeat our half-hour concerts many times on all five stages throughout the day. Wow! We had never done anything like this before. We made plans. We appointed a chair.

We were eighty members at that time, and so we divided ourselves into five groups. Each group created a unique stage setting with different songs and different costumes—it was like five different choruses, each singing their own half-hour performance, again and again. Some members sang in more than one group, changing costumes between shows. One stage was formal. We chose a program of familiar songs with beautiful melodies. Our formal costumes were perfect for this stage. Then there was the casual stage. Our fun songs fit well with this stage. We used our more casual outfits with flat-heeled shoes. The most challenging stage was the one with a "down-home country" theme. What to sing? Our brainstorming sessions were noisy. Everyone shouted out crazy ideas. Someone said that she had, and could play, a gutbucket. Another said that her father had a saw that he played, and she would learn from him. A washboard appeared, then a ukulele. We had a fun quartet in the chorus who knew some country songs. They volunteered to be a part of this group, to put a twang in their voices and add other hillbilly songs to their repertoire. Off they all went to work on their half-hour performances.

The Gutbucket Band (as they were now called) came to me for coaching. They were too civilized, they said. They felt that they needed to act more uninhibited. I wanted them to chew gum, but they insisted they wouldn't be able to sing with a wad of gum in their mouths. One of the quartet members was having the most trouble. She felt too prim and proper for this band. It was hard for her to act like a mountain gal. I finally picked up an old hillbilly hat that was hanging on my hat rack by the door. I threw it on her head. She was a sunflower in bloom. She changed her whole personality and became a different person. Yay! She was set free. And she liked it. So did we. As they performed each half hour, they became crazier—more creative with the hillbilly personas. She never lost that part of her personality. We were sorry when the concert was over, and the Gutbucket Band was no more.

The one mishap that we remembered during that long day at the Harrisburg Fair happened with the formal group that sang all our beautiful, full, rich Valley Forge songs. When the pitch pipe was blown for our last song of the day, it was three notes higher than it should have been. We started anyway. We knew that the end note of this finale song was a very high one. We didn't realize just how high it was until we approached the final chord. As the director, I saw it on the faces of the high tenors. Their eyes screamed, "No way!"

Looking around I saw Lee in the center of the chorus, a tenor who can sing very high. As we approached the final chord, I stared at her and she knew that this note was all hers. Her eyes told me she understood. And she sang it—a high C—at full volume. What a way to end the finale! This day was one of our most challenging performances—five different stages, five different costumes, half-hour performances all day long. And we did it!

Music Educators National Conference

It was late spring, and the weather was unusually warm. The regional contest that year was held at a hotel on the Atlantic City boardwalk. We were the winning chorus and had sung last on our Saturday night champion show. The Music Educators National Conference (MENC) was also held that weekend at a hotel several blocks from ours. We were invited to perform for them after their Saturday night dinner and speeches. Tight fit for time, but we couldn't say no.

That night, immediately following our champion show performance, all sixty of us, in our costumes and full hair and makeup, quickly ran to the boardwalk, where several tram cars waited for us. We piled into the many little open-sided cars, which were all hooked together. It was nighttime, and our blue dresses with sparkles shone in the lights of the boardwalk. As we rattled along toward the MENC hotel, we could smell the salt air and hear the waves crashing on the shore. It was intoxicating. It was almost midnight, and we laughed and sang in the nighttime air as we bounced along, hanging on to the bars of the tram cars.

This is one of the few times many of the MENC members heard the sound of four-part a cappella harmony—sung by women. We chose our program carefully. We wanted them to hear the beautiful sound of barbershop harmony. Ann Gooch was a teacher and a member of MENC. She asked us to sing one of our non-barbershop repertoire songs that George Avener had given to us. It was his arrangement of "Do You Love Me?" from *Fiddler on the Roof*. The song is a conversation between a man and his wife who had been in an arranged marriage for twenty-five years. We ended our performance with this song. Our basses portrayed the man, Tevya, and our tenors portrayed the woman, Golde, as they sang the words to each other. The other chorus members created the background of music.

Tevya (basses) softly asked Golde if she loves him. Golde (tenors), shouting over the dishes she is washing, wondered if she heard him correctly. Tevya sofly repeated the question. And the dialogue continued as the wife reminded him of all the things she willingly had done for him and then said that after all these years, yes, she loved him. And he answered quietly that it was nice to know. We felt especially happy with the performance and hoped that the music teachers would soon embrace our a cappella sound.

Our tram was waiting for us, and sixty tired singers rode back to their hotel. No party that night.

"Fame"

Sometimes music tugged at our heartstrings. The Variety Club summer concerts did it every time. In 1927, the Variety Club was founded as a social club in Pittsburgh by eleven men in the entertainment industry. In 1928 they rescued a baby left in a theater. From that beginning, the Variety International Children's Fund has grown to serve children with disabilities resulting from injury, illness, or congenital conditions who are between the ages of birth and eighteen.

This was the ideal group for Valley Forge to support. The Variety Club summer camp was located in a town close to our own. Every year they invited us to sing for them—first for the young children and then, immediately following, again for the older kids. The counselors brought the children into the large recreation room and sat them, as best they could, in rows facing the space where we had set up our risers. They positioned the children who used wheelchairs so that everyone could see the stage. These children had disabilities, some of them extreme. Some children were missing limbs. Some were unable to walk or to hold up their heads. Some were completely non-responsive. We sang our fun, exciting music—songs that we hoped would make the kids laugh.

"Fame" quickly became their favorite. They loved our choreography and, after our many performances, they learned our motions and mimicked us from their seats. They clapped and swayed their hands and arms (as best they could) to keep time with our music. Even the counselors were involved—some actually ran up to join us on the stage. The kids loved it. So did we. Year after year the kids waited for "Fame." When they got impatient, they would holler, "FAME! FAME! FAME!" As soon as we began the familiar introduction—"doo, doo, doo, doo"—the kids erupted in cheers. Year after year we performed for the Variety Club kids. When the song left our show repertoire, we had to revive it for the Variety Club performances. Most of us remembered the song, but it didn't matter if all of us didn't know all the words. The kids still clapped and laughed and even shouted the word *FAME!* with us at the appropriate time. That shared joy, isn't that what music is all about?

Mighty Macs

Most of our self-produced shows were held at the Immaculata College auditorium in Malvern, Pennsylvania. At the time this college was a small women's school located a short distance from our rehearsal hall. It was perfect for our shows—beautiful and with excellent sound and lighting equipment. We used it often.

The school had hired Cathy Rush to be the head coach of the girls' basketball team. They had no gymnasium and no uniforms. It was 1971. Under Cathy's coaching the girls started to win. The school cheered them. The nuns attended their games. Excitement was everywhere. But the girls needed everything: they needed money for outfits and travel. Valley Forge Chorus wanted to do something to help. The school agreed to donate their auditorium to us to recreate one of our shows, and we did. We gave all proceeds to the Mighty Macs basketball team.

They won the championship in 1972, and in 2011 a movie was released that told the story of this girls' basketball team and the coach who believed in them. We cheered them, we watched them win that championship, and later we watched the movie. The Mighty Macs were our team.

Beer Park Performance

Picture a beautiful park on a delightful warm Sunday afternoon—walkways, large trees, shrubs, and pathways; a beautiful open-air theater with huge white pillars on each side of the stage. Now picture an all-women's chorus being invited to sing for a men's group who were having their annual picnic at this park. Add lots of beer. Note that the ladies' room is down a narrow pathway, through the trees at the edge of the park.

Assessing the situation, we made two rules.

1 It is two-by-two to the ladies' room.
2 Give our best performance and then head to our cars fast. No standing around and socializing as we usually do.

We had a very good time and sang well. However...

♪ There was no stand for the emcee's microphone, so they taped one to the inside of one of the pillars. Our emcee talked into the microphone and all she and the audience saw was either side of the large white pillar.

♪ During one of our songs a strange person appeared in the middle of the back row—singing his heart out. I don't know how he got there. He had to have gone around to the back of the risers and climbed up to the top step. (I wonder if someone helped him.)

♪ One of the men came up on stage to nibble at the neck of the director (that's me). He disappeared into the audience before we reached the end of the song but not before the chorus lost it and started laughing so hard they had a hard time singing.

After a huge standing ovation, we gratefully left the stage, hurried to our cars, and took off for home.

Muff's Dress

Imagine this. You enter the stage with seventy other ladies, all dressed in a see-through jacket over a strapless blue gown with elastic around the bodice to keep it up. You don't need to wear anything under it because you are thin and petite. We were singing "A Pretty Girl Is Like a Melody" as we entered the stage from both sides of the top riser. The chorus stepped down each riser as they walked, catty-corner, to the bottom of the risers, one behind the other, like showgirls on a runway. From the top, the rows crisscrossed at the center of the risers.

Suddenly, as you step down, your foot catches the hem of your dress. And your dress stays put as you begin to walk right out of it. Hopefully, only the person directly behind you sees the result. Recovery is swift. The show goes on.

Mimi's Bow

We were learning the choreography for one of our big production numbers, "Rock-a-Bye Your Baby with a Dixie Melody." For the end of our song, the front row came forward and together got down on one knee. With arms spread, they sang the finale. Their thigh muscles ached from all the rehearsals. At our first performance, Mimi, one of our front-row dancers, apparently lost count and stepped forward—way before the rest of the front row.

And there she was, center stage, on one knee with arms spread. All by herself.

I laughed hard—it looked so funny. She held her pose until the rest of the front row joined her. We finished the finale. After the chorus's bow, I motioned for Mimi to take her own special bow. She gave it her all, and the audience loved it.

Shag's Eyelashes

What do you do during a performance when one of your singers on the front row sits down on the floor because she isn't feeling well? You stop and wait while several members help her up and make her comfortable. And what do you do when you look into her eyes and realize she has her false eyelashes on upside down? You want to giggle but you can't. Laughter will happen later. We never stopped teasing Shag. We still remember.

Marji and "Undecided"

Summer concert series performances are fun and relaxed. Often there is spontaneous laughter on stage. The emcees are able to speak to the audience with an easy dialogue. Strange things often happen in that relaxed environment.

One of our favorite songs is "Undecided." It is the song we took into contest when we won Regional for the first time. Our choreography is fast-moving and creative. During one part of the song, rows one, three, and five take four sidesteps to the left and then four sidesteps to the right. At the same time, rows two and four do the opposite—four to the right and four to the left. We finish by dividing the chorus in half, with each half taking four steps toward their outside and then four steps back to the center. This leaves a rather large opening down the middle, about four feet wide, for maybe ten seconds.

We were performing at the new Rose Tree Park for their summer series. The stage was nestled against a slope. Our risers were placed very close to the back of the stage. Our two tallest women, Jean and Marji, stood on the center back of the top riser. In the middle of the performance, Marji felt a little dizzy and decided she'd better sit down before she fell down and stopped the whole show. She took advantage of the time our emcee talked and jumped off the back of the risers, climbed up the hill directly behind the chorus, and sat down on the grass to rest. No one noticed.

This would have been fine, but the next song was "Undecided," with the empty riser space down the middle. When the chorus moved to the outside of the risers, exposing the middle of the empty space, there she was—on the hill behind the risers—staring at me and at the audience. Our gazes met; it was pure shock for both of us. Then just as quickly she disappeared as the chorus stepped back together. The chorus had no idea what I had just seen. She and I both knew it was going to happen one more time during this song and we were ready for it. On stage, I started to laugh but since I was the only one who knew what was funny, I quickly gained control and continued with the song and the intricate choreography. Laughter came later when backstage, after the show, we shared with the chorus what had happened.

Here's to the Winners

Not too many months after we won our first-place international medals, our neighboring men's barbershop chorus, the Bryn Mawr Mainliners, won their district championship competition. This was quite a year for Philadelphia—everyone was winning. The Mainliners held a celebration show with Valley Forge for our friends and families. They called it "Here's to the Winners." Both choruses shared the stage. Quartets sang, separately and with each other. The joint choruses performed the duet from *Music Man*, "Lida Rose," and "Will I Ever Tell You." A quartet from both chapters joined together to sing an eight-part arrangement of "Royal Garden Blues." Even our Gutbucket Band was on the stage with their jug and spoons! By this time, they'd been renamed the Down Home Jug Band. We all thanked our parents, children, aunts, uncles, and neighbors for the support they had given us through the years. We ended the show with the combined choruses singing an eight-part arrangement (by John Peterson) of "Let There Be Peace on Earth."

Printed right after the front page of the program was this message:

A MESSAGE FROM THE PRESIDENT
OF THE MAINLINERS

Tonight it is my pleasure on behalf of the Bryn Mawr Chapter to honor a great organization, the Valley Forge Sweet Adelines and their talented director, Jan Touring Muck.

The accomplishments of Valley Forge under Jan's leadership are truly impressive. She has taken a group of talented singers and molded them into a chorus that consistently performs with both disciplined precision and vibrant excitement. These are the qualities required of an International champion and they reflect the personal qualities that Jan brings to everything she does. These include patience, determination, persistence, a dedication to perfection and a lot of love and enthusiasm.

While Jan's accomplishments with Valley Forge are well chronicled, her contributions over the years to the Mainliners and her status as an honorary member of our chapter are not so well known. Jan's involvement with Bryn Mawr began over ten years ago when our directors began calling on her for technical advice and a critical ear. In recent years Jan has been invited to coach the chorus as we prepared for competitions. Two years ago, Conrad Keil, our competition director, asked Jan and the stage presence committee of Valley Forge to design a choreography package to go with our competition number, "Somebody Stole My Gal." Jan's winning ways proved to be infectious since the package helped us win the Eastern Division Chorus championship this June for the first time since 1969, and most recently place third in the Mid-Atlantic District Competition.

Tonight marks the first time that the chorus Jan directs and the chorus she coaches will perform together on a show. It provides an occasion for each organization to express the admiration and affection we feel for this remarkable person. Join with us in this salute to a winner.

Kent Wood
President

And printed on the back page of the program they had written this story.

THE VALLEY FORGE CHORUS

On October 28,1983, in Detroit, Michigan The Valley Forge Chapter won the coveted title of INTERNATIONAL CHORUS CHAMPIONS. They competed with twenty-six other choruses from the United States, Sweden, England, Canada and Holland. The Valley Forge Chorus wove a spell over the audience and judges with the intensity and confidence of their performance characterized by high levels of accuracy and dynamic contrast.

This 100-voice chorus is acclaimed for their championship performances. They have appeared on The Mike Douglas Show, Evening Magazine, The Variety Club Telethon, The Johnny Mann Great American Choral Festival, The Upper Darby Forum, Longwood Gardens and The Rose Tree Summer Music Festival.

This chorus has placed in the top five during all its international competitions over the past ten years. Within this multitalented group lies their very own chorus line; a gutbucket band; comedy acts; jazz dancers; several quartets; tap dancers and soloists. All numbers are performed with exquisite costumes and dazzling choreography. They have a versatile repertoire, everything from Broadway to Basin Street.

Sweet Adelines, Inc. was founded in Tulsa, OK in 1947. It is the largest women's singing organization in the world with over 33,000 members and 750 chapters representing seven nations. There are chapters in the U.S., England, Sweden, Holland, Canada, and Australia, with prospective chapters in Germany, Japan and New Zealand. The members are trained in the art of singing four-part harmony, barbershop style, without instrumental accompaniment. Each year the 750 chapters compete in twenty-seven regional contests throughout the United States, Canada, England and Sweden. The twenty-seven Regional winners then compete at the International competition.

15

Coaching and Teaching
Other Sweet Adelines

Join Sweet Adelines and See the World.

THE SWEET ADELINES WERE going global. They had chapters in Canada and now they had established their first chorus in England. The English chorus requested that we send faculty from the United States for their first regional meeting. Music schools are good, but attending classes is for the general audience. Individual coaching by an outside expert is the way to learn the craft and improve the chorus. A personal coach can address the specific needs of the chorus they are working with. And the English chorus wanted experienced coaches to help them get started. The Sweet Adelines chose a young director, Ginny Fog, and me to travel to England to teach and coach. They provided us with scripts for our classes. I quickly realized why they chose us to be the first faculty. Most of the teachers and coaches from Sweet Adelines were from the western half of the country—Chicago, Oklahoma, Phoenix, and California. They were far more experienced than either Ginny or me. We were both from the East Coast: smart, friendly, experienced, and low key. We wouldn't frighten new and inexperienced Sweet Adelines. We were just what the English needed.

The classes and coaching went well, and we partied with them in the evenings. Ginny and I both felt the weekend was a success. Sending us was a good decision. And then Sweden joined the Sweet Adelines, and SAI headquarters asked me to be the visiting faculty. The script that they gave me was "American English—Diction." Go figure.

Visiting Sweden was like visiting a whole new world. At 3:30 in the afternoon, the sun went down, it got dark, and all the car lights automatically came on. The food was healthy and good. Too much was never piled on my plate. Wonderful. I had a whole chorus of trim bodies to coach. And all of them were taught singing in their schools. I was gone long enough that the size of the average American was a real shock when I deplaned in Philadelphia.

♮

Many years later, when Australia and New Zealand were exploding with Sweet Adelines, two choruses on the North Island, Auckland and Whangārei, wanted to hire a coach to spend two weeks with them. These were small, new choruses and my low-key manner was appealing to them. I went to New Zealand, and for two weeks I traveled back and forth, coaching the two choruses. This was another new world. I visited in December and January, which was mid-summer for them. Philadelphia is cold in winter. Deplaning was a shock.

Lessons Learned

The more contests Valley Forge won, the more I was asked to teach and coach. And the more my wineglass collection grew. Glasses from the UK, Sweden, New Zealand, and Australia joined my broken and repaired glass from Paris.

Being a championship director does not necessarily make you a good coach. The skills are different, and I had to learn them—by trial and error. The chorus director that you are coaching needs to hear what you are hearing and understand what you are doing. How else is the director to reinforce what you have done when the session is over, and you are gone? I've heard of directors who won't attend a coaching session. Therefore, no follow-up. What a waste of time and money. I don't know what I would have done if it had happened to me. I hope I would have taught the chorus to sing *without* a director—ha! Sometimes you are asked to coach a chorus three weeks before a contest. This doesn't allow time for the chorus to own any changes you suggest. About all you can do is to fix a few of the places that will raise a red flag for the audience and judges. These places are easy to find if you sit back to enjoy the music and suddenly you stub your toe while listening (that's what we call it). Something needs fixing. The chorus will love these changes (now called *enhancements*) and fix them quickly—so long as there are not too many of them. No one ever gets a perfect score, so don't try to make the chorus perfect. It sounds ludicrous, but it works. You'll have a relaxed, excited, confident chorus who will sing and look wonderful. There is not much more you can do at the last minute.

Finally, there comes a time when you have rehearsed long enough. That's when you take what you have and sprinkle pixie dust on the final song, mistakes and all. Be aware that the chorus must sing for the director, not the coach. It is the director that the chorus wants to please. As the coach, you have to step back and get out of the way. Always bring your bag of pixie dust.

Island Hills in Los Angeles

It was July 1978—just three months before the Sweet Adelines International quartet and chorus contest in Los Angeles. The Island Hills Chorus was our winning regional chorus in 1977, which made them eligible for that year's international contest. Their director, George Avener, had chosen the contest songs and was preparing them well. But then he decided to step down from being the director of the Island Hills chapter, effective immediately. Whoa! Panic!

Their completely qualified assistant director, Estelle Grau, took the reins. As is usually the case, she hadn't had much time to practice directing the chorus. Island Hills chapter called Renee Craig for help, and she graciously agreed to coach them. George had chosen two songs that were risky according to the arrangement rules of the contest. Renee was worried about the song selections, and rightly so. They were marches. Marches don't have many built-in places to add "love and finesse," which are point getters. The Island Hills music team discussed the suggestion and ramifications of changing songs two months before competition. They made the decision to use the songs they had been practicing and not worry about whether they would lose points. They loved the songs, they loved singing them, and they felt good about putting both songs on stage. Decision made. Go with the original risky songs.

Renee came in for a rehearsal on Thursday night, September 15, too close to contest for in-depth coaching, but Renee has magic in her hands, and Island Hills wanted (and needed) a little of her fairy powder sprinkled over them.

In the meantime, the Island Hills music team contacted me to come for a Saturday session on September 17. They had been watching me direct for several years, and they liked what they saw. In fact, they said that when Valley Forge performed, they watched me as much as they watched Valley Forge. On stage, they wanted to have some of what I give to my chorus. It was an exciting opportunity for me, and since Valley Forge was only a few hours away, it was easy for me to come for a Saturday coaching session. I arrived Friday night and had a get-together with some of the chorus members, so I was ready to work with them on Saturday. We spent four hours together. Even though we all knew it was too close to contest to make any changes, I still tried to fix some of the mismatched vowels and made them sing with support and to hold out their phrases—all things that were in the judging category and that I hoped would be easy to remember.

But the ending of the song (the *tag*) didn't go anywhere. I felt I *had* to change it. I knew the contest was only three weeks away, but I took a chance that they would like another ending well enough to remember it. Here's what we did. We took the melody line (leads) and asked them to hold their note, by themselves, until the end of the song, sneaking a breath if needed. The entire chorus was to look involved as the leads were "hanging out there." Then they joined the leads for the ending of the song. All parts were to put some support under their tone and keep it strong until the director cut them off. Animated faces were important, as was freedom of body motion, as the sound grew stronger and stronger. It had to look, and feel, like the whole chorus was going to march right off the stage. To better describe the idea, we likened it to a jazz band that yells, "Bring it home!" as they end their song. We loved it. And the more the chorus sang it, the better it sounded.

Three weeks later we were all heading to Los Angeles for the contest. During the three days in the hotel, before the contest, Island Hills rehearsed. I looked all over for them. I wanted to drop in to wish them good luck. I couldn't find them. (There are eight thousand attendees at a convention.) Contest day had arrived. I finally discovered what time Island Hills was competing and decided to try to locate them. They were already in the traffic pattern—leaving the hotel, getting on the bus to the contest, getting their picture taken, checking makeup, making the last trip to the rest room, and then to the final warm-up room and contest stage. That's where I found them—in the final warm-up room.

The traffic pattern at contest was supposed to allow a ten-minute warm-up period before entering the stage. This backstage crew had run into a timing snag and sent the chorus, in their bus, back to the hotel—and then recalled them a half hour later (this is when I found them). The wait had caused a slight change in their firepower. Island Hills wanted one last run-through of their two competition songs—like shaking up the champagne bottle before you popped the cork. They positioned themselves on the warm-up risers, getting ready to sing one last time. Then they were told, "No singing in this room."

What? We can't sing?

I felt for Estelle—a brand new director being caught in this dilemma. They hadn't sung for about an hour. You can't go on the stage cold. I felt the panic of not having that last run-through. We normally sing softly in the last warm-up room and pop the cork on stage. But to not sing at all? No way! I said to myself, "Think fast, Muck. They don't have time to waste." So we did it this way. They mimed the whole six-minute contest package. Estelle directed. They sang, danced, and accepted the applause. And they never made a sound.

Island Hills couldn't wait to get on that stage and actually sing. Ya gotta know your chorus, think fast, and trust your gut feelings. Sometimes you have to make lemonade out of lemons.

I wanted to hug them all, but I knew I'd spoil their makeup, their hairdo, or worse, their costume. It was just lots of, "You look great! Good luck! Have fun." We didn't have much time together, so as I turned to leave, I said, "Bring it home!" And they did. They nailed that ending and had the audience up on their feet.

Smashing! And they won the contest. 1978 international chorus champions! I watched them from my seat in the convention center and, immediately after the announcement, ran backstage to get my hugs. I didn't care about the makeup and hair. It was crazy.

You know what they said? "Thanks for coming to the warm-up room. It gave us so much confidence." They said that they went on stage saying to themselves, "Bring it home."

Three weeks before contest is just not long enough for muscle memory to take over. Did Island Hills remember the matched vowels, breath support, and ends of phrases that I had taught them? Nope. Did they remember to smile, and bring it home? You bet. Did they win the contest anyway, even though they had forgotten the little coached corrections we had made? Yep. No one gets one hundred percent scores on the contest stage, so don't make changes at the last minute just trying to get yourself one more point. Use pixie dust.

Last Minute Change

Here's an interesting example about what "last minute" can mean. I worked with a chorus as they climbed the contest ladder until the year they won Regional. With my blessing, they changed coaches to take them to their first international contest. With eighteen months to prepare, the new coach found two better arrangements for them to use for the contest. Unfortunately this chorus was too inexperienced to learn two new songs for their first international contest in that timeframe. They came in last. I hadn't worked with them for well over a year, but I knew them. For their first rehearsal after returning home, I took my daughter for company, and we made the two-and-a-half-hour trip to their rehearsal hall. Nothing needed to be said—I just had to be there to share their pain.

Don't Interrupt a Teacher

As a teacher, I find one of the hardest things to do when I'm sitting in a classroom setting is to not interrupt another teacher when, in my opinion, it's obvious there is a solution to the problem she is trying to explain. It happened to me at an International School where the lesson was how to design choreography to match the song. A championship chorus stood onstage in a ballroom with a top-notch coach working with them as a demonstration. I sat on the front row. The chorus sang three of their songs, all with choreography. They were smashing. So good! But the chorus felt that all the movements looked the same. It was obvious to the audience that they were the same. The chorus wanted more variety between the songs. They were looking for a solution to this "problem."

All three songs had the same rhythm and the same message. It's no wonder the choreographer used the same steps—it was just what the songs needed. The steps fit with the music, and they were creative. The coach was on the spot. I could sense she was having trouble. When the choreography is good and it fits the music, how do you solve a problem when you know there is no problem? This class was supposed to teach solutions. There were about two thousand people in the audience. Help!

I wanted to stand and holler up to the stage "It's the music!" The audience would have paid attention to me because everyone knew I was the director of the Valley Forge Chorus—a chorus well known for its choreography. I had a heated discussion with myself, and by the time I decided not to interrupt, the coach had somehow changed the direction of the class. I was so glad I had kept quiet. It would have been a terrible thing to do. But I knew the choreography was right for the music. The solution was to change the music.

You just don't interrupt a class in front of two thousand people.

Carolina Harmony

Coaching Carolina Harmony Chorus, located in Raleigh, North Carolina, was one of my special times. We were together, coach and chorus, for almost five years. I developed close friendships with the director and members of the chorus. The director was a talented musician; her best friend in the chorus was Debra Shapiro. For the weekend, I always stayed with one or the other of them. Debra has a beautiful soprano voice and is a master of the piano. In the evenings, after our coaching session, we would have dinner together and Debra would play the piano for us. We would enjoy a glass of wine and listen, talk, and laugh. My husband and I would stay with Debra as we traveled through Raleigh on our way to visit our son in Jacksonville, Florida. We bought our furniture for our new home in High Point, North Carolina, and visited with them for the weekend. Debra played the piano so beautifully that her teacher wanted her to become a concert pianist. She preferred being a professor at the University of North Carolina. Debra eventually accepted a teaching position at the University of Maryland. We kept in touch. It was through my friendship with Debra that, many years later, the idea for this book was born.

Was It Me?

Being a coach isn't all international trips and nights playing piano with friends. It's a lot of responsibility and second-guessing, too. I will carry these decisions with me forever. Was it me?

One beautiful chorus was poised to win their regional contest. I had coached them many times and was attending the contest. I visited them during their last rehearsal, and they sang their songs for me. The ballad was beautiful, but the uptune had a spot in the middle where the chorus's energy lagged, and it sounded as though they might be slowing down the tempo. I mentioned this to them—reminded them to keep the energy going when they approached that spot. They went to the stage and I went to the auditorium to listen to them. The ballad was beautiful, but the uptune was just a little frantic. Too much energy and not sung together. Had I been too specific? The chorus lost first place by two points. Had I done it? Had I broken one of my own rules by making changes the day of the contest?

The next year they won the contest, but I wasn't their coach.

♮

One chorus was new and small. I had coached them the year before, and they had done well. I was invited back the next year in hopes that they would continue to improve. For two weeks we worked on all the technique necessary to score well. We fixed their vowels and carried out the ends of phrases. Working hard to improve, we perfected a few changes in volume, corrected their diphthongs, and added a motion or two for the showmanship score. They needed a lot of warm-up to go from "gang singing" to "unit sound." I knew this.

The contest weekend was hectic. I didn't give the chorus enough time to warm up. They went on stage and sang every vowel, every phrase, perfectly. I was very proud of them. But they never tuned a chord. They were gang singing and scored quite low. I learned a lesson. Don't sweat the small stuff. Sing in tune.

I wasn't their coach anymore, either.

♮

And finally, one chorus was good, they were seasoned competitors, but not used to singing together. I was taking them to the contest as a favor. They wanted to score well and had the knowledge to do so. Just before we competed, word came back to us that there was some unexpected noise on stage. I opted not to tell the chorus because I didn't want them distracted.

We sang, and they sounded distracted. Was it my mistake?

16

Stepping Out of Our Comfort Zone

Stepping Out with the Stars, 1984

THE TIME HAD COME to make our first (and only) recording. We were entering the big time and we were ready. We needed twelve songs for the tape. Sweet Adelines International would not allow us to record our contest songs, because the original recordings of winners were still for sale at headquarters. We looked for other songs in our repertoire to fill the time.

A room at the church in our neighborhood had just the right amount of natural reverb. They said OK to our request to use their facility, and we contacted a recording studio to record us. Our name for the cassette was *Stepping Out with the Stars*. We had just acquired an arrangement of the song "Steppin' Out"— and we *were* stars, having won the international contest. But we had to learn the song first. It had an enormous number of words to memorize and lots of verses to sing. The scheduled date to record came before we had it all learned. The many verses all began with different words and not all of us could remember which words came first. We almost had it memorized. It was the signature song of our cassette, so we *had* to record it. On the Saturday of our recording session, there appeared two large sheets of paper with the first word of every verse printed in bold black letters, in order of performance. It was an honest-to-goodness cheat sheet. They were placed on easels at either side of the room so all members could see them. Thanks to these sheets, and the member who brought them to rehearsal, the recording of "Steppin' Out" didn't have any hesitations at the beginning of every verse where you could swear you heard someone say, "What's the first word?" In the middle of recording this song, the chorus was sounding a little unglued, so I stopped them, and without using the pitch pipe to tune up, we solidified our sound, then continued. On the final recording it sounded as though we had made a key change. As our session came to an end, and we had some extra time, we decided to add one more song. Without any extra rehearsals, we were able to record "Battle Hymn of the Republic."

It's amazing that we were able to record twelve songs in one day. It was my job, as we finished taping each song, to put on earphones and listen and approve each take. It's hard to believe that we were so well trained that each song only took one or two takes before it was OK for the cassette. Next, we decided in what order to present the songs. It was like putting together a twelve-song performance for an audience. The order made a difference.

None of us knew what to expect from this recording. Our first recorded song was "Steppin' Out." We put "Something in the Way He Moves" as our second song. It was beautiful, and the emotion in the lyrics was evident. The tears poured out of each of us as we listened to our brand new tape. It was so beautiful—and such a relief. We had done an outstanding job of recording our music. *Stepping Out with the Stars* was a huge success. Years later, when CDs were introduced, many of us had the cassette transferred to a CD so that we could play it in our car. The musicality of the chorus was extraordinary. To this day, I am awed at how talented we all were.

Two of our members were vacationing at a seaside resort about a two-hour drive from the church. They decided not to leave the beach to come up for the recording session. They felt it was going to be a flop, and they didn't want to be a part of it. That was not a good thing to tell a director. And another thing not to tell a director is that you are going to stay home from rehearsal because you have to wash your hair. Not good. It really happened.

Philadelphia, 1986

For the international contest in 1986, the Sweet Adelines added a semi-final day to the chorus contest. As usual, all the choruses would compete on Thursday by singing two contest songs in the barbershop style. The new part of the contest, the semi-finals, would be held Friday and the finals on Saturday night. The top five choruses from the semi-finals would sing a fifteen-minute performance package. Two of the songs had to be in the barbershop style and would be judged accordingly. Ten more points would be awarded for the performance style.

For the choruses that expected (or just wanted) to be in the top five, this more than doubled the workload for competition. There were now four songs that had to be competition ready—two for the semi-finals and another two songs to be judged in the finals. Then you had five or ten minutes to add emcee work, sing more songs, or do a dance routine if you wanted—10 points for that.

This was the first contest for us after winning the gold medal and we were reasonably confident that we would make the top five again this time. We decided to present a clown package for the finals (my favorite idea). There was music to find and costumes to design. And we had to learn how to make our faces look like clowns without losing our individuality. Good grief! Our first few attempts at makeup were pretty scary. The audience (and judges) wanted to see our expressive faces, so we kept downgrading our makeup until we had only enough to give the illusion of a clown face.

Our plans were coming together nicely. We chose to sing two ballads for the contest part of the finals, "Laugh, Clown, Laugh" and "If I Had the Heart of a Clown." We added some fun songs like "Make 'Em Laugh." The choreography team was hard at work. They designed a three-ring circus on stage with a make-believe tiger in the middle of each circle. We moved the entire chorus down to the stage, using only the floor and the lower three riser steps. Two of our tallest members acted as tightrope walkers. They started at each end of the top riser and slowly wobbled toward each other along the imaginary tightrope stretched along the back row of the riser. For balance, they each carried an empty, broken umbrella covered with shiny silver pipe cleaners.

"Be a Clown, Be a Clown" was our finale, and the front row (including the director—nineteen of us in all) headed to the front of the stage and did somersaults toward the audience. We ended the song, sitting on the stage floor, legs outstretched in front of us, laughing at the audience.

Ta-dah!

♮

The summer before the contest, Sylvia Alsbury came to coach us. We were having trouble finding just the right clown feeling. Sylvia asked us to pretend we were in the circus and to enter the stage as circus people. She sent us out of our rehearsal hall and said, "How would you enter the tent? What would you do? Now come back in." The chorus went nuts. We pretended the rehearsal hall was the stage and we laughed and skipped into the room.

One of our members did cartwheels across the floor to her riser position. One stood on her head. One went to the front of the room, sat on the floor, and talked to the make-believe audience. Two girls grabbed hands and danced around each other. It was all off the cuff, all ad lib. It was bedlam. Sylvia loved it. It was perfect.

But we couldn't remember what we had done. We tried to do it again. It was a fiasco. We just couldn't duplicate it. That night, after rehearsal and after Sylvia had gone back to Tucson, one of our members sat down and made a flow chart assigning specific activities and locations to all the chorus members. She brought it to our next rehearsal and explained it all to us. It worked. We were able to rehearse the entrance. From then on, when we entered the stage for the clown act, it was an organized activity. Everyone had a place to go and no one crashed into another person.

Three months later we were driving our own cars into Philadelphia for the contest. How nice not to have to take a plane. We were tired from rehearsing—even before we went onstage. We placed fifth overall, but our performance package placed second (the ten points helped). That was the first time the top five choruses presented a performance package. We didn't realize how much work had to be done to put on a fifteen-minute performance. But it was worth it—our staging was magnificent.

That year we were the only chorus who put on a performance for the finals. Everyone else did a parade package with emcees. The judges liked us. After the contest, the executive secretary sent a letter to Valley Forge saying that our performance in Philadelphia was exactly what the executive board had envisioned for the new performance package requirements. It took many years before all choruses would create a complete finals package—a performance, not just singing four songs and using an emcee to tie it all together. It was a lot of work, but so much fun to perform.

International Education Symposium—Summertime Classes

As international faculty members, Ida, Lennie, and I were often asked to teach at our International Education Symposium (IES) schools. These were held at universities throughout the country during the summer months. There were often eight hundred attendees. We slept in the women's dorms. We had visiting faculty from the outside world—professional singers, university professors, and so on, who came to teach us. One year the entire school was divided into choruses named for different colors. Mine was the blue chorus. Each chorus had a director, a stage manager, and a choreographer. With Valley Forge having three members on the faculty, we were split up and each given separate choruses—director Jan, choreographer Ida, and stage manager Lennie. Each chorus learned two songs, choreographed them, and performed them on the Saturday night show.

On the final night, after the blue chorus had performed, I went into the auditorium to listen to the other groups. Ida's chorus was just about to sing, and I sat down next to her. Afterwards, Ida turned to me and asked what I thought of the choreography of this chorus. She had worked with them and had helped design the choreography. I was honest. "Ida, it looks like two different people worked on the choreography. It doesn't hang together." I will never forget her response.

"The director added her own staging to our design."

I didn't answer Ida. I knew what she was thinking. We didn't need to say any more to each other. The understanding was there. Without any knowledge of what had happened, and just watching the chorus on stage, I could pick up that there was something not right about the staging. It "stubbed my toe." And then I thought what a blessing it was when the director and choreographer had the ability to weave together music and staging.

Directing by Greg Lyne

Several years after we had won the international contest in 1983, our IES main speaker was a wonderful gentleman from the men's Barbershop Harmony Society, Greg Lyne. Greg was well known and highly respected and soon to be a Men's International Champion Chorus Director (1990). One of his classes was devoted to the art of directing. Of course, being only five foot two, I chose to sit in the front row so I could see and hear. This made me a prime target to be a "volunteer" for demonstration purposes. I'm sure I had my gold medal around my neck. In front of a class of three hundred people, Greg called me to the front and began to work on my directing style. For twenty minutes he helped me to become more effective with less work. His suggestions were very subtle, and very hard to adjust to after my twenty years of directing.

When he had completed his demonstration, I sat down to quite a bit of applause. I remember thinking, "Whew! I've just won International and here I am being taught how to improve my directing." Amazing. And I was OK with it. When I reviewed the videotape of our winning performance, I saw what Greg had been trying to teach me. As best I could, I tried to make my hands perform as he wanted them to. The lesson that I learned was that you never stop refining your directing. You never stop learning.

Houston, 1988

Valley Forge's membership grew by about fifteen people just before we competed in Houston. One of our neighboring choruses was having trouble keeping members and decided to disband and join Valley Forge. They were all good singers and we welcomed them, but this was a major adjustment for the chorus. As the director, I felt like I had two different choruses to direct at the same time. We were preparing to compete in Houston, Texas, and we had work to do. It was just going to take time—like moving into a new neighborhood and attending a new school. By the time we arrived in Houston and had many rehearsals, the feelings of togetherness as a single chorus finally returned. We placed third.

San Antonio, 1991

The San Antonio contest was like being on vacation with ninety of our best friends. We stayed at the Marriott on the Riverwalk and spent most of our free time visiting the restaurants, taking boat rides, and buying cowboy hats. We wore our gold medals from previous contests all the time. No matter where we walked, we met a friend. One evening I arrived back at the hotel with only a gold chain around my neck—no gold medal. It was somewhere on the Riverwalk. I had to go home without it. About a year later, the medal arrived in my mailbox in an unmarked package—no name or return address. Apparently, a Sweet Adelines member found it and returned it to headquarters. I had engraved my initials and date (1983) on the back. Someone at headquarters must have gone through the roster of Valley Forge in 1983 and found the one person with the initials JLM. I felt whole again.

17

Bits and Pieces

OVER A TWENTY-FIVE-YEAR CAREER, a lot of things happen that just don't quite fit anywhere else. This is a collection of some of my favorite stories while I was a part of the Valley Forge chapter of Sweet Adelines International (1967–1992).

The Berwyn Tavern

We almost always ended our weekly rehearsals with a beverage at the local pub. Our rehearsals were over at 10:30, and we had found a tavern that had a private room in the back that stayed open till 2:00 a.m. At this time (in the early seventies), there were twenty-five to thirty of us who met at the tavern. The private room was too small for all of us, but we squeezed in anyway. The tables and chairs were so close together that there was no room between them. We learned very quickly that we should order two drinks at once instead of just one, because the server couldn't worm past those of us in the front to give us all our seconds.

At the end of the evening, when it was time to go home, many of us slid to the floor, and crawled under the tables to get to the other side, where there was room to walk. Since this was a private room, and it was late in the evening, we were free to laugh out loud or even sing. One evening, we marched in a line around the room singing the "Stars and Stripes Forever" march. We followed the leader (whoever it was) as she marched over chairs, around tables, and back over the chairs. One of the other songs we liked to sing was "Turn Your Radio On." It was a solo with chorus accompaniment. One evening it didn't take much to convince Marji, our soloist, to sing her song. She stood on a table, held a spoon for a mic, and belted it out as we all accompanied her. Those days we sometimes didn't get home till 1:30 or 2:00 in the morning.

But then the tavern was sold, and the new owner asked us to leave. He wanted to upgrade the restaurant. We moved on, but our new after-rehearsal eatery didn't have a private room. We had to stop singing and dancing around the chairs, but we did continue to get together after rehearsals. Even now, years later, many of us continue to meet for dinner once a month.

The School System

Many of our members were employed as teachers. Every other year they had to put in a request for a week away from school to come with us to international competition. This was usually held in the early weeks of the school year, September through November. Sometimes the school said no, and we had to compete without one or two of our members.

1983 was the year we all knew we had a good chance of winning. No one wanted to be left behind. What to do? One of our teachers "got sick" that week in the fall. She was with us as we won the blue ribbon. It was the year Philadelphia was winning everything—basketball, baseball, and ice hockey. We were celebrated as another winner for Philadelphia, and the local TV station filmed us arriving at the airport waving our blue ribbons and signature three-cornered hats. And of course, we had to sing for the cameras. Oops! There she was, our sick teacher, waving her blue ribbon and three-cornered hat. Her disciplinary action was a two-week unpaid "vacation."

Colored Underwear

Summertime is a good time for outdoor corn roasts and barbecues, and we were preparing for one of our best picnics ever. The sun was shining, and the air smelled of summer flowers. Everyone was arriving, saying hello to friends, and finding their way to the bar. We are party people, and the anticipation of a good time was high. Oops! We all stared at Dan. The material of his white slacks was so thin that you could see he was wearing colored underwear. Only his best friends would care about this. We turned to Ken and asked, "What color is your underwear?"

Without a hesitation he answered, "White."

"Change with Dan."

"What?"

"Change underwear with Dan. You have on dark slacks and you can't see through them. Dan has white slacks, and you can see the colors of his underwear. Switch."

"Yes, ma'am."

So they disappeared into the men's room to switch underwear and came back looking great. White under white, colors under black. Problem solved. The men probably didn't care, but we knew that all our friends would giggle at Dan's underwear faux pas. And we cared about that.

The Banner and the Song

We had our own banner—it was a large banner with the words VALLEY FORGE in the red, white, and blue colors of our chorus. We were proud that we carried the name of Valley Forge. A

friend of ours is a graphic artist, and he designed our banner. We had a professional seamstress in our chorus who made it for us. We brought it to all our contests—regional and international. We hung it over the balconies of the convention centers, so it was seen from the auditorium *and* the contest stage.

It was with us in Detroit. From the stage we saw our friends and parents standing up in the balcony. They held the banner over the edge of the balcony and shouted "Val-ley Forge! Val-ley Forge! Val-ley Forge!"

Norristown State Hospital

We were on our way to perform at the Norristown State Hospital, the local, active, state-funded psychiatric ward. We were told that the stage lighting was bad and there was no room to change clothes. We had to arrive in costume and full makeup. On our eyelids was blue eye shadow. Under our eyebrows was a thin line of white powder. Black eye liner and false eyelashes completed the eye makeup. Rouge highlighted our cheeks, and fire-engine red painted our lips.

Jeanne and Barb got lost on their way to the performance, so Jeanne pulled her car into a gas station for directions. A young, male gas station attendant approached her open window and asked if he could help.

Jeanne answered, "We're on our way to Norristown State Hospital and we're lost."

At that moment, Barb leaned over Jeanne and said in a loud voice, "I don't wanna go!"

Jeanne immediately picked up the charade. "Now, Barb, you promised when the time came, you would be good."

The attendant was last seen backing away from the car.

Eight to a Room

In the early days of attending our regional meetings and conferences, we were careful of our household's money that we spent on our hobby. We slept four to a room, bringing our food with us— sandwiches, fruit, sodas, chips and dip, and an electric skillet to cook our dinner. One weekend we must have lost count as to how many of us were staying in the room because when it was time to retire, we had eight members ready to spend the night. What to do? Well, we took the mattresses off the beds and put them on the floor. We used the box springs to make four more beds. This worked well. Everyone had a reasonably comfortable place to sleep.

Except no one thought to leave the bathroom light turned on as a night light. What an obstacle course at three in the morning when someone had to head for the john. We tried not to step on heads.

Glow Necklaces

Four in a hotel room on a Sweet Adelines weekend creates fun. One time, in one room, someone brought some glow necklaces with her, those long flexible tubes filled with a fluorescent chemical. The four roommates were playing with them late one night—making hairpieces and bracelets and just being creative. One of the women wound up her flexible tube into a tight circle and stuck it in her mouth. She turned off the hotel room lights and in the darkened room, she began to talk. Light shone out of her mouth and then disappeared again when her mouth closed. The more she talked, the harder they laughed.

After a while, the necklaces broke from the continued flexing (but not in anyone's mouth), and the result was a spray of glowing (non-toxic) fluid on the bedspread and carpeting. At this point, they completely lost it. They imagined the next morning when the housekeepers would tidy the room and think aliens had visited them during the night.

The Had-tos

When we went to competitions and put four women in the same hotel room, we learned to stake out a corner for our clothes and use only one fourth of the countertop in the bathroom. Living so close with people you've known for years creates a unique form of intimacy. We don't usually talk about kids and husbands on our trips, but one year, one foursome shared their stories. One by one, each mentioned that their first child was born somewhat less than nine months after their weddings. Four identical stories. From then on, the roommates called themselves "The Had-tos."

The Support Circle

Hidden among all the fun and struggle to be champions was a small group who discovered that they had something special between them. Each woman had a child who was addicted to drugs. Before rehearsals, on Tuesday nights, they came together in the kitchen of the rehearsal hall to just talk about their kids. All the chorus knew why they met, and we let them be—but they often heard us say, "If you ever need me, call me." They didn't care that we knew about their troubles. During one summer coaching session with Ann Gooch, we were outside for our lunch break. The "druggie group" (as they called themselves) were together on the lawn sitting on one blanket. The chorus knew they were talking and left the group alone for the lunch hour. If we had help to offer, we joined them. If we didn't, we just let them be. One member was new to our chorus and didn't want anyone to know she had a druggie, too. She just sat close by the druggie group and listened. This group lasted over a year, and they still say how much it helped them to share with people who understood.

Sue and Tootie

Tootie had lost her fifteen-year-old daughter Lisa to a drunk driver. We started singing a new song, "Six Weeks Every Summer." Each time we performed our song, Tootie thought, "I would take my daughter for six weeks every summer if I could have her." At a performance, standing together on the front row, Sue noticed that Tootie was in trouble. Tootie couldn't hold back the tears. Sue reached down and took hold of her hand. Tootie's mother and children were in the audience, and her mom also noticed that Tootie was in trouble. She noticed that Sue reached for her hand and held it for the entire song—something she wanted to do but couldn't.

Sue came to me with the story and asked me not to have the chorus sing "Six Weeks Every Summer" anymore. She told me about Tootie's daughter and explained how it was impossible for Tootie to perform this song. Done. We never sang that song again. That same year, 1973, we were scheduled to compete in Washington, D.C., our first International. Tootie wouldn't go. It was the anniversary of her daughter's death, and her family always had a mass said for Lisa. Kathi took Tootie aside and said, "My brother is a priest, and he will have a mass for Lisa." For the entire week-end, someone was always beside Tootie to make sure she made it through. Many years later, she said to me, "Thank God for music and laughter. Without those in my life, I would not have made it. During my very bad times you brought music into my life, for which I endlessly thank you."

Kick-a-Poo Party

From the beginning of the Valley Forge chapter, many of our hus-bands, boyfriends, and brothers enjoyed being a part of our cho-rus life. We included them in much of what we did, although we did have an unwritten understanding that we would not sing at our family gatherings. When we had our annual installation of new officers, we made it special by celebrating someplace other than the rehearsal hall where, after the ceremony, we shared food, drinks, and friendships. We also made sure to choose an *after-glo* location following each performance, a place where the men would enjoy going out with us for something to eat and drink. We made sure our men were a part of all that we did. We wanted them to feel like part of the chorus. (We also wanted them to know where we had been when we came home late at night. It was nice to hear a sleepy, "Did you have a good rehearsal?")

One year we bought our men ties with the Valley Forge logo on them. We also had dinners and lawn parties at chorus members' homes—corn roasts at the Bosnas' and a pig roast with Bloody Marys at the Allens'. Many friendships between the men were started during these evenings. The party that will live forever was one that Lennie organized as a thank you to the guys for all the help that they gave to us with all our activities. It will forever be known as the kick-a-poo party. Kick-a-poo joy juice is a drink

---

Kick-a-Poo Joy Juice

Ingredients
- ½ gallon Fleischmann's Preferred Whiskey
- 2 bottles pink champagne
- 1 large can pineapple-grapefruit juice
- 1 large can orange juice
- 1 lg. bottle ginger ale

Preparation
Mix above ingredients together in a large punch bowl. Add ice. Stand back—there's a kick.

---

with a powerful kick. When the men heard that we were serving a drink in a punch bowl at *their* party, they wondered if we had lost our minds. They pooh-poohed the idea. We served it anyway.

It was so delicious that we kept drinking it. And drinking it. And drinking it.

It was hard to go to work that entire week after our first kick-a-poo celebration. Our men became good friends with each other while filling their glasses with kick-a-poo. To this day, Sue and her husband can't remember which one drove home that night. They made it safely—thank God.

WWWW

After one of our many rehearsal gatherings, Mimi mentioned to us how boring the months of January and February were. Kathi chimed in with an idea. "I have a cabin in the Poconos that we could use." It took us a while to realize what she was really saying. A sleepover! With four bedrooms and extra spaces, the cabin could sleep twelve. We suggested a date, Kathi approved, and the planning began. We needed food, drinks, pillows, and blankets—some of us brought sleeping bags, snow boots, and directions to the Poconos. Soon twelve members were ready to go, including three husbands. Having the husbands along was a welcome idea. It was a mountain cabin, and any wildlife we encountered wouldn't be friendly. We had such an incredible time that we did it again for a couple more winters.

Many years later Janet W. bought a cabin in Betterton, Maryland—a couple blocks from the shores of the Chesapeake Bay. She couldn't wait till she could invite all the gang to her place. It became a tradition. Summer or winter, it didn't matter. Sometimes there were four of us and sometimes fourteen. The cabin had three bedrooms, and we had blow-up mattresses, reclining chairs, couches, box springs, and mattresses to sleep on. We brought food for meals, plus snacks for afternoon board games on rainy afternoons. We ate at the cabin for breakfast, lunch, and the first evening's meal. But Saturdays we went into Rock Hall or Chestertown to visit the town, shop, and have a Chesapeake Bay dinner. In winter, we quickly learned not to put our wine and Bloody Mary mix on the back porch to stay cool. At seventeen degrees, the bottles cracked and made quite a mess. In summer we took walks along the beach.

We started out in the Poconos calling ourselves the Sacred Sisterhood of Wonderful Wacky Women of the Woods, and soon we became the Wonderful Wacky Women of the Water. Janet got us T-shirts with the logo WWWW spread in an arc over two crossed wine glasses.

Lamb Tavern

When all three of my kids were in school all day, I wondered if I could hold down a daytime job. In my town, there was a nice restaurant called the Lamb Tavern. They had a busy weekday lunchtime crowd. Did they need a daytime hostess? I learned a new trade. It was my job to make sure all the servers had an equal number of customers. The restaurant had a bar, a large dining room, and a special room at the end for big parties.

One day I took a reservation from a Mr. Forge, who was bringing a party of eight for a luncheon at one o'clock. Could they have the back room? I should have seen this coming. At one o'clock on their day, as I approached my hostess desk, I saw eight society ladies out to lunch, waiting to be shown to their table. They were dressed to the nines, with hats, gloves, fur stoles. One had a long cigarette holder, which she held high in the air.

Egad! This was my chorus.

With a straight face, I escorted these ladies to their table, proudly walking them right down the center of the main restaurant. They strutted boldly to their private dining room. We all dissolved into peals of laughter once inside our private room. I should have known that "Mr. Forge" meant Valley Forge. They got me.

Guardians of Humility

Our chorus was attending a retreat weekend, a Friday night and Saturday escape for education and fun. It's filled with singing and classes and sometimes fun, crazy contests. We arrived late afternoon Friday and checked into our hotel room. I'm-in-charge-Lennie was not around. She was off somewhere else, being in charge.

The temptation was just too much. Her nearest and dearest friends went into her room with rolls of toilet paper. They started at the top of the room and draped the paper all over everything— on the windows, mirrors, around the bedposts, back up over the table lamps, and across the room to the bathroom door. They didn't miss a thing. The room was covered. When Lennie came back from her chores and opened her door, we heard her famous expletives all down the hall. And then we also heard the sound of satisfied laughter. Job well done.

Who Did I Sleep With?

How else can I phrase this? My Sweet Adelines friends from California were in Los Angeles for their spring competition. I was in San Diego for a Thursday–Friday–Saturday noon business meeting of a company I had joined. The Sweet Adelines Show of Champions was Saturday night in Los Angeles, and I was only two hours away. These were the winners of the contest—some of the best choruses and quartets were performing in the show. I wanted to go.

I called the Los Angeles hotel. They put me in contact with the chair of the competition. Yes, there is a ticket available. Yes, we will find a bed for you. Yes, one of the members from the San Diego Chorus will drive you back on Sunday, if you can leave early morning.

Yes, I can do that.

Buses or trains to Los Angeles was an option, but fortunately one of my friends from the meeting in San Diego heard about my plans and, having nothing to do, drove me to L.A. Perfect. On Saturday after lunch, I grabbed my toothbrush and pajamas, and we were off. After the performance on Saturday night, I picked up the room key from the hotel desk. I quietly let myself into my room, took the empty half of the bed nearest the door and slept well. In the early morning I left money on the table for my half of the bed and slipped out to meet my ride back to San Diego.

Who did I sleep with? I don't know.

18

The Quartets

VALLEY FORGE ALWAYS FIELDED a quartet or two from within the chorus. Here are *some* names of our many chapter quartets: Better Halfs, Parfaits, Soliloquy, Troubadours, The Neat Arrangement, TNT, High Voltage, The Revolutionary Sound, The Generation Gap, Paoli Local, and Never Say Never. And this list doesn't include the many quartets that had only one or two members from Valley Forge.

The Better Halfs

The Better Halfs were charter members of the Valley Forge Chorus and our first quartet. They were fun to watch, natural when they performed. They laughed and made fun of life. Every time the chorus was together, they sang for us. When we partied in a private room, several of our members sat at their feet to listen to them sing. Much of the personality of the Better Halfs became the personality of the chorus. They sang well and looked good. They were gutsy and had fun with their music. They loved to entertain—just like Valley Forge.

Through Connie's husband, Alex, the Better Halfs became good friends with the Philadelphia Men's Barbershop Chorus. The Better Halfs asked one of the men if he would coach them. He said no but he recommended they ask a boy in his chorus, just eighteen years old, to be their coach. His name was Roger

The Better Halfs

Blackburn, and he was a trumpet major at the Curtis Institute of Music. His father was a barbershopper, which made Roger a "barbershop brat." Roger said yes and spent many Sundays with the quartet, as their coach and arranger. The Better Halfs "adopted" Roger. His own family was many miles away, and he quickly had four other mothers to take care of him here on the East Coast. He enjoyed many dinners with the families. We never got tired of hearing the Better Halfs sing his arrangement of "Frankie and Johnny." Several years after Roger's graduation, he accepted

a position in the Philadelphia Orchestra. He also became the
director of the Philadelphia chapter of the Barbershop Harmony
Society.

The Busy Bees

Alex and Connie, the baritone of the Better Halfs, had eleven
kids. Four of their girls sang together as the Busy Bees. (Yes,
their last name began with a B.) The youngest Busy Bee was

The Busy Bees

the lead at only eight years old. The tenor, Claire, was eleven. She's the same Claire who later became my star pupil. The Busy Bees were well known in the area and were invited, along with Mayor Frank Rizzo of Philadelphia, to celebrate the opening of the huge shopping mall being built in the neighboring town of King of Prussia. Valley Forge held their first rehearsals in that brand new shopping center. The Busy Bees often sang for us.

The Paoli Local

The Paoli Local was a new quartet, and I was their coach. It was contest time, and we were together at the hotel, warming up just before they competed. I asked them where they wanted to place, and they answered, "First!" Oh, my goodness! I swallowed hard. That's a dangerous goal for a novice quartet. (They were a first-time competitor.) I must have looked at them with a "You've got

The Paoli Local entertaining at an after-glo.

to be kidding me" look. They ignored me and repeated their goal. We said good luck as they left for the traffic pattern. I went into the auditorium to listen.

They announced the next contestant, the Paoli Local. They walked on stage with such confidence. Their performance astounded me. When they left the stage, I jumped out of my seat and ran to the backstage entrance to meet them. They have told me that I came running down the hall with my arms flailing, yelling, "You did it! You did it!" I hugged them all.

Later, when they announced the Paoli Local as the Novice Quartet winners, the quartet went crazy. They ran on stage to receive their novice award medals. As they started to leave the stage and go back to their seats, one of the stagehands said, "Don't go away." Puzzled, the quartet hung around backstage. When they heard the announcement of fifth through second, and they were still standing backstage, the thought was...maybe we placed sixth. Nope. This novice quartet from Valley Forge had just won the entire quartet contest. Valley Forge went bonkers.

Growing Girls

In Sweden the Growing Girls were members of the Rönninge Sweet Adelines Barbershop Chorus. They were eleven when they started singing together. In 1986, at sixteen, they came to Philadelphia to sing in our international quartet contest—for evaluation only. They stayed the week at Lennie and Ken's bed and breakfast. Lennie was out of commission with a sore back, so Ken took the girls to the CVS for makeup and to the new King of Prussia Mall to shop.

One evening, Darrel and I took them to his Mainliners men's barbershop rehearsal, and afterwards we joined the chorus for

With the Growing Girls. © *1990 GerryOHalloran.*

something to eat and drink. Did I mention these girls were absolutely gorgeous? I'd never seen the Mainliners smile so much.

The girls had a free day here in the Philly area, and the weather was perfect for a trip to the Jersey Shore to enjoy the sun and sand. I asked my son John if he would like to invite a buddy of his to take the four girls to Ocean City, New Jersey, for the day. They could use our car (and a little of our cash). It's not hard to envision two good-looking eighteen-year-old boys taking four gorgeous sixteen-year-old girls to the shore for the day. They spent the day on the beach. Later the boys took them to a nice restaurant for fish and crabs. Ann, from Valley Forge, owned a beach house in Ocean City that they used to wash off the sand and clean up for dinner. In the quiet after the evening meal, the girls started to sing a love song to the guys. The restaurant

The Mainliners welcome the Growing Girls. © 1990 GerryOHalloran.

became quiet as the diners listened and watched. The boys were speechless. They had never been sung to before. The other diners applauded at the end of the song. On the way home, they stopped in Philly, and the girls shopped on South Street. John still has a sweet, faraway look in his eyes when he tells me the story.

♮

The Swedish-owned store IKEA was opening in North Jersey. Lennie couldn't resist introducing them to the Growing Girls. Her idea was for IKEA to spotlight them during their grand opening while they sang impromptu performances in locations throughout the store. IKEA was contacted and Lennie provided them with a video of the Growing Girls gold medal performance at the international quartet contest. IKEA liked them, and days before their grand opening, the Growing Girls arrived in Philadelphia.

I picked them up at the airport and dropped them off at Lennie's home. On opening day Lennie and I drove them to the IKEA store. This was a two-and-a-half-hour drive. First performance was at 2:00 p.m.

Traffic! Traffic! Traffic!

We were afraid we would be late. We suggested the quartet put on their makeup and warm up in the car. The parking lot at the store was overloaded. We drove around. No place for us to park. The clock was ticking. I'm-in-charge Lennie pulled up in front of the security guard and said, "I have four singers here that have a 2:00 p.m. performance and there's no place to park!" They found us a parking place right by the main entrance. We got the quartet set up to sing but they had no mics. Lennie to the rescue. Mics were provided for all of their performances. We left them in the good hands of the IKEA personnel. Two days later we came to pick them up and where did we find them? We found them at the IKEA Swedish grocery department helping to sell the Swedish food to the customers. They were having a wonderful time.

The Growing Girls came to the United States often to sing for chapter shows, including Valley Forge. Lennie became their agent. She helped book their shows and kept up to date with their calendar. They were about nineteen by then. Several years later we heard that they were again hired by IKEA to open a new store in California.

And with all this, they still had time to win the Sweet Adelines quartet contest in Miami in 1989.

The Revolutionary Sound

One cold winter Saturday my husband's company (the PQ Corporation, a chemical company) hosted a hospitality room at a convention in Washington, D.C. Many of the convention's other vendors had entertainment at their hospitality rooms to encourage attendance. Darrel, my husband, thought it would be a good idea if his company invited a quartet from Valley Forge Chorus to be the entertainment for his hospitality room—just what was

The Revs sing for the PQ Corporation

needed to bring the mostly men attendees into the room for food, networking, and to learn about PQ.

The Revolutionary Sound (a lovely regional champion quartet from Valley Forge) was contacted. They had asked Darrel if he would like them to write a parody about PQ for one of their songs. He agreed—if they would use words like *Q-cell* and *microspheres*. They were available and agreeable, and they accepted the gig. On the way to D.C., it began to snow. Twelve hours and eight inches of snow later, the quartet finally arrived at the hotel. It was late, and after a stop at the coffee shop, Darrel helped them get registered. They just made it in time to sing at the Friday night cocktail party. They sang their parody about chemistry. The following day, when word got around the hotel that there were four young girls singing about chemistry in the PQ hospitality room, it was crowded all day. It was wonderful being snowed in at a hotel in Washington, D.C., and singing all day long. By Sunday, the roads were clear of snow and they made it home safely.

But Darrel had a story about their arrival that they didn't know about. On Friday night, as he was standing by the desk helping the girls to register, Vittorio, attending the convention from Italy, came up to him and said, in his Italian accent, "Hey, Dar-elle, which-a one is-a mine?"

PQ Hospitality Song

Here's the song the Revolutionary Sound sang for PQ's hospitality room. Our thanks to baritone Jean Brooks for the words.

> If it's quality that you would like to see
> Here's where you get the best deal
> PQ is a name new to the plastics game
> Here's where you get the best deal

Q-cells, microspheres
Innovative peers
Research through the years
You're invited to compare the rest
Then you'll see we're the best
Here's where you get the best deal

Tag:

Here's where you get the best
Here's where you get the best
Here's where you get the best deal

19

Deciding to Retire

December, 1991

I WASN'T THINKING ABOUT LEAVING the Valley Forge Chorus. I just wanted a new goal—something unique and a little risky. I thought I'd like to come to the rehearsals around nine o'clock and just direct the fun part of the evening. My chorus had extremely talented and capable members who would love to take over the first hour and a half of the rehearsal. They could do the warm-ups and teach new music. They could even teach musical craft. But I needed to look further into the future.

The plan was for me to come at break time and direct all the songs that the chorus was learning. I wanted to be in charge of sprinkling the pixie dust—the finishing touch that creates fun and beautiful music—with none of the more routine work. I hoped that this would revitalize me. But almost every week someone in the chorus asked me to attend something "very important" before the rehearsal, anything to keep me involved. I finally gave up on the idea of taking my much-needed break.

It seemed the tigers that usually pulled this chorus were just strolling along and, of course, the chorus began to stray. Many of my strong leaders, either musically or emotionally, had moved to other cities or backed away from contributing to the chorus management. I was one of them. The rehearsals didn't have that wow focus. I had trouble finding good music for the chorus to sing. The Valley Forge fire was slowing down for me. There were those who wanted to step in and help out. One member wanted to organize our rehearsals like she did for her teaching job:

Warm-up	10 minutes
New music	20 minutes
Craft lesson	20 minutes
Repertoire review	10 minutes
Break	15 minutes
Announcements	10 minutes
Etc., etc., etc.	

This was not the Valley Forge that I knew. We were a chorus with high goals, but we traveled where the wind blew. A rehearsal by the clock was not how we operated. I had a goal for every rehearsal—but not a time commitment. I needed the freedom to improvise. One day, in December 1991, we were rehearsing for a performance. My eyes drifted over the ninety women who stood in front of me on the risers. I saw many, many good friends, and memories of our fun times came into my mind. And suddenly it was clear to me—I had an epiphany. It was time for me to retire. I was losing the Valley Forge fire, and I couldn't give what I didn't have.

Our trip to Russia was scheduled for June. I would step down after our return.

20

Russia

IN 1988, IDA WAS invited to become a showmanship judge for the Sweet Adelines. This was a big deal. The training is intense. The time commitment is enormous. The responsibilities are awesome. Not only must judges know what makes good barbershop harmonies, but they must also be able to quickly fill their judging sheets with the reasons for their numerical scores. There are opportunities to become judges in music, sound, showmanship, presentation, and expression. Each category has multiple judges at competition time—between two and five per category. There could be a total of four to fifteen people sitting at the judges' table looking up at you from the front row—pencils in hand.

It often takes years of training to become a qualified judge. When Ida called me and told me that she had received the invitation, I laughed. She still reminds me about this. From the time I became the director of Valley Forge (back in 1969), Ida and I worked together (almost daily) as we both put our heart and soul into the Valley Forge Chorus. We filled our time with performances, shows, and contests. We were on the international faculty and taught throughout the country and soon after that throughout the world. And Ida has five kids. She was busier than a one-armed paperhanger. That invitation was an acknowledgment of a job well done. I laughed because I knew she had reached a pinnacle in the Sweet Adelines world, and I was happy for her.

She had just received the ultimate compliment. I also knew how much busier she was going to be.

In 1990, Ida was required to trial score other regional competitions for her certification. Ida was in Grand Rapids, Michigan, trial scoring their regional competition, when she met Ann Jarchow, the director of the Grand Rapids Chorus. Ann shared with Ida how, in 1989, her chorus had spent two weeks on a concert tour of the Soviet Union. They were one of the first women's choruses to visit the Soviet Union and the first to sing at Tivoli Gardens in Copenhagen. The organizer of the tour was in the audience for the competition. Less than a week after Ida returned from Grand Rapids, she received a call from the promoter, New Olympians International Show Teams. I don't know how they heard about Valley Forge, but I know they found Ida's name listed in the competition program as a trial scorer. They asked if we were interested in going to Russia for a concert tour.

Ida was immediately suspicious. What a way to market a trip to Russia! She quickly called Ann Jarchow, and they talked for forty-five minutes. Ann raved about the trip and the organization that sponsored it. She said, "We'd go back in a minute." Ida became more and more excited and was convinced that this would be a wonderful opportunity for the Valley Forge Chorus. Next she had to present the idea to the Valley Forge governing board. She did and was immediately appointed chair of the Russia trip.

At first, there was doubt among the chorus members. The first hurdle was the cost. This trip would be at our own expense. It was $2,250 per person for an eleven-day concert tour to Russia. Did we have enough singers who could go to even attempt the trip? We sent a survey to the chorus that asked for each member's availability. When the results came in, there were forty-four singers and twenty-two guests who said yes to the trip. This number included friends, husbands, daughters, sons, sisters, and one retired Valley Forge member who flew in from California so she could join her mother on our trip. We also had a member from another chorus transfer to us so she could sing in Russia. First hurdle overcome.

The second hurdle was the sound. Could these forty-four singers create a good, strong, balanced sound? Would they be performance ready in time? Combined with the sound was the final hurdle: the music. Could we represent the USA with a strong barbershop sound?

Ida and I spent several hours putting the names of our forty-four singers and voice parts on small squares of color-coded paper. We placed these named squares all over my dining room table on imaginary chorus risers. Before we started, Ida said to me, "You know, if we can't make this work, we don't go." We looked at the balance of sound, the height of individuals so that they could be seen, the songs we would sing, and the staging we would be doing. We moved these little pieces of colored paper around the table until we were satisfied that we had a good sound and a good performance presence. Finally, we felt that this group looked good and would sing well. The trip was a go. The final two hurdles overcome. It took us two more years to plan and implement this trip to Russia.

The timetable looked like this:

First week of May, 1990. A video of our May show and the 1988 Houston competition was sent to New Olympians International Show Teams for our audition.

Early July, 1990. We were approved by their international show director Bonnie Hood to present an eleven-day show tour in the Soviet Union during the summer of 1992.

August 14, 1990. We received the official invitation.

We were to begin and end the trip at Copenhagen, Denmark. We would fly to St. Petersburg for our first performance, then on to Sochi for back-to-back performances numbers two and three. The fourth performance was in Moscow. And our final performance was at the Tivoli Gardens in Copenhagen. Eleven days, June 21 to July 3, during the White Nights Festival.

We were getting excited!

♮

We formed a committee to help with the expenses. We applied for grants but quickly found that grants were not available for travel expenses. We were financially on our own. Our biggest surprise came from the Bryn Mawr Mainliners. A large corporation with headquarters near us in Wilmington, Delaware, had hired the Mainliners to perform for one of their corporate events. The CEO of this company had been a member of the Barbershop Harmony Society and was generous with his support. The Mainliners asked us to share their performance time and gave us one third of their fee for our part in the show. At the end of the performance, Ida walked up to the CEO to thank him for having us at his company. She mentioned that we were going to Russia. He questioned her as to how this all came about and what we were going to be doing in Russia. He then offered us a large lump sum toward our trip.

♮

We wanted to wear something that would distinguish us as a single chorus while we walked around in this foreign land. Anything red, white, and blue would be our "walking outfits." We ordered baseball caps with red-and-white stripes and blue stars. We ordered lightweight, flannel-lined, red rain jackets to keep us warm on cold nights. We had them embroidered with our Valley Forge emblem. In addition to our walking outfits, we needed a costume for our performances. We wanted to bring only one, to save on luggage space. It had to be wrinkle free—something we

On our jackets.

could leave rolled up in a ball while traveling—and easily slip it on before our performances. This was one of our easier choices— our white dresses with the hot pink trim.

One of my special joys was having the chorus learn a Russian folk song, in Russian, to sing with the women in the audiences. We asked a barbershop friend to arrange "Moscow Nights" for us. "Please make the music simple," we begged. "And leave lots of room between the lines for the Russian words." We wrote the Russian words phonetically on our music. I started night school classes to learn Russian. One of our members' parents was from the Ukraine, and she had learned Russian from them. We helped with the spelling and pronunciation. Our plan was to sing their song for them, first in English then in Russian. My Russian teacher wrote an invitation to the women in the audience to join us on stage. I used it to invite them to sing "Moscow Nights" with us. (Our guides warned us that they would be too shy to do this.)

♮

A good friend of mine came with us to Russia. Her husband, my husband's best friend, had passed away the preceding September. Pat became my roommate. It was a good choice. She was not a member of the Valley Forge Chorus, but she was a musician and past director of the Lynchburg, Virginia, Sweet Adelines chorus. She understood how to be my roommate for this trip. It was good for her to be with us!

♮

June 21, 1992. Forty-four singers and twenty-two friends and family board a plane from Newark Airport bound for Copenhagen. Our guides for the entire trip met us at the airport in Copenhagen. Marita and Rinsophia were both from the Netherlands. They were experienced Russian travel guides and spoke fluent Russian and English. They were also about our age and full of fun, like us. They were with us for our entire tour and soon became friends as well as guides. Ida, as our chair, worked closely with them. (Our favorite call during the trip was "Where's Ida?")

Our guides gave us suggestions as to how to behave while we were in Russia:

♪ Accept whatever changes are made to our performances or venues. It's their country and they know best.

♪ Avoid eating certain foods, but taste all the food that we are served.

♪ If you want to eat American, stay home.

♪ Make all unpleasant side comments in the privacy of your hotel room.

♪ Direct all questions to our two guides—not your stateside "management team" (the husbands).

♪ Stay together. Never go out alone. Proceed with caution.

♪ Bring gifts to give as a thank you to those who help you while in Russia. Some suggestions were cigarettes, chewing gum, dollar bills, and the lotion, shampoo, and conditioner that you find in most American hotels.

Our first two-night stay, in Copenhagen, was wild and crazy. Their soccer team had just won the semi-finals, making them eligible for the championship match, and they were celebrating in the streets all night. We heard and saw them from our hotel rooms. A couple of our more adventurous women joined them on the street outside of our hotel.

While we were in Copenhagen, Millie—our Angel Fund creator and mom to Ginny, our Gospel Train tambourine player— fell and broke her hip. One of our husbands, Dr. Sheldon Sax, was with us and he helped take Millie to the hospital. Ginny stayed behind with her mother while the rest of the chorus went on to St. Petersburg and Sochi, minus two singers. As we left the hotel to take the bus to the airport, Ginny was at the door holding it open for our luggage and saying goodbye to us all. We knew she now had to survive for a week on her own in Copenhagen. Everyone was handing her money, saying "Here, I know you are going to need this for your hotel bill." Fives and tens were tucked into her pockets until we felt confident she had enough to last the week.

The trip to St. Petersburg on Aeroflot was an experience. At the airport the military was everywhere, in uniform and with guns. Natasha, from Russia, joined us there. Our emcees were able to talk to our audiences because Natasha translated all our emcee material for our Russian performances. As we left the St. Petersburg airport and were on our way to our hotel, our bus driver pulled over and stopped along the Neva River. With an empty bucket in hand, he ran to the edge of the river to scoop up some water. He took it back to the bus and added it to a very hot radiator. We were wide-eyed as we drove along the streets while two proud Russian guides described the architecture of the buildings of St. Petersburg.

Our American ways became apparent when we arrived at our first hotel in St. Petersburg. One of our members was vocal about the fact there was no coat rack. I had to remind her that we were not in the USA, and finding fault was not a very smart thing to do in a foreign land. That was the end of that. Unfortunately, we were told that another large group (the Seventh Day Adventists) had not checked out. There were no rooms for us at that hotel.

We had a performance that night and we needed a place to unpack and change—not to mention a place to sleep for the night. Not to worry. Our guides found a Luxury Line tourist ship docked on the river. They had rooms. Understandably, those rooms weren't ready for us, so we had to change and put on makeup in the one small bathroom that was available. However, it didn't have all that we needed. No toilet! (I didn't even ask how that was handled.) We ended up using all our extra time playing musical hotels and had only twenty minutes to get ready to perform. Most of our makeup was applied as we traveled in the bus to the venue.

Switching hotels became the second challenge of our trip. We had many men with us, and true to form, they were the take-charge type. We love it when they take care of us while in the USA, but it made us uncomfortable while we were on an organized trip to Russia. Taking charge was the guides' job. With sixty-six people in our group, we used two buses for our travel. On our way to our first performance that evening, I asked that all the guests be put on one bus and all the singers in another. This was the time to ask the chorus to remind their guests (mostly our men) to let the guides make all the decisions and for them to just enjoy the trip, not try to manage it. It worked. From that day forward we had the most wonderful time. The guides were able to freely travel the country with us while our men made sure we were safe.

It says Valley Forge Chorus Jan Muck.

They surrounded us wherever we went. They were looking out for us, keeping us together. There were always at least two men at the back of the pack as we traveled.

We were on our way to our first performance and it was thrilling. The venue was the Jazz Club and it was packed with people expecting jazz. Natasha was always on stage with us as our translator, and she introduced us to the audience. She turned to us and said that the audience wanted to know more about us. They wanted to know what we did in the States. Natasha took a few minutes to ask us questions. We held up our hands when they asked for teachers, then moms, then computer engineers, and our one lawyer. How old were we? Our youngest held up her hand: twenty-six. Our oldest was seventy-two. We could hear the audience talking. They were surprised when they found out we had paid our own way for the trip. We added this information to our next performances. The Russian folks wanted to know us better.

In Russia, when a member of the audience likes your performance, they come up on stage and hand you flowers...whenever they want to...even in the middle of the song. Can you imagine being handed a bouquet of flowers while you are performing on stage? At first, we didn't know what to do. But we all felt the love that was in the bouquet, and the chorus members who received them held the flowers close to their hearts and continued singing (as best they could).

We had planned to sing "Moscow Nights" and invite the women in the audience to sing with us on stage. Our finale, "One Moment in Time," would follow. After that first performance, we quickly learned that this didn't work. The women first hesitated—and we remembered one of our guides saying they were shy. Both our guides were the first to join us. Then the women of the audience rushed to the stage. "Moscow Nights" was so emotional with the Russian women singing at our side that there was no way we could sing anything after that. Our finale that night was anti-climactic. We reversed the order of songs for all our remaining performances and made "Moscow Nights" our finale. One of the Russian women who had enjoyed being on the risers with us noticed how we laughed and enjoyed ourselves. She said, "We have to learn to smile like you Americans."

That night we stayed up till after midnight. We found the lounge of the cruise ship–hotel and filled it with singing. Three of our members had each purchased a balalaika at the local market, and they pretended to play it. There was a baby grand in the middle of the lounge, and my friend Pat sat down to play. We

The Balalaika Three.

sang everything we knew. That night the sun never set. Between midnight and one o'clock the sky turned a soft gray and then back to blue again. It was the White Night.

Some young men from Syria were on the tourist boat listening to us sing. They became our groupies and followed us on our travels through Russia. It might have been the music or maybe just forty-four women laughing and having a good time that made them follow us. Our younger women were enjoying the attention, but our men were worried. By the time we were in Moscow, the Syrians were gone. In St. Petersburg, we visited the Hermitage Museum and were faced with what looked like thousands of people standing in line to enter. This is where we experienced the respect the Russian people have for the arts. Our guide, Natasha,

Pat at the piano at midnight.

went straight to the door of the Hermitage. Within minutes she returned and ushered all of us to the front of the line—all sixty-six of us.

A young man in St. Petersburg said to us, "Young American women are beautiful. Young Russian women are beautiful. Old American women are beautiful. Old Russian women are not."

♮

In Sochi, we enjoyed the beautiful gardens and wonderful Black Sea waters. We were interviewed on their TV station and performed several songs for them. They had found some risers for us, but they must have been for little people. The four steps were about half the width of our feet and about twice as high as the ones we usually use. It was a challenge to do our choreography. We had to hang on to each other to keep from falling off the risers, but we did it. The Sochi people deserved to see the best that we could do. And they did. We spent two nights in this wonderful resort town. Our audiences for our two Sochi concerts were young and on vacation. This was the only venue where we had a curtain. As we waited on the risers for the curtain to open, we noticed how quiet it was on the other side. No audience noise. We didn't know if there would even be an audience. There was. Close to 600 people. They just didn't talk before a concert. They were excited to be seeing American women singing for them. When they applauded, they raised both arms above their heads and, in unison, clapped their hands together. This was the ultimate approval. At the end of the first performance, we invited all the women to come to the stage. There was nothing shy about them. They left their seats and headed for the stage. They brought their mothers and their young daughters with them. They all came.

They outnumbered us on the stage. Our chorus made room for them on all the steps of the risers (including the back row) and they squished in among us. In front of the first row were all the little girls, standing with their moms. We were dressed in our white and hot pink costumes. And it was a beautiful picture.

We started to sing together. This time we were all singing the Russian words, and as I directed them I noticed some of the chorus members in the back row had put their arms around their Russian neighbors. Slowly the touch worked its way down the risers, through the chorus. Everything was in slow motion as we sang. Hands reached for hands, arms went around the backs of neighbors. Those in the front row had their hands on the shoulders of the children in front of them. Soon they were all swaying with the music. And then the Russian women continued to sing the second verse. We sang with them in harmony, without the words. Tears streamed down our faces. As I watched this happening, my heart was full of love for my chorus and love for these

Singing "Moscow Nights."

Russian women who gave their hearts to us that day. We will forever feel that love.

As we loaded our buses to go back to the hotel, an elderly gentleman ran up to the open windows of the bus and handed us flowers. Then he ran back for more flowers and brought them to us, all through the open windows. The bus driver waited for our gentleman to complete his gift of flowers, and then we drove away. We performed again the next night, and an artist who had attended the first concert returned with an individual painting for each of us to take home—over forty paintings in one day. They were beautiful and easily fit into our suitcases. You'll find them framed on the walls of our homes.

The next day we had time to walk around Sochi and chanced upon a cathedral. There were beggars outside. A very old woman, unable to climb stairs, was on her hands and knees as she worked her way up the ten steps to enter through the doors into the church. It was a beautiful moment. We stayed quiet and watched.

The Baptisms.

As we walked around outside the church, we came upon a courtyard. A priest and two altar boys in their vestments moved through the crowd. At least seventy to one hundred people encircled the priest. Infants and very old men and women were participating in their first baptism. We were awed and speechless. Seventy years of communism and still they came forward to be baptized. We couldn't talk, we didn't want to break the spell of witnessing this first baptism. It was so emotional. Each of us was offered a little silver cross as a memento of the day. I still have mine.

Our two Dutch guides had told us never to travel alone. However, things happen. One of us opened her money pouch and gave some money to the beggars in front of the church. Somehow she became separated from our group. Someone had noted where she kept her money. It didn't take long before she was approached by some kids. They grabbed her money belt and cut the strap, cutting into her, too. They escaped with her money.

She had a terrible knife wound across her upper arm. Dr. Sax once again was called into action. He preferred to treat her with the medical bag he had brought with him. He cleaned her wound, stitched her arm, and she was good to go for the rest of the trip.

Back we flew to Moscow. Ginny joined us from Copenhagen. She said she was scared to death flying alone on Aeroflot. When she arrived, we were gathering in the lobby of our hotel in our red, white, and blue walking outfits. We were to take a subway ride to Red Square. The trip on the subway was the only time our members did not all travel together. Our guides said we had to have people who could move quickly and stay together. They had to follow directions, no questions asked. Ida talked with everyone individually and some of the chorus self-selected not to join the subway ride.

The train doors opened and closed very quickly. We could not bunch up at a door or we wouldn't all get onto the train. We had to enter by different doors of the same cars. We joined arms so that we wouldn't become separated. We were told that if we lost someone, we'd never find them again. It was obvious that the guides were worried. The subway stations were full of statues and beautiful artwork. We had never seen anything quite like this. We made several transfers. Every time we got off the subway, we joined hands. Again, the men took care of us. They were the last off the subway, watching to make sure no one was left on the platform. It was twilight when we left the subway and walked up the ramp to Red Square. The first thing we saw was the lights of Saint Basil's Cathedral. Then we noticed Lenin's Tomb. Red Square was huge, with many tourists strolling through the square. A group of women approached and asked where we were from. They were music teachers visiting Russia. "Would you sing something for us?" they asked.

Natasha was concerned. She told us to wait and left in a hurry to talk to some of the soldiers who were in Red Square. She asked if we could sing. It may have looked a little suspicious having a bunch of people congregating in the middle of Red Square. She was afraid they would try to separate us, but they gave the OK. So we sang "American Bandstand" and "Moscow Nights." We drew quite a crowd of international visitors. Can you imagine the

Singing in Red Square.

Valley Forge Chorus, all dressed in red, white, and blue, singing "American Bandstand" in Red Square? Wow!

We headed to Lenin's Tomb. "Keep your hands out of your pockets, put your cameras away, and do not talk." Some of us went into GUM, the department store on Red Square. The downstairs was the American dollar store.

Moscow was a beautiful city with shops and restaurants and nice hotels. It was our last time in Russia, and everyone was buying souvenirs. We attended the ballet as a group, wearing our red, white, and blue walking outfits, with jeans and tennis shoes. At the intermission, a gentleman came out on stage and announced that there was a performing group from the United States in the audience. Would we come up on stage and sing for them? Yikes! No warm-up, no costume, no planning. But we hopped onto the stage and sang. And we were invited to come back onto the stage after the ballet to meet the dancers. After the performance, they brought two large posters to the stage and spread them on the floor. Each member of the dance troupe, on their hands and knees, signed their name. And then they gave us the posters. Mine is framed and on the wall of my family room.

We visited the Kremlin, believing that we were one of the first groups ever to be allowed to go inside. We saw the history of Russia—paintings, monuments, jewelry, all centuries old. Awesome! It's been said that this collection is unequaled in the world.

And then it was time to go home. As we packed our bags for the long trip home, some of us gave all our extra clothes to the housekeepers at the hotel. We could tell by their faces that these gifts meant a great deal to them, so we found more things that we didn't need to take home, mainly jeans and sneakers, but also underwear and lipstick. This left room in our suitcases for all the mementos we brought home from our trip, jewelry, decorations, and matryoshka dolls.

We were sad that the trip was over so soon. We said goodbye to our guides. Natasha had become a real performer as she emceed our shows. Marita and Rinsophia were part of us. We actually had them singing with us in the hotels. We all were changed by the love shown to us by the Russian people. We had thought when we first went to Russia that we were just going to sing and sight-see. We turned out to be ambassadors of the American woman's way of life. At that time, Russians had not really been exposed to women who had enjoyed a lifetime of living in a free world. They saw women singing with a joy of life. They said to us, "Now we know what to work for; you have shown us what it is like to live free."

♮

We flew to Copenhagen and our Millie (with the broken hip) joined us. Hugs all around. She was in a wheelchair but healthy and healing. We insisted that she join us on stage that night for our performance at Tivoli Gardens. We pushed her all over the streets of Copenhagen and up onto the stage, wheelchair and all. Millie sang her one performance with us.

We stopped off in London to change planes. We had several hours to wait. Off to a restaurant we went. We brought out the wine we had bought in Russia and, making sure the bottles were in a paper bag, we poured the wine into our water glasses, hiding the process under the table. We celebrated. It was a surreal time, we all felt different. We had developed a close bond with each other and felt the sadness that it was soon to end.

We also knew that I was soon to retire.

Valley Forge in Baltimore, 1992

Home from Russia and things changed at our rehearsals. We became a divided group, those who had been to Russia and those who had not. Everyone was aware that I was retiring. By this time, I had been directing Valley Forge for twenty-three years. Plans were being made for a new director.

The international convention that fall was in Baltimore, just a two-hour drive from our hometown. We were not competing that year. Instead we were asked to give a twenty-minute presentation of our Russian trip for the Tuesday night international variety show. That meant those who could not go with us learned the notes and most of the words to "Moscow Nights." We came together as the Valley Forge Chorus. All our members were on stage for this special performance.

We chose songs that we had sung in Russia and wove a story around them. We decided not to make it a travelogue but instead share the emotion and friendships that we had found in Russia. Our pictures were made into slides, the script was created, and rehearsals began. Two of our travelers were the emcees. They reminisced about the trip and talked back and forth between themselves as the pictures and music began.

"And remember when we went to the Russian Ballet?" (Picture!)

"Yes. And the dancers were magnificent."

"Can you believe that during the intermission they invited us to come on stage to sing for them?"

"We had never before performed in our sneakers and jeans. At least we had on our red, white, and blue casual walk-around outfits."

Starting out with the song "Sentimental Journey," we continued with songs and pictures that shared our feelings about the people and the country that we had visited. We sang "American Bandstand" to the picture onscreen of Valley Forge in Red Square. As we sang "Moscow Nights," we showed the picture of the Russian women holding hands with us on the risers. Sometimes we would sing softly as the emcees spoke, and sometimes we just sang the music.

As the finale approached, one single emcee, Lennie, stepped up to the mic. We began to sing "One Moment in Time" very softly. She shared with the audience the love we felt for the Russian people, the warmth of our new friendships, and the respect that was shown to us for our music. As the chorus heard her speak, they began to pour all their love into their song. Lennie spoke of the time a young Russian child turned to her mother with a question.

The mother translated for us.

"She said my daughter asked how you came to be here, and I told her, God sent you."

On stage, the chorus was unstoppable. "One Moment in Time" exploded in emotion. On the screen was a picture of a five-year-old Russian girl sitting on the lap of one of our singers, with their arms around each other, hugging. The audience was on their feet.

The performance was over, the curtain closed, and we came backstage. There were many people waiting for their turn to speak, and they were crying. Ann Gooch was there. With tears in her eyes, she said, "Your chorus destroyed us."

I had directed my last performance with the Valley Forge Chorus.

21

Retirement Party

August 2, 1992

THE CHORUS PREPARED A surprise retirement party for me. I thought I was going to a late Sunday brunch with my husband, Darrel, and with Lennie and Ken. Ken worked at the Hilton Hotel. The hotel had just opened this room and they wanted me to see it. That's what I was told.

This "Sunday brunch" was in a big private dining room in the ballroom section of the Hilton. I thought that strange. I opened the door and immediately backed out because the room was occupied by another large group. Lennie shoved me back into the room.

"SURPRISE!"

The chorus had invited everyone we knew, including those we had asked to coach us. And my kids. Marion, from the chorus, had put together a scrapbook of events in our life. She included comments from the chorus and cards from those who couldn't attend. There were pictures of the chorus from every contest I was part of. Many stood up and talked about our time together and what it meant to them. My son did the same. Someone turned to me and sang "Wind Beneath My Wings." I cried.

Some of My Favorite Comments

♪ "Except for the births of my children, the most exciting times of my life have had to do with music. Thanks for the memories."

♪ "Singing for you in this chorus was a dream come true. I shall truly miss you."

♪ "Thanks for putting up with us all these years."

♪ "You are an inspiration to me. Thanks for the memories."

♪ "Thanks for helping me learn how to express myself."

♪ "I shall never forget your champion spirit."

♪ "I'll always remember our musical moments of excellence."

♪ "You have always been a champion with me. You are Valley Forge, and it won't be the same blowing the pitch pipe for someone else."

♪ "I love you for being Jan and so wonderful. Will miss you much."

♪ "May your 'one moment in time' be yet to come."

♪ "You are a special lady with lots of flair and class. Please come back often and sing with us."

♪ "All the very best for our classy director. You're a loyal and good friend."

♪ "Many thanks for turning my late descent on the risers in the '91 show into a hit."

♪ "You made the difference in my Sweet Adelines life and I wish you peace and happiness."

♪ "I am thrilled to be a part of Valley Forge and to have sung under you."

♪ "It's been the happiest five years of my life, singing under you."

♪ "You've opened up a fantastic part of my life."

♪ "Thanks for being a great teacher."

♪ "Thanks for all my medals."

♪ "I certainly enjoyed my time with you and the chorus, and I especially enjoyed my time with you as a quartet coach. You had wonderful insight."

♪ "Thank you for the many years of friendship. I miss making beautiful music together and hope that in the years to come, you will fondly remember the joys, tears, love and, most of all, the laughter that we shared. With music always in my heart..."

♪ "In the past six years I have grown to love an art form I never knew existed in the musical world. Music has been an important part of my life since I was a child, but never before had I been challenged and inspired to do and feel so much, while either rehearsing or performing. Your direction has given me a musical fulfillment that I only wish I'd known was possible many years ago. Thank you for giving me so many opportunities to grow...Your dedication and commitment to Valley Forge and to each of its members has been an inspiration to us all."

♪ "My world grew much larger in the last seventeen years, thanks to you. It's been wonderful."

♪ "Your devotion to the chorus and the members was obvious and strong. You had no self-interest. You were for the chorus and not yourself....no ego. You were unselfish."

♪ "My sincere thanks for our years of association through Sweet Adelines and your foresight in seeing a talent in me I didn't know existed. When you told me you were recommending me for the judging program, I couldn't have been any more surprised if you said you had sent my name in to NASA to become an astronaut! Thanks to you I've had some great experiences, accomplished a lot and proud of what I've done in the judging program because of your insight."

What Made Valley Forge Great?

A Letter from Linda Johnson to Jan Touring Muck

I've often thought about the magic you created with Valley Forge, and I believe it came from your style of leadership as much as your musical expertise. All individuals want to be part of something extraordinary, but few are exceptional or disciplined enough to attain it. Valley Forge, under your direction, allowed chorus members to experience and sustain excellence.

Many directors want complete control, but you didn't need or want that. Only a rare leader can release control, and still retain control. You taught us that each person's contribution, from section leaders to choreographers, hostesses, music collators, and even sequin sewers was essential and valuable. All tasks had to be done, and done well, so all could concentrate on the music.

At one change of officers, Lennie suggested the new officers and board members consider themselves gardeners. Each one had their own plant to tend and should not mess with the other person's flowerpot. That idea came from your leadership model.

In rehearsals and performances, you asked us to put our individual voices in your hand. When we did, the result was magical.

The bond you fostered remains firm over the years. I'm glad I sang with Valley Forge under your extraordinary direction.

Jan, thanks for the love, leadership, and hard work you gave to Valley Forge and to each member whose voice you held in your hands.

Linda Baten Johnson

♪ "I've always admired you and your work with Valley Forge. I remember listening over and over again to "Undecided" and "Painted Lips." I feel privileged to have been present and up front at your fine International performances."

♪ "Your joie de vivre, your sense of the novel, and your commitment to strong, basic barbershop techniques were always an inspiration to me and to many others, I'm sure."

♪ "It will be sad not to see you, spunky and strong, at the front of Valley Forge. With a song of admiration and loss..."

♪ "Great things happen to those who get off their butts and go for it....and you did! Congrats! And do you still owe me a steak dinner or is it the other way around?"

Leaving Valley Forge, A Legacy

The members of Valley Forge Chorus became leaders in our international organization. We had three international board members, two of which became international presidents. We had three international faculty members, two international judges, one regent and a regional director of musical activities. Seven of our members became a director of their own chorus. At one contest we counted eighteen of our past and present members who were competing on the international stage in choruses or quartets. One of our members, by singing with Valley Forge in every contest and competing as a tenor in many quartets, collected twenty-nine medals.

22

What Do You Do When the Music Stops?

1992

OUR NEW DIRECTOR JOINED us shortly after my retirement luncheon. For many of us, this was the end of twenty-five years of enjoying a life together. Some moved on to join other singing groups or tried their acting skills with the Narberth Community Theatre. Some opted to take time for themselves and their families. All were looking for the challenge, fun, and friendships they had as a Valley Forge Chorus member. It was not to be easily found.

For me, it was strange being without the ninety-two women who shared my life for twenty-five years. Who would have thought that loneliness would be part of the feelings that developed around me? The phone didn't ring, no one asked my opinion about anything anymore, and my evenings were free.

It wasn't long before those of us who had left the chorus realized how much we missed each other. We didn't want to lose touch. Someone came up with the idea of a monthly dinner, and it sounded like fun. We found a restaurant that we all liked, and when they promised they would enjoy our rambunctious style, we organized our email distribution list and set up our calendar. From September to June we checked off one Thursday each month and sent out postcards with the dates. July and August

Valley Forge veterans.

were home pool parties, and Ida and Marji took turns as hostess. It was an open house for anyone who wanted to join us. We called ourselves the Valley Forge Veterans, and yes, at this writing, almost thirty years later, fifteen of us are still laughing, reminiscing, and sometimes singing together at some restaurant. We never know who will join us or when an out-of-town member will drop in.

It took a long time for my life as a barbershop director to fade into my past. It helped that in its place I fielded teaching and coaching requests from all over the country and even Canada. This was wonderful, as they required no preparation, no classes to design. Everything I needed I already had.

The Sweet Adelines International organization kept me busy when they included me in a group of coaches that were sent to small- and medium-size choruses who wanted help singing good barbershop music. Usually it was for a weekend, which meant Friday night, Saturday all day, and Sunday morning. SAI also invited me to be a personal mentor to barbershop directors who requested some one-on-one help. And there were teaching responsibilities at the annual IES summer conferences. It kept me busy.

1993

American barbershop was gaining recognition across the seas. England, Sweden, New Zealand, and Australia were all beginning to develop choruses to sing our barbershop music. Imagine getting a phone call from some unknown Sweet Adelines member in New Zealand inviting you to spend four weeks on the North Island to coach two new choruses. They were preparing to enter the New Zealand area competition in June 1994 and were looking for someone to help them with their songs. I was recommended to them. I said yes, of course. My style was good for the new competitor. (I *was* one once.) I liked working with choruses as they reached for a gold medal at the regional competition level. This was a good fit.

When the time came for me to leave, it was November—summertime in New Zealand. I packed my bags with summer clothes and started on the thirty-six-hour flight from Philly to Auckland. There was a nine-hour layover in San Francisco, so I put my carry-on in a locker at the airport and took the trolley to the waterfront. I toured the art shops, watched the seals from the boardwalk, and had a delightful lunch of wine and shrimp. Too soon it was time to head back to the airport to collect my luggage and board the plane for a thirteen-hour flight to New Zealand. The plane landed at the Auckland Airport at 5:00 a.m. Thirty-five women waited for me inside the terminal. They waved and cheered as I walked toward them. Then they sang hello to me. What a glorious welcome!

For four weeks the days were full of travels back and forth between the two groups, coaching both the choruses and their quartets, and even giving private individual vocal coaching sessions (the dreaded PVIs I thought I'd never do again). We worked hard on the competition songs, but we also talked about chorus management, the music staff, and choreography. And they found time to take me sightseeing.

The two women who were my hosts, Jan and Marilyn, took me all around Auckland and the wonderful places along the North Island. They shared their home and their favorite music with me. We listened to the recording of Malcolm McNeill, the New Zealand popular recording artist, and Dame Kiri Te Kanawa, the famed New Zealand opera star, singing their album *Heart to Heart*. I fell in love with the title song. This song was special. It was written by Malcolm McNeill and sung as a duet with Kiri. We played it all the time. Jan and Marilyn gave me a copy of the album when I left for home. It would be fifteen years before that song would again become a part of my world.

I came to New Zealand to help them with their music, but it seems they taught me how to live a calmer life. I learned to be patient as I waited for traffic to clear the one-lane bridges so we could pass. I learned that it was nice to bring flowers to every family that had me for dinner. And I learned that if I ever forget to take something out of the freezer for dinner for the family, I know I can always stop and get fish and chips and a blanket and go to the beach to sit and have supper. I also noticed that as they drove along the two-lane roads to show me the countryside, they often pulled over to the shoulder to let the line of cars behind them pass by, and then we would go on our way. They also drove on the left side of the road. That took some getting used to.

♮

I made one more coaching trip to the land Down Under, a combination of Australia and New Zealand for six weeks. I took Darrel with me this time as we traveled the eastern coast of Australia. We spent a week together, sightseeing and coaching. He visited the Barbershop Harmony Chorus in Sydney while I coached the Sweet Adelines choruses. One evening he stayed home with the seven-year-old son of the director while I coached her chorus. When it was time for me to fly across to Western Australia to attend and teach at a weekend seminar, Darrel flew home.

Coaches from the United States work very hard when they visit this world. There were special classes in the morning and lots of PVIs during the daytime hours. Every quartet had their focused time with the visiting coach (me). The Australian and New Zealand choruses knew that barbershop harmony began in the United States, and they wanted to gain as much knowledge as they could from United States coaches. During that time, I was privileged to be able to coach the magnificent Perth Chorus as well as another group south of Perth, in the Margaret River area. A carload of chorus members took me on a winery tour in the region and then drove me to the Perth airport for my trip to New Zealand. There were two wonderful wineries before our lunch stop and one gorgeous one after. Although I didn't take any samples with me on the plane, I certainly did enjoy a good amount of delicious Australian wine.

Back again in New Zealand I spent four weeks traveling both islands of this beautiful country, teaching and training their choruses. Along with the work, they showed me their volcanoes, their caves, their beautiful farms, sheep, green mountains, and rocky shores. And they shared their wonderful food. I loved spending two of those weeks with the Christchurch Chorus.

1994

Let me introduce you to Katie (not her real name). In 1983, the Valley Forge Chorus was competing in Detroit. In the audience of eight thousand was a brand new Sweet Adelines member who was attending her first international competition. Katie had come with her husband and many of her friends from the New England Chorus. Typical of our contest life, quartets were singing all around their hotel lobbies and in all the restaurants they visited. Chorus members hurried to find their scheduled warm-up rooms. In and out of the elevators came fancy costumes, makeup, and false eyelashes. It was organized bedlam. Excitement and anticipation were everywhere.

Soon it was time to go to the convention center for the chorus contest. Katie and her husband wound their way past the many people standing in line for the hot dogs and ice cream and finally found their way to the steps that would take them to the contest hall. Everything was new to them and they were enjoying the crowds and the music. They watched Valley Forge Chorus compete. Katie's husband commented, "Man, these girls have it!" Katie saw and heard the best of the best—the Valley Forge Chorus won the contest that year. She still remembers the songs we sang and the costume we wore. I didn't know Katie at this time; we met much later. Through the years she developed into an excellent quartet singer and a section leader for her chorus. Eventually she began to arrange music for her quartet and chorus. And after that, other choruses asked to sing her arrangements.

♮

In 1994, I was coaching and teaching at IES. Katie came to the school that taught singing, stage management, and choreography. She was assigned to my blue chorus, and for three days—six rehearsals—I was her director. I still hadn't met her personally. She was just a part of my chorus. Years later she told me that she "worshipped me from afar," which means "I learned a lot from you."

"What did you learn?"

"You get right down to the underwear," she responded.

"What on earth do you mean?"

"You make us sing the right way. We carry out the end of the phrases, we sing in sync, we use the same vowels. You teach us to sing musically. You make us do all the little things that make our music beautiful."

And I thought, "Sure, if you don't have the basics, how can you build your music to be beautiful? Some strange sound will always destroy the harmony if you aren't singing as an ensemble."

1996

Katie's chorus had won their regional contest and was going to compete in their first international competition. Their director, Helen (not her real name, either), was looking forward to taking her chorus to Salt Lake City for five days in October 1997. She was excited to be directing her chorus on the international stage. As a schoolteacher, Helen had to request three days for a leave of absence. They said no. They would not approve her request to be absent a few days in October 1997. She began to look for someone to direct her chorus in the contest.

Katie recommended me to Helen. She knew that I would be good for the chorus and thought that I might enjoy a return to full-time coach and director. I did. Helen and I had a long talk. I could really empathize with her. Bringing a chorus to First Place Regional and then not taking them to International? Not a good thing. My only request was that I become their *interim* director and teach and train them for the contest. I didn't want to join them two weeks before the trip and wave my arms just so they would not get out of sync. I wanted to work with them and get them ready for the stage. I wanted them to be the best they could be, with my help. Besides, a chorus has to know and trust their director on a contest stage. It is apparent to the judges when there is a disconnect. We had to build this trust.

Helen attended every rehearsal. She sat behind me to observe what I was doing. Her chorus responded to my directing. I loved the control I had over what they were singing. Whatever I asked them to sing, they returned it to me with all the energy and attention they could give. It felt good to be competing again. Every week, they were ready and excited to know what they were going to learn this week. We were becoming a family, pulling together to reach a goal. I held nothing back. They could handle it all. As I directed them, Helen's chorus watched her intensely; they wanted her to be pleased. This chorus was hungry to learn and was going to take all this to the competition stage. I pushed them as hard as I could. They responded.

I did not realize how difficult this was for the chorus and for Helen, but somehow, we survived. I believe that Katie made sure things ran smoothly. She was always by my side. Our friendship began to grow.

♮

Contest time came quickly, and we had everything ready. The costumes were done, and the staging was perfected. Musically, I felt that they were more than ready for the trip. It had been several years since I had directed a chorus on the contest stage. I really didn't think I missed it. After all, I had already competed more than twenty-five times. Even attending the yearly international contests didn't tempt me. I loved hearing the quartets and choruses and seeing my old friends—but my directing days were tucked away in my happy memories folder.

Or so I thought.

1997: Salt Lake City

We arrived in Salt Lake City. We were excited and confidant. We settled into our rooms and unpacked. Before we started our rehearsal schedule, I had a chance to visit the convention center. It was not time for the contest; the hallways were empty. I found myself walking alone in the backstage area. Passing by an open stage door, I saw that the stage crew was setting up for the next session.

Taking the chance of being stopped, I entered and made my way around the heavy curtains, stepping over wires and ducking under backstage drapes. There was the familiar smell of equipment. The lights were low. No one stopped me, so I pushed back the side curtain and walked onto the stage. There it was—spread out in front of me—the entire concert hall. Four or five levels with empty narrow staircases just waiting for people to climb to their seats. Thousands of neatly placed chairs lined the sides of the hall. Thousands more covered the convention floor—all in a semicircle around the stage. Moving downstage slowly, to the center-front, I stopped. Looking around at the thousands of seats, memories of performing took over my body. My shoulders went back, my rib-cage lifted, my chin went level with the floor, and my face felt like it was radiating. I took command of the stage. I slowly looked all over the room. I could hear the applause. I could see the standing ovations. This is where I belonged. I had come home.

I stayed there until my head and heart were full. Leaving the stage, I never thought I would ever have this feeling again. I was grateful that I hadn't met anyone I knew. I wanted to savor the feeling for as long as I could.

Little did I know!

♮

Contest day. Makeup. False eyelashes. Unscented hair spray. A chorus breakfast (this was our only meal until late in the day). We sang together as we finished eating. The chorus made me stand on two chairs so that I could direct them. They were sitting and standing all around me. Love was everywhere. We sang one of the love songs that Katie had arranged for them, and I motioned for her to come and stand by me. With one hand on her shoulder, my other hand gently directed her song. She softly cried.

Later that day, when it was almost time to leave the hotel and go the concert hall, we gathered together—dressed, made up, and hair sprayed. We opened our bottle of cold duck, poured it into our oversized wine glass (compliments of Valley Forge), passed it around for each to take a sip, and we were ready. We were taken to the convention center, to the warm-up room, the photography room, and then to the backstage area.

The chorus competed. They were wonderful. The biggest challenge for a competing chorus is to put on stage what they have rehearsed. They did this. They did the best they could do, and out of about thirty other contestants, they placed twelfth. This was remarkable for their first time on the international contest stage. There were choruses there from all over the world—many had competed before. They felt as if they had won—and they had, against all odds.

We said our goodbyes at the Salt Lake City airport. Mostly hugs, kisses, and tears. It was a beautiful experience for everyone, and it was over. But never say over forever.

Mix the Choruses?

Something had been swirling around in my head for many years. It had started in 1972 after the Valley Forge Chorus had won their first regional contest. The Mainliners (The Bryn Mawr chapter of the men's Barbershop Harmony Society) had won their division contest. Valley Forge Chorus was invited to sing as guests on their spring show. We didn't sing together, but we thought about it. We all wanted to—at least all the women did.

Years later we performed with the men of the Orpheus Club (1986), and again I thought about how much I would like to direct a mixed-voice barbershop chorus. It would be an a cappella chorus of men and women singing the rich, joyful sound of happy music that people would enjoy singing and audiences would love to watch and listen to and be entertained by. I wanted a chorus that had a good time rehearsing and performing for the enjoyment of the audience. Our music would always be fun and uplifting. There would be no competitions.

The dream was taking shape. But the timing was never right. At that time, the men barbershop singers and the women barbershop singers were two separate groups. Mixing them did not bring favor to the world I was living in. Eight-part barbershop harmony with 200 voices—that's what I wanted to do. That was all I knew. It was an awesome idea but not very well received. There were only a handful of eight-part mixed-chorus arrangements available.

Then in 1998 the Mainliners needed a new director. They were a good chorus, well over seventy-five members. The chapter had known me as their coach since 1972, and I had just worked with them in the spring of 1992 preparing them for their spring competition. Every year they would win their division contest, and sometimes their scores would qualify them for their international competition. I applied for the position of full-time director. I was entering the men's world, and I hoped to bring them to the international stage more often. I did a great deal of soul-searching because I knew exactly what I, personally, would have to do—the time commitment, learning where to find men's arrangements, learning their contest rules and how to perform as a woman on stage in front of a chorus of all men...and I really wanted to do this.

So did someone else from out of town. An experienced male director, Kirk Roose, was moving to the Philadelphia area and had heard that the Bryn Mawr Mainliners were searching for a director. He applied. The personal interviews for the position of director were held at Conrad Keil's office in downtown Philadelphia with the two applicants and the governing body of the Bryn Mawr Mainliners. This included several of my good friends, Tom Halley, Eric Jackson, and Conrad Keil. This meeting was held in their boardroom, and I loved the whole process. They questioned us in depth. It felt like a group of strong individuals trying to solve a problem, each suggesting solutions and then discussing them. It was great. I wasn't nervous, just excited.

Then, later, Kirk and I auditioned in front of the whole chorus. We each took our turns directing one or two of their complete rehearsals. What fun it was for me to be in front of seventy men singing their hearts out. I was enjoying the thought of being a director of a men's chorus. It was a happy time.

And then the chorus voted.

Oops! It wasn't me. It was OK. I was disappointed, but it was more like, "Well, that didn't work...what's next?"

Soon I would have *Bits of Broadway* to fill my days with music.

Bits of Broadway

1998

Mimi Brown had joined the Narberth Community Theatre. The Valley Forge Veterans went to all her shows and watched her sing, dance, and act on stage. She was putting together a *Bits of Broadway* show to give the members of the theater a chance to sing the Broadway show music that is seldom performed. It was to be bits and pieces from Broadway show music sung by soloists and a large mixed chorus.

Mimi was the creator and producer of the show. She chose her favorite show music and made all the necessary arrangements for procuring the rights to the orchestra, soloist, and chorus scores. She was able to hire the Rose Tree Pops Orchestra. But then she hit a roadblock finding a qualified theater person to be the choral rehearsal director. All the people from the Narberth Community Theatre who she asked said no.

Over a delightful dinner at a quiet restaurant, she said to me, "The Narberth Community Theatre is putting together a *Bits of*

Mimi Brown Producer/Director Bits of Broadway (Photo by Pat Sinclair).

Broadway show. I am the producer. I have picked the musical director and the orchestra, but I need a person to teach the chorus numbers. Do you think you could be the rehearsal director? Could you teach the music and work with a piano accompanist?"

I thought of the challenges. Two things: I had never directed a mixed chorus and I had never used a piano during a rehearsal. On stage the chorus would sing with the orchestra, and I would direct them. The fun for me would be in directing the rehearsals of this great show music. In two seconds my answer was yes. I was heading into a new life with men, women, and a piano. I was even able to sing in one of the acts—as one of the four old ladies who put on crazy big hats and sang "Pick-a-Little, Talk-a-Little" from *The Music Man.* Fun!

Word went out about the show. We immediately began our auditions. People from other choruses and choirs came to audition for *Bits of Broadway.* Many were members of the Atrium Singers, a lunchtime choir from one of our neighboring businesses. We ended up with about fifty voices in our show chorus. Our accompanist, Pat Gaul, was an experienced pianist. (Her son joined the chorus.) She had been involved with area theater groups as musical director and as a performer. I learned how to work with her as a piano accompanist. We stumbled along for a while, but with her help we soon became a working team.

We needed many soloists, and they, too, had to be auditioned. An ad was placed in *Stage Magazine* asking for soloists who wanted to "sing the songs that you never get to sing in little theater." Listening to the auditions for a chorus was familiar to me, but auditioning soloists was like actually being involved in a Broadway production. The auditioning team was formidable. Mike White, the driving force from the Narberth Community Theatre and a mentor and personal friend of Mimi's, joined us. They were looking for the right voice for each of the songs. I was able to hear the style and quality of each soloist and soon realized what Mimi wanted for each song. It was thrilling and rewarding to be involved with this team. After each person auditioned, we would thank them and say, "We'll be in touch," just like the big-time shows. Discussion between us followed.

During auditions, the most amazing experience happened, and we still talk about it. An unknown man appeared at the auditions. He wanted to sing "The Music of the Night" from *The Phantom of the Opera*. As he started to audition, our pencils slowly fell from our hands. We just looked at him while listening to his wonderful voice. We were mesmerized. He asked if he could sing one more song from *Les Mis*, and he sang "Bring Him Home." Again we were transfixed by the beauty of his voice. We were awed. We couldn't talk. Discussing the audition was useless. We didn't need to vote. He was the only one to have two solos in our show. His name was Lou Shaw. He brought the house down at each of our two performances. Our entire cast was smitten by his voice.

Everything was new for all of us—the members and the directors. As we learned the music, we became friends. This was becoming fun. We were excited to sing these show tunes. We worked for four or five months on Wednesday evenings learning and memorizing the songs from *Showboat*, *The Desert Song*, *The Phantom of the Opera*, *Mack and Mabel*, *A Chorus Line*, and *Les Misérables*. What better way to end a concert than with a finale of "Do You Hear the People Sing" from *Les Mis*?

♮

None of us will forget the petition that went through the chorus about a week before the first performance. Mimi wouldn't hear of singing while holding our music. But "Master of the House," from *Les Mis*, had difficult words. The chorus wanted to read their words for this one song. Her response to the petition was, "You had five months to learn this song. Now you have five days." Of course we did it. We sang it from memory.

Mimi did the research and wrote the script to tie it all together. We had a full house and rave reviews.

1999

Never in our wildest dreams did we expect to create another Broadway show. And yet, less than two years later, we put together a sequel, *Bits of Broadway II*. Friendships were renewed, new singers were auditioned, and rehearsals were scheduled. From our opener, "Another Op'nin', Another Show" to our closer, "Strike Up the Band," we were again singing songs most people never get to sing in little theater.

Another full house with rave reviews.

♮

Mimi says she learned how to be a leader from being president of Valley Forge three times. She organized the group travel to our contests. She chose the support people. Her drive for excellence was what made us want to produce *Bits of Broadway II*. The designs of our *Bits of Broadway* programs and our T-shirts were both done by Pat Sinclair, a professional advertising designer and a personal friend of Mimi's. Mimi chose Dean Tyler as the narrator of our show. Dean was a friend of hers from the days she worked with him at WIP Radio. Mimi learned to listen to all sides of a discussion and then make a decision as to what was best for the whole chorus.

Her acting ability, in part, came from being on the front row of Valley Forge. Her face, body motions, and timing were all part of the perfection needed for performing with this award-winning chorus. (It was Mimi who stepped out from the front row before everyone else.) There were singers from many groups who made up the chorus of Narberth Community Theatre. Singing with mixed voices to the accompaniment of a full pit orchestra was quite a new experience for most of us. And after two performances of the first *Bits of Broadway*, in two short years, many of us would once again be together in song.

♮

It was three years before I heard from Katie again. She asked me if I would be interested in working with a new chorus. I listened. Twenty-one members of her original chorus had decided they wanted to get together and start a different kind of barbershop chorus. No one in the group felt confident enough to be the director. I didn't want to direct again. I listened some more, becoming interested in what she was saying despite my misgivings. I finally realized that they didn't want me to direct. Yay! Katie wanted me to help them develop their new chorus, Millennium Magic.

The more Katie explained to me the goals of this new group, the more excited I became. This was something very new to our world: a chorus that didn't want to sing with a director. This had never been done before, and they wanted me to guide them. They felt that we knew each other well and they liked the way I had worked with them in the past. What an opportunity! This was creative and unique. We would be blazing a new trail and singing the music we loved. And it was with the women I had come to love when we went to Salt Lake City. It was the perfect fit. Women who were crazy enough to try something new, and a coach that was crazy enough to drive four hours each way just to step back out of the way when they sang. That's crazy.

I said yes.

♮

The family was back together again. We rehearsed together once a month. I acted more as a coach than a director. I started with the "underwear:" holding the ends of phrases, singing the right vowel, using good vocal skills. It wasn't long before we started learning special techniques: fine tuning, more volume variations, more vocal styles. Soon I was able to step back while they sang. We worked on listening to each other, rather than watching the director. This allowed the chorus to connect with the audience, which enhanced their staging. We were creating a performing ensemble. And we developed the chorus's personality.

We always went out for food and drink after the rehearsal, and I would get to socialize with the chorus. Then Katie and I would come back to her home for the evening and just share our feelings—with a martini. We both wanted the same thing for this chorus, and it created a very strong bond between us. It always helped me to talk candidly with someone I trusted, going over the program and making sure we were moving forward all the time. We were creating this unique and powerful chorus: twenty-one women with a single goal, working together.

Finally, they were ready. I took Millennium Magic to contest that year; but from then on, they would be announced this way: "Contestant number x, under their own direction, the Millennium Magic Chorus!"

The results that first year were first place, small chorus, and fifth place in the entire contest. Millennium Magic became famous. They won the small-chorus award year after year at the regional level. Soon they qualified to compete in the Harmony Classic small-chorus contest held yearly at the international level. They knew who they were. They knew where they wanted to go. And they knew how to get there. It was time for me to let them go. So I did. I am very, very proud of them.

Katie and I still meet once a year at International and spend a few moments together, just being friends.

23

Shorty, Tom, and Me

1998

WHEN A WOMAN MARRIES a member of the Barbershop Harmony Society, it is presumed that the two of them will always attend the Men's Competition held each year during the Independence Day holiday. This was true for Darrel and me, and also for Pat, the widow of Darrel's best friend. (Pat was my roommate in Russia.)

It was the July 4th weekend in 1998, and Pat was with us as we attended the annual international convention. As we stood on the balcony of our hotel, admiring the view, we talked about our mutual love of music and how it affected our lives. She knew of my dream to start a new chorus; she turned to me and said, "So what are you waiting for?"

Ouch! It was a simple and direct question. One I had no answer for. The timing for Pat's question must have been right. It was not the first time I had been scolded for not starting my new chorus, but now it felt like it was time to check it off my bucket list—or forget about it entirely. Since I didn't want this to be one of my deathbed regrets, I decided to investigate this idea.

The first person I contacted was one special friend, Shorty Yeaworth. I knew him as the producer and director of the Wayne Concert Series in our neighboring town. Shorty invited lecturers, soloists from the Philadelphia Orchestra, and a four-organ concert as his guest performers. The Valley Forge Chorus performed for their final event of the season, called Friends and Family. Shorty and his wife lived about half a mile from my home, and we had known each other for about ten years. We worked together with a network marketing company.

Shorty's bio says he was born in Berlin, Germany, the son of a Presbyterian minister. He was a member of the American Society of Composers, Authors, and Publishers (ASCAP) and is remembered as the producer and director of the science fiction movie *The Blob*, staring Steve McQueen. He worked on the *Billy Graham Crusade* television broadcasts. A trek to Israel to direct one of Pat Boone's Christmas specials led him to a love of traveling to Israel and Jordan, and he soon became a travel guide for that area. At that time, he was designing an entertainment complex in the kingdom of Jordan.

He was the perfect person for me to talk to about this new chorus that I wanted to create. Was this a viable project? Could it be done? Was I on the right track? I was looking for validation of the concept, not the particulars. Shorty, his pianist wife, Jean, and I spent many hours just talking together about what was going on in the entertainment world. I told them what I wanted to do and why I was so excited about starting this new chorus. Shorty encouraged me. He felt there was a market for this kind of entertainment. Their interest was just what I needed. They added a road map to my scattered thoughts and gave me the support that I needed. The most profound suggestion Shorty made at that time was for us to have a party before the first rehearsal so that all the singers could get to know each other. At the end of our talk, Shorty invited my new unknown chorus to sing in the spring concert of the Wayne Concert Series for May 13, 2000. I didn't have a chorus and we had yet to sing a note, but we had our first performance.

My original thought was to put together an a cappella chorus of both men and women to sing eight-part barbershop songs. But something much bigger and unique was evolving. I talked to someone from the Mendelssohn Club of Philadelphia about administration, their finances, and how they maintained good singing. (Mendelssohn is Philadelphia's oldest chorus, having been founded in 1874.) I talked with Shorty about sponsors, grants, rehearsal halls, mixed-chorus rehearsal techniques, and more, and I researched the availability of eight-part songs that had already been arranged (not many) and how to get them.

Choosing the Co-pilot

I am not a do-it-alone person. I knew I needed a buddy, someone to help me organize this project. I am a musician, and I needed a "let's get it done" person. This had to be Tom Halley. Tom was an active member of the Mainliners Chorus. He was a quartet singer performing with a mixed quartet called The Philharmonics. He owned his own company. He was a wonderful singer, well known, loved, and respected in the barbershop world. He was a fun person to know, and he was organized. He also had a flair for the performance stage.

Would he do it?

1999

In April, while attending the women's Regional Barbershop Convention and Competition in Ocean City, Maryland, I spied Tom in the middle of our hotel lobby. Wasting no time, I ran up to him with this request: "Join me in starting a mixed-voice a cappella group. I can do the music. I just need a man who can organize." He paused. For a very long time. Then he started asking me questions. My answers were vague. I wasn't sure just what kind of chorus it would be, so I said, "A contemporary performance group, singing all kinds of happy fun songs. We would sing good music and have lots of performances." The best way I described this new chorus was to say that in ten years, I'd like to sing on stage with Peter Nero and the Philly Pops.

And then he said, "Let me think about it."

Sigh. At least it wasn't a no. I knew without Tom I wouldn't be able to do it. He was the perfect match for me and this new chorus. It was Tom or no one.

Our email conversations went like this:

Tom: "I'm not sure what to do. I'm working ten hours a day right now, and I wonder what good I will be to you if it continues. I am very interested but need to be careful what I promise. I must deliver whatever I promise, so tell me what you need, and I'll say yes or no. I want to play but absolutely don't want to overcommit."

Jan: "I'm going for it. I've talked to directors, fundraisers, sponsors, suggested rehearsal halls, and even possible arrangers. We have our first performance in May of 2000. All I need is you!"

Tom: "That's what I like about you—you go for it! Give me the rest of this week to think about it."

I waited. One week later...

Tom: "OK, let's do it. By June I want to have a business plan ready—you know, policy, mission, entrance requirements, budget, all that neat stuff."

Tom was on board.

Two weeks later, in May 1999, we teamed up to start a new and exciting chorus. We talked together a lot. This was something new. It hadn't been done before. We both were excited about the uniqueness of our idea—a mixed-voice a cappella chorus singing all kinds of different music. Tom felt the drive and passion within me. He said this about me: "At the helm of this venture, you burned. This takes somebody who burns." Soon we both burned.

It was a huge undertaking. A ton of effort. A ton of decisions to make. We could steer the boat wherever we wanted to steer it. We talked about the need to hold barbershop at arm's length. I was concerned that we were going to be thought of as the ugly stepsister of the barbershop world or that we were draining voices from the Sweet Adelines or the Men's Barbershop choruses. Our friends thought we were going to be a barbershop chorus. They were worried about losing performances to us. That's all they knew. There were a lot of people who wanted to pull us off of what we thought was the way to go. We held firm. We chose Wednesday night as our only available evening when most of our friends were not already singing in a barbershop chorus (Monday and Tuesday) or a church choir (Thursday). We were determined not to make people choose between this new a cappella group and their own choruses. Tom chose the first Wednesday of January 2000 as our starting date—our first rehearsal.

We had our mission defined, and now it was time for each of us to get to work.

Choosing Our Music

While Tom was busy with the administration and membership of this chorus, my challenge was to learn where to find the music for us to sing and for audiences to enjoy. What kind of music was out there for us? I had no idea. But I did know that I wanted to direct all the kinds of music I liked—a little bit of everything. The first target for my questions was music educators from high schools, colleges, and community choirs. I called the head of music at

Miami University. He said that he spends two hours every day looking for music for his choirs. My heart sank. This was not what I had in mind.

I learned that the Moses Hogan website had spiritual sheet music available. There was a phone number, so I called. Moses Hogan himself answered the phone. He sent me a cassette tape of all his arrangements and the music to "Elijah Rock." This arrangement seemed to be too difficult for my new chorus to learn. Maybe next year. I was learning. It was later that I found out that Moses Hogan was a well-known pianist, composer, and arranger. I didn't know that when I called. And he actually talked to me! Wow!

Searching the Internet for music publishing companies, I found J.W. Pepper and Son. Their home office and warehouse were in my hometown of Malvern, Pennsylvania. It was so easy to browse through their books and files. I found the music for "I'm Beginning to See the Light (SATB)," and it looked like a simple arrangement. The warehouse had electronic pianos for you to use. You had to use earphones to hear what you were playing. I put on a set and sat down to play. It was so easy and so much fun. This song sounded good to me. So I purchased one copy.

It was July and time for the Men's Barbershop Convention. This time we went to Anaheim, California. I had an entirely different focus at this convention. I talked to everyone I knew who would give me guidance: Joe Liles, Conrad Keil, Brian Beck, Jay Giallombardo, and Renee Craig.

I had heard of a group of accomplished barbershop quartet singers who called themselves Fanfare. There were sixteen of them—four quartets—and they had joined together to sing other kinds of music. Fanfare had been together for about four years, but I had never heard them. I kept my eyes open for them and finally found Ken Gibson, one of their members. I introduced myself and asked, "Where do you find your music?" He recommended I look at J.W. Pepper.

So I pulled out my one copy of "I'm Beginning to See The Light" and asked, "If by singing this, am I on the right track?"

"Definitely!" was his answer.

My one comment to him was that I needed a beautiful, easy-to-learn song that I could introduce to the chorus on the very first rehearsal, and they would be able to sing it that very first night.

"Of course," he said. "I have just the right song for you. I'll send you the music for 'All the Things You Are.'"

Onward!

For our first performance in May we needed five numbers with a variety of styles, including a fast, peppy song; a fun, crazy song; and a good closing number. The search was on. I met Don Gooding standing at his booth at the convention's marketplace. He was the owner of Mainely A Cappella, "the largest source of a cappella music in the world" (later renamed A-Cappella.com and now out of business). With him was Deke Sharon. Don and Deke were business partners in the publishing business. Deke had founded the nonprofit the Contemporary A Cappella Society (CASA). Deke is often considered the father of contemporary a cappella.

I was able to spend time talking with them at this convention and later over the phone. Tom and I became friends with Don and Deke. They were genuinely interested in what we were doing. Deke made suggestions of other a cappella groups and the music they sang. Listening to the music of these other groups helped me to decide what kind of music I wanted this chorus to sing (or not to sing). It was then I decided to sing everything that I liked and only what I thought would fit the Pops image. I also talked with Brian Beck, who wanted to arrange "Satin Doll" for us. I went home flying high with the support I had received at the men's contest. About a week after we came home from the convention, "All the Things You Are" arrived in the mail. This was exciting for me. It was a gorgeous ballad that was only a page and a half long. It was also a song that I could direct with lots of love and emotion, something I wanted this new chorus to have. It was perfect for our first rehearsal.

Now, with the addition of "I'm Beginning to See the Light," we had two songs. We needed three more for our first performance. Soon "Satin Doll" arrived from Brian Beck, plus a piano recording of the arrangement. J.W. Pepper had an arrangement of "Short People," and Renee Craig sent me her two-chorus arrangement of "Do You Hear the People Sing" from *Les Mis*. It was the perfect closer, the finale.

It was during this time that I was told that what I was trying to do was impossible. I said that my chorus was like a very large Manhattan Transfer. This truly would have been impossible— you can't fine tune forty voices—but I wanted to try to come close to this sound.

Shorty had offered this new chorus an opportunity to perform on the final Friends and Family Concert in early May. We had chosen our five songs for our first performance. We had to have these five songs off the paper in three and a half months. Tom was on board. We had our mission defined and we were building our chorus. My idea of a two-hundred-voice barbershop chorus disappeared, thank goodness.

Choosing Our Membership

We put out the word that we were starting a new chorus. Tom wrote these emails to send to some special people explaining what was happening and inviting them to audition. It was selective recruiting. He chose the singers we knew would want to rise to the challenge that we planned to present to them. All had left their choruses, and we knew they would like this idea. Every request was a personal invitation. Our friends invited their friends; couples came to us because they wanted to sing together. We scheduled two days in October for auditions. Here's the invitation:

From: Tom and Jan
Date: September 22, 1999
Subject: Join our new chorus!

Dear Singer,

You may have heard the exciting news that there is a new mixed-voice a cappella chorus being formed in the Philadelphia area. Well, plans have been underway for some time, and we'd like to tell you about it and invite you to be a part of it. It's here!

Here's a summary of everything you'd want to know about the new chorus, and how to be a part of it.

Purpose

The new chorus will be a high-quality auditioned group of singers that are committed to singing exciting and unique arrangements of progressive music—mixing the sounds and styles of barbershop, jazz, folk, Broadway, and gospel. We will perform as often as possible: in our own produced shows, as guests on other shows and festivals, and as paid performers.

This will be a chorus like none other in the Philadelphia area.

The Music

The music will be exciting, and the arrangements will mix men's and women's voices in producing a unique and wonderful sound that will be a joy to be a part of and listen to. We already have commissioned several arrangers around the country to begin work on music for us.

Unique Characteristics

♪ No risers—multi-leveled staging of individual singers/ groups of singers

♪ No choreography—emphasis on excellent musical performance

♪ Multi-part modern and custom musical arrangements

♪ Possible combined performances with orchestration

♪ Special group opportunities—duets, trios, quartets, octets, etc.

Chorus Name

Our members will determine the name of the new chorus, soon after our first rehearsal.

Affiliation

We have no current plans to join any musical organization. We will be independent as a singing organization, to pursue endeavors that will meet the needs of the chorus.

Musical Director

The director of music is Jan Muck, internationally known Sweet Adelines, Inc. director, and chorus and quartet coach.

Schedule

Auditions

Mon and Tues, October 11 and 12, 1999, by appointment
    As needed after the initial group, by appointment

Rehearsals

Wednesdays, weekly. Beginning January 5th, 2000

Auditions

Membership to the chorus will be by audition only. Singers will be given a vocal audition that tests vocal quality and musical accuracy and ability. Above average singers who are committed to contribute to the high quality of the organization and the chorus will be offered membership. Ability to read music is not required. Members WILL be expected to prepare and learn music on their own between rehearsals.

    To schedule a 10-minute vocal audition, contact Tom Halley.

Rehearsal Site

Rehearsals and auditions will be in the Great Valley, PA area, off the Rt 29 exit of Rt 202. Directions and maps will be provided upon the scheduling of an audition.

Performances

The first performance has already been booked for May, 2000.

    Well, that's it! We hope you'll join us for a very new experience in mixed a cappella chorus singing. We're so excited, and we have some great music for you to enjoy and a chorus setting that will be a new and challenging experience for us all – making mixed harmony the wave of the future!!

Thanks for considering us. We look forward to hearing from you! Please call or email us if you have questions.

Oh, and tell your friends about it!!

Tom Halley, Chorus Manager
Jan Muck, Musical Director

The Auditions

The most difficult part of auditioning our friends was when we felt they were not suited for the sound and activities we envisioned for this new chorus. Tom was always saying, "Protect the product." This new chorus was the product—and we always kept that in mind. Tom and I asked singers to sing some scales to hear where their voices sounded free and full. We played a short phrase on a keyboard and asked them to repeat it. "Happy Birthday" is a great test for pitch accuracy. Before they auditioned, we asked the singers to prepare to sing, a cappella, a song of their choice. This is where we were able to hear their true performance voice. We were looking for quality of voice, accuracy of pitch, and the ability to blend the voice within the ensemble. We were starting a chorus, not a group of soloists with vocal accompaniment. We recommended they sing the part we thought sounded the best, but in the end, they chose to sing the part where they were happiest.

We were also aware that we needed people who were positive and self-starters. We did not want to spoon-feed the notes to each member. Pops would sing without holding the music, so the ability to memorize was an important aspect of our selection. I didn't want to teach basic singing (previously known as "the underwear"), so we looked for people already skilled. Tom and I had clearly defined goals for this chorus. We both conveyed the same message: We were looking for good singers who wanted to do something extraordinary. We didn't care what they did for a living or whether they were tall or short. They just had to be excellent singers with a desire to be with something new and exciting, and they had to trust Tom and me to lead them.

Some singers did not pass the audition, and some were encouraged to get voice lessons and come back again for another audition. One person did just that, but after he auditioned again and passed, he quit his voice lessons. He sang with us a year and when it came time to re-audition for the chorus, we had to remove him. His voice just didn't blend with the other singers. At audition time a singer rushed in, out of breath, and immediately began to audition. This was a good singer, and I knew the voice, but after hurrying to be on time, the singer had no breath support. Ever hear a good singer without breath support? This person was asked to come back and try again but never did. I was brokenhearted. An unknown walk-in had a good voice, but when we questioned her about how she learned the music, we heard that she never looked at the music. Worse, she hadn't even learned music by listening to people standing nearby. Fear struck my heart. Declined.

Fortunately, it was almost a self-select situation. Our biggest concern happened when an excellent singer visited us one evening and he was obviously a heavy smoker. We all knew he had just smoked a cigarette before he entered the room. Fortunately, there was no return visit, and no audition was necessary. Whew!

By mid-October we had forty auditioned members. Tom sent out this letter:

From: Tom
Sent: 10/13/99 4:18:54 PM Pacific Daylight Time
Subject: Mixed Chorus Audition Results

Dear Singer,

Congratulations! We are pleased to announce that you've passed the audition for the new mixed chorus!!

We have to say again that the talent of the applicants has been nothing short of amazing. We are so excited, that we can hardly stand it!! You will be very pleased at the quality of singers that are becoming a part of this endeavor, as we are. You are a part of something very special, something very new and unique, and we're only now beginning to see just how special and talented the players are. The possibilities are endless.

We will be sending you a package concerning the next step for membership in the coming month. Our plans for music and voicing and all the other aspects of the chorus will be taking place in the coming months, as we prepare for January, when we finally get the chorus together for the first time. It is going to be wonderful.

For now, we ask you to continue to look for other talented singers that you think will add to the quality of the chorus. Spread the word.

Also, remember to keep your calendar free on Wednesdays, starting on January 5th, 2000. That is when the magic will begin.

And it WILL be magic.

The Best to You,

Tom Halley/ Jan Muck

Tom and I were like a fast sports car driving down a racetrack, hanging out the windows while cheering and beckoning all good singers to hop on our dream. This chorus was growing, and who knew where we would end up?

We followed the suggestion Shorty made to us and had our party in my home between Christmas and New Year's. Many of the singers knew each other; all the singers were friends by the end of the party. I sometimes wonder if that didn't set the tone of our entire chorus life. To this day, we laugh and say, "We party well and also sing." We had over forty people ready to start our new chorus. We had the May 2000, performance deadline, and Wednesday, January 5, 2000, was our first rehearsal. Happy New Year!

24

The Launch of Pops

THE MORE TOM AND I worked together, the more the goals of this new chorus took shape. Between us we knew that this was going to be bigger than even we imagined, and we were excited to make it happen. And so were our forty new singers. A new set of tigers was emerging.

- ♪ Ann was with me at Valley Forge. She had been treasurer of several women's groups and volunteered to handle our money accounts.
- ♪ Dan was a quartet barbershopper and the first baritone of Darrel's quartet, Harmony Springs. Tom's letter came to him at just the right time. He was ready for something new. As webmaster for the Mainliners, it was a natural that he would do the same for the Pops. Dan quickly became the glue for the Pops. He was the third leg of the stool. Dan added a little arranging, a little management, a little directing, and anything else when needed. He gave Tom's letter to his next-door neighbor Pam, who auditioned and joined.
- ♪ Pam was our theater actress and quickly took over the staging and emcee duties.
- ♪ Pam's husband, Ken, joined Pops so he would see his wife more often.
- ♪ Marji volunteered to find a restaurant close to Siemens for us to share our after-glo after each rehearsal.
- ♪ Marilyn couldn't wait to get her hands on the scheduling of our projects.

Marilyn worked at Siemens, a company located near Great Valley, Pennsylvania. She sang with the Atrium Singers of Siemens and also sang with us in *Bits of Broadway*. Now she was with us for this new chorus. It was she who found our rehearsal hall. Her workplace had a large education room on their lower floor and made it available for us. It was the company's donation to the community—in other words, free. But every singer needed to sign in to the office building and then take the elevator down to our room. Siemens asked us to wear name tags at all times while in their buildings. We also had to have an employee of the company with us at all times. This was OK because twelve of the company's Atrium Singers now belonged to our chorus. Most of them had sung with us in the two previous *Bits of Broadway* shows.

Whatever the chorus needed—at any time—someone would step up to help. We heard comments like "I'll do it" and "What do you think about this?" We needed music, costumes, boxes to stand on, and a name. All this would come, in time.

Our First Rehearsal. Jan 5, 2000

We brought the music for our five songs to that first rehearsal, enough for everyone, plus a few extra copies in case we had unexpected guests. I wasn't sure how this chorus was going to learn the music. After warm-ups, we handed out the music to "All the Things You Are."

My mixed chorus from *Bits of Broadway* had used a piano to learn their music, so someone brought a keyboard to our first rehearsal. The singers in this new chorus were good sight-readers and were ahead of me as I used the keyboard to introduce the music. I sensed that they were getting annoyed with the slow progress because the keyboard was just getting in the way.

Besides, a cappella singers don't tune to a piano, and they were having trouble. I tried it for several rehearsals and then put it away.

The one story I remember about the results of this first rehearsal was from a couple, Deb and Owen, who had heard that day about this new chorus and decided to come to investigate. After hearing the first run-through of our ballad, Deb thought the people singing must have had the song to practice before rehearsal. They didn't. It was an easy song, and the members were sight-reading it (just what I wanted). Deb said to me, "The first rehearsal just left me in awe. There was this cacophony of voices singing their parts and you took it and broke it apart and said, 'Do these eight measures.' You made them sing it three or four times and it was music then—and it was stunning. I felt so excited that we just happened to be there for this first night. And that we could do it together, as a couple. And having the rehearsal at a corporate setting was also very impressive. It indicated that you were very serious." They joined.

Every member left rehearsal that evening with the music to five songs—to be learned for the Wayne Concert Series in just three and a half months:

"I'm Beginning to See the Light"
"All the Things You Are"
"Satin Doll"
"Short People"
"Do You Hear the People Sing"

♮

We were moving fast. Thank goodness I only had the music to worry about. Tom had everything else. Shorty was staying visible during this time, and we talked of him many times as we rehearsed for his show. We all knew of his movie *The Blob*, and

for want of a better name we began calling ourselves The Blob
Chorus. We needed our own name—fast. We asked the members for ideas and got 179 suggestions. Some were really good,
like *Philly Sound* and *Octavox*. But then there was *The Necktie-
Petticoat Chorus*. No way.

At a meeting of about ten of us, we looked at all the names,
talked about them and then took a vote. We decided upon A Cappella Pops. A Cappella because that's the kind of chorus we were,
and Pops because that's the kind of music we sang. In future days,
we began to refer to our members as Popsters. I think Tom coined
that word. I loved the name. It was my favorite choice.

I myself was in awe of the sounds of the chorus. After we
had rehearsed for about two months, Shorty came to visit our
rehearsal. (I'm sure he was checking us out before the big concert
in May.) He listened for about an hour and then got up and left
without saying a word. The Siemens member who escorted him
to the front door tactfully asked him what he thought about the
rehearsal. And he said, "They are already better than my Wayne
Concert Choir."

A quick costume was decided upon before our Friends and
Family Concert on May 13. Everyone wore black slacks. The men
purchased identical black shirts with shiny silvers buttons. The
women wore a different colored jacket—red, yellow, bright blue—
over a black shirt. If they didn't have a colorful jacket, they found
one at a local thrift shop.

The venue for the Wayne Concert Series was a large church
that had choir risers on the stage. It was perfect for us at the time.
Our boxes would come later. The rehearsals were going well, but
the arrangement of "Satin Doll" was way beyond our abilities at
that time. As the performance date got closer and closer, we knew
we were in trouble. We didn't have any other song to sing and we
had agreed to do five—and "Satin Doll" was one of them.

It was much too difficult for this new chorus, but we had to do it. The chorus was not used to singing close-harmony jazz chords and hadn't yet learned to listen to each other. It was hard to tune. We had a guest visit us at one of our rehearsals one evening as we were learning "Satin Doll." To give you an idea of how difficult this song was for us, our guest got up and left when we finished rehearsing the song. We affectionately began to call the song "Satan Doll." Brian Beck (the arranger) had sent us a learning track to help us get a feel for the sound of the arrangement. I asked Shorty, "Could we sing along with the music at the concert?" Shorty said it could be done. So at the concert, we played the tape over their sound system and sang along with it. It worked.

♮

The Wayne Concert Series was over for the season. This Friends and Family performance had many local groups, which performed along with the Wayne Concert Choir. This was our "fifteen minutes of fame" and we found out we really loved performing together. Shorty had all of the performers sing together as the finale of the two-hour show.

Jean Yeaworth remembers that first concert at the Wayne Concert Friends and Family performance. We were only four months old and had learned five songs for this concert. Jean remembers watching me warm up the chorus as I said to them, "You won't remember the notes and words, so you have to remember to entertain the audience. Stomp your feet, wave your arms, and smile so that the audience knows you are having a good time entertaining them." (Did I really say that?) The Popsters did just that. Our performance was fun and the audience seemed to enjoy us. Of course our singers remembered the notes and words, but if not, they didn't look like a deer in the headlights while they tried to remember. They just smiled and kept right on mouthing something. Jean said that she had never seen a director with more sincerity than I had when I directed them. She said that my whole body led them. And they followed. She called me an encourager, a cheerleader.

This was a wonderful venue for our first concert. And it was just the kind of performance we had envisioned for the Pops. When it was over, we realized we had had our first "Wow!"

♮

We were ideal guest performers on upcoming barbershop shows that first year, because we were something new and unique. The Greater Harrisburg Chapter of the Sweet Adelines, now directed by Claire, from Valley Forge, invited us for their June 8 show. Our five songs were perfect for this gig.

The Christmas season approached, and we received invitations to be guests on the Mainliners Christmas Show and another local men's barbershop chorus, the Bucks Mont Squires of Song, from Bucks and Montgomery County. We spent the fall learning Christmas music. Our first Christmas concert was for my church, St. Peter's Church in the Great Valley. My love for A Cappella Pops Christmas music started here—our first Christmas together.

My church had a new guitar-playing minister who had only been with us since the summer months. Occasionally he would bring his jazz group, Sweet Lou and the Jay Hawks, as entertainment for events. Knowing he loved music, I had no problem asking him if Pops could sing for the Christmas dinner planned in early December. Of course, he said yes, but he also asked us to sing only a few songs. He took a chance on us as he had never heard us perform. I was a parishioner, and he may have had a hard time saying no to my request.

The event was a light supper for about sixty people, and we were to sing four songs. We had to squeeze into the corner of the room, but only after we had moved a table or two out of the way.

We sang two familiar fun Christmas songs, "The Most Wonderful Time of the Year" and "Rudolph, the Red-Nosed Reindeer." The third was a Christmas carol, "Angels We Have Heard on High." But the fourth (and final) song was "In the First Light" from the popular jazz group GLAD. It had a huge, big glorious ending. We pulled out all the stops. Almost before we finished the last chord our minister was up on his feet, jumping up and down. He ran up to me. I will never forget the look on his face as he threw his arms around me to give me the biggest hug. He couldn't even talk. He didn't need to. With only four songs, we had reached out to our audience with the message of Christmas. I wanted to duplicate that feeling at every Christmas performance from that day on.

♮

Years later we performed the Christmas program for a retirement village. We talked to the audience as we left the room. I was stopped by a lovely woman barely five feet tall. She grabbed both of my hands in hers and thanked me for the wonderful performance. And then she said, "I've been here two years and I've hated it. Now I know it will not be my last home. There is a better one waiting for me. Thank you."

25

Sam, the Jam Man

IN OUR NEIGHBORING TOWN of Phoenixville, Pennsylvania, a beautiful old theater had fallen into a terrible state. "Run down" would be a compliment. The Colonial Theatre had been built as a vaudeville theater in 1903. Mary Pickford (1913) and Harry Houdini (1917) had performed on its stage. In 1917 a Wurlitzer organ was installed under the floor, mounted on hydraulic lifts. It could be raised to the center of the stage for organ concerts. As years went by, movies were added. *The Jazz Singer* was shown there in 1928. In 1958 the movie *The Blob* (directed by Shorty Yeaworth) used the theater as a set, and we watched the Blob as it oozed through the projection opening of the Colonial Theatre and began to attack the town of Phoenixville. It was a small theater, and Shorty made it seem more frightening as his actors ran out the front door in fear, returned by way of the back alley, entered the back door of the theater, and ran, in fear, out the front door once again.

The theater went into disrepair—you couldn't sit in the seats, the bathrooms didn't work, there were holes in the walls, and you couldn't go up to the balcony because you might fall through the floor. You could almost sense the mice had been living there for many years. It had been a beautiful theater, with red and gold velvet drapes. In 1996 a group from the local town decided to start a foundation to restore the theater. Mary Foote was the manager of the restoration, and in 1997 the Association for the Colonial

Colonial Theatre organ.

Theatre (ACT) was able to purchase the theater. It was reopened in 1999, predominantly for films. Mary Foote's real interest was to have the community feel that they were part of the renovation of the theater. Most of the work was done by town volunteers. It was at this time that Marilyn, a member of the newly formed A Cappella Pops, knocked on Mary's office door. This was Marilyn's town, and she saw an opportunity for Pops to support a worthwhile charity.

"I'm from A Cappella Pops. We would like to do a performance in the theater and donate the proceeds to the building fund. Is this possible?"

And Mary responded, "It sounds like fun, but it is terrifying. I know nothing of live production."

They had only a twenty-by-thirty-foot stage in front of a movie screen. The ACT knew they wanted to have live entertainment, but they just weren't ready for it. A Cappella Pops knew we had the experience necessary to put on a show, but we were only one year old. This was a major project. Marilyn set up the initial meeting with Pops and Mary. I have no doubt that our passion and experience played a big part in their allowing us to use the theater. It must have gone something like this:

Mary: "You'll need dressing rooms. We have no dressing rooms."

Pops: "That's OK. We'll clean up the second floor, fix the lighting, patch the walls, and put down rugs."

Mary: "But there are neither lights nor sound equipment for the stage."

Pops: "That's OK. We'll rent them."

Mary: "How can we sell tickets?"

Pops: "We'll pre-sell them and have our people collect them at the doors."

The association agreed and a date was chosen for our show—April 8, 2001. Of course, we asked Marilyn to be in charge of all the arrangements. Both the performance and the restoration were major projects, and we began to design the program. We were not quite a year old and didn't have the repertoire to perform for an hour and a half. We decided to have an A Cappella Jam and invite five groups from the surrounding area to perform with us, as a fundraiser. We sent out invitations to all the a cappella groups that we knew or that were recommended to us. We asked for a tape (or CD) of their performance. In some cases Tom and I visited them during a performance or rehearsal. We were looking for variety—an entertaining performance and a good musical product—and we were looking for groups willing to volunteer their time and effort. Tom and I listened to the tapes and watched the performances and extended the five invitations.

We knew what costume to wear—the only one we had.

Costumes meant that we had to have dressing rooms for our guests. The second floor of the Colonial Theatre was being used as their junk room, with a kitchen full of boxes, three rooms with broken walls, a bathroom, no lights, and no curtains on the windows. The floors were covered with dust. We took over the second floor. We had some major cleanup work to do and as the show date approached, we turned our attention to the job ahead.

One Saturday in March we all gathered at the theater and attacked the second floor, armed with mops, pails, electrical equipment, spackling, and anything else we needed. We repaired the walls, fixed the lights, and moved boxes and anything else we couldn't use to the third floor, the new junk room. We cleaned the kitchen, mopped the dust, and repaired the bathroom. The next Saturday we brought in our old rugs and lamps, and shades for the windows. We lent our personal clothes racks for each room.

With cleanup completed, we focused on dress rehearsal next. We had to rent the lights and the sound equipment. We could only afford one spot, so we positioned that on the balcony to shine on center stage. It could be moved...a bit. Our newly found tech man Ross stayed up there and moved the spotlight around the stage to light the emcee and the soloists. He was the only one allowed upstairs, because it was dangerous.

The spot was wide enough to cover a quartet. The stage lights would have to do for the chorus. For our tech rehearsal—setting the lights and checking the sound system—we asked a couple of our tallest and shortest people to stand on the boxes to help us set the lights. This was all new to me, and I was fascinated watching the A Cappella Pops team go to work. I didn't know we had such talent. Between Tom and Marilyn we had the team working on every aspect of getting the theater ready for us.

On the day of the show, there was no room big enough for us all to gather at the theater, so we used the empty bar and grill next door. We changed in their small bathrooms and warmed up our voices in the large room that used to be the restaurant. The wife of one of our members stayed in the back of the theater auditorium waiting for the cue that it was the last song of the performing group. Then she came to get us.

There was no backstage. The street was the only way to enter the auditorium. All performers would come to the stage from the front door and line up along the sides of the theater so they would be ready to enter the stage. We didn't want any dead time between performers.

Tom put together a logo for our show: Sam, the Jam Man.

We put Sam on all our promotional materials. We made sweatshirts with Sam, the Jam Man, on the back and *A Cappella Jam 2001* on the front. Mary Foote had Sam, the Jam Man, shining on the movie screen at the theater for weeks before the show. And there he was, on stage, as our audience entered the theater.

Sam, the Jam Man (courtesy A Cappella Pops)

We sold out the show. There were people outside in the street waving their money in the air to purchase any available tickets. A Cappella Pops opened the show singing only one song, "Good Old A Cappella," arranged by our friend Katie. We quickly left the stage to let the show begin. The group called Key of She was first. They were six women who had formed after their original group disbanded. This was Key of She's second stage performance. For many of us, it was our introduction to vocal percussion. And it was done by a woman. A wonderful way to open the show. Next were the Madrigals, from West Chester University, with their lovely long dresses and beautiful sound, singing madrigals. Quite a change from the Key of She. Two gals and two guys, The Philharmonics, ended the first half with a standing ovation. Our Tom was the tenor, and everyone in the audience personally knew each of the other members of the quartet. They received whoops and hollers for their wonderful performance.

The University of Delaware was the home of the Y Chromes. They were the perfect group to begin the second half of the show.

Sold Out! (courtesy A Cappella Pops)

Yep, eleven college men in painters' coveralls having a wonderful time clowning around on the stage. When the emcee asked, "Aren't they great?" the audience yelled back and cheered for them. And for our barbershop friends, we had Night Magic, four women whose quartet had placed in the top five at the previous Women's International Contest. They were getting ready to compete again in the fall for that gold medal. And our own Renee Walsh was the baritone. A Cappella Pops closed the show with five of our best songs. As a finale, we brought all the performers on stage for their applause and to thank the audience for sharing their day with us. We had a standing ovation.

The party afterwards—the after-glo—was at the Black Lab Restaurant across the street from the theater. Food, beer, and song. We had our picture in the Phoenixville paper as we donated a check for $3,700 to the Colonial Theatre. It was an amazing

Pops presenting our gift.

experience for such a young singing group. We filled the auditorium, and Sam, the Jam Man, came back for eight more years.

In later years, we learned that the theater's electric bill had been close to $4,000 and they didn't know how they were going to pay it. Our donation had gone straight to the electric company.

We had a wonderful relationship with the Colonial Theatre. It soon became a restored movie theater with two new bathrooms in the lobby and a balcony that held more than 180 extra seats, making it a 658-seat theater. For the Pops to continue to perform on their stage, we needed to use the entire theater for two nights and an afternoon dress rehearsal. The Colonial Theatre felt that even with our donations, they were losing revenue from two nights and an afternoon. Our philanthropy mission was accomplished, so we moved on. They put our name, A Cappella Pops, on a plaque on the back of one of the new seats as a remembrance of our total donations of over $20,000.

Along with the original five performing groups, those who donated their time and talents for our jams were:

♪ The Foundation Singers, Philadelphia
♪ High Five Quartet, Baltimore
♪ Eight to the Bar, Drexel University
♪ Svitanya, Philadelphia
♪ Lunatic Grove, Philadelphia
♪ Round Midnight, New York City
♪ Norristones, Norristown, PA
♪ DaVinci's Notebook, Mid-Atlantic Area

Coda

It is now 2021 as I write this, and Mary Foote is retired from managing the Colonial Theatre. They have purchased the bank building adjacent to the theater and built two movie–performance auditoriums. There is a thirty-foot concession stand in the lobby and a rooftop deck. Phoenixville is alive with restaurants, outdoor decks, and specialty shops along the main street. During the summer months, you can't find a parking place on First Friday. And the Colonial Theatre stands tall in the middle of it all.

26

Building Blocks

Tax-Free

SWEET ADELINES INTERNATIONAL IS a nonprofit organization, and all chapters, like Valley Forge, fall under this umbrella. I knew that many members of Valley Forge used its nonprofit status to deduct items from their income taxes. I felt that the Pops members would want the same option. Therefore, one of our first duties for the Pops was to set ourselves up as a nonprofit organization. Ann, now our treasurer, took Tom and me to her lawyer, and we did the paperwork to make this happen.

Costume

We knew Pops was going to be different from our traditional choruses, and that meant the outfits that we wore while singing had to be different. I had a vision but no knowledge of how to make it happen. I tore out a clothing advertisement in a magazine that showed many different ways to wear black and white—scarves, ties, short or long skirts, vests, and so on. That ad showed the variety that I thought we could use on the stage.

Mary Ellen David, from the Valley Forge Chorus, was now living in New York City designing clothes for off-Broadway shows. She was thrilled when we asked her for help with our chorus outfits. Tom and I and Eileen Kelly (our volunteer costume chair) drove from Philadelphia to Manhattan to meet with her. Eileen brought colors that we liked. Mary Ellen lived in an apartment right next to the site of the World Trade Center. When we arrived, she took us to the roof of her building, where we looked down into the remains of the subway system. We took her to lunch.

We started out with pictures and colors and ideas. *Mary Ellen* started out with, "If you had to pick three or four words that you wanted Pops to be known for, what words would you chose? What's the vision?" We decided on *sophisticated, cool, fun,* and *musical.* It was a good day being with Mary Ellen. We chose the colors for our outfits. They would be black, gray, and silver with very big chunky silver jewelry. Each Popster would choose the clothing style that best suited them.

We brought this idea back to the chorus with some guidelines: no white shirts or all-black suits for the men, and only dark stocking for the women who wore skirts that showed their legs. Boots were OK. We encouraged outfits that pushed the edge. They had to be flashy. I wanted the men to wear funky silver necklaces, but that didn't go over too well. Maybe it was a little too far past the edge. At holiday time we asked the members to change their outfits to black and gold with lots of sparkles—Christmas cocktail party clothes. For the summertime, we again called Mary Ellen for costume colors. She suggested using orange, chartreuse, hot pink, and royal blue—we added just a few white slacks. The Pops enjoyed being comfortable in sundresses and Hawaiian short-sleeved shirts, as long as they were in the summer colors. This idea was successful. I think it added to the freedom to be ourselves as we performed.

Boxes

I didn't want to use choral risers. I wanted more flexibility for our performances than risers would allow. When using risers was suggested, I was heard to say, "Over my dead body." Tom, Dan, and I talked about making individual risers that could be moved around as we changed staging. We wanted the chorus members to move from box to box, or to put two boxes together to make a seat. Members needed to see and to be seen. Dan put together a design. At first he made the boxes collapsible but soon decided they would be safer if they were glued together. We made a small number of boxes in three sizes: four, eight, and sixteen inches high. We didn't make one for everyone.

When Dan finished, Ann took them to her garage and painted them all black. Little handles were put inside to make them easy to carry. We had originally thought to store them in one place and haul them together in a member's truck, but we eventually decided to have members take them home and individually bring them to rehearsals and performances.

The boxes were an excellent idea and we put them to good use redesigning our staging to fit the venue and the music. As the boxes got slammed into car trunks, they started to break down along the edges. One year we collected all the boxes, cleaned up the edges and corners, repainted them, and kept going.

After-glo

Marji found the ideal restaurant for our after-rehearsal chorus gathering—the Cedar Hollow Inn. We had our own private dining space. Our rehearsals ended at 9:30, but the kitchen closed at 10:00, so we had to hustle to get there in time to place our food

Dan and Eileen.

order. When each of us arrived, we went straight to the service
bar and ordered our drinks. Our server was Lois, and she immediately took our food order. She had talked to the kitchen staff
and they agreed to stay open a few extra minutes until we all had
ordered.

There were usually ten of us there every week. Friendships
developed. One evening, I sat across the table from Dan, who was
seated next to Eileen. I kept noticing that Dan used his right
hand to lift his drinking glass. Eileen used only her left hand
to hold her glass. I watched this for the whole evening. It never
changed. The next morning, I couldn't resist an email to Dan.
"CAUGHT YOU!" I typed. He fessed up and told me that they
were dating. Later, we were all invited to their wedding.

Logo

The chorus wanted a logo. We were being hired for gigs and we had contracts to sign. Dan, who had a degree in computer science, developed a website for us. It was time to have a logo. A couple of Popsters got together and searched the internet for graphic designers. They chose a woman from Virginia Beach, Virginia, who gave them several ideas. The choice was easy. One design looked just like what we were—singers who had fun singing and looked sharp. The words they decided to put beneath the design were the words that Pam, our emcee, used every time she opened our performances. "Ladies and gentlemen! We are A Cappella Pops! Nothin' but Voice."

I was busy with the music while all this was developing. When the Popsters showed me what they had decided on, I was thrilled. That logo was everything A Cappella Pops was and wanted to be. That was wonderful. Later, we trademarked the name with our logo.

A Cappella Pops
...nothin' but voice

Pops logo.

Auditions Every Year

It was my idea to have all Popsters re-audition every year, and
Tom agreed. It wasn't to "fire" someone from the Pops; it was
more a feeling that we wanted everyone to keep up with their
voice quality and not to slough off after they joined the chorus.
Every January we re-auditioned everyone. Every ten minutes
from 6:00 p.m. to 7:30—by appointment—we listened to our chorus members sing something they loved. It was really an easy
re-audition, but not too many Popsters looked forward to singing
alone for Tom and me. We asked that they sing one song for us.
It could not be a song in the Pops repertoire. It had to be different. They brought guitars with them or pre-recorded music (kara-
oke) to sing with. Anything was OK. It gave me a chance to hear
everyone's voice singly, which helped me choose the chorus music.

Renee sang a ballad for her audition, "When I Look in Your
Eyes," from *Doctor Dolittle*, and it was beautiful. I said this and
she told me she had an a cappella solo arrangement of it and
would I like to see it. Of course. It was a great song, and I decided
to have the chorus sing it. And who had the solo? Renee, of course.

Janet W. brought puppets with her to her audition, and they
sang to each other. I wanted to put Janet and her puppets on our
stage, but it never happened. I don't know why. Maybe we didn't
get the arrangement. Sad.

Having re-auditions every January also made it easy for
those who wanted to leave the Pops. They simply chose not to re-
audition, no excuses or apologies necessary.

The Sound

Most of our performances needed no amplification. We were performing at small retirement gatherings, dinner meetings, and

such. When we performed at larger venues, they had their own sound systems. Our Pops members helped set up those systems for our performances. But if the sound stopped working, they would be singing on stage and couldn't do anything. Ross came to our rescue. Ross operated the audio and video systems for the company where we rehearsed. When we produced our first jam at the Colonial Theatre, we asked him to operate the rented sound system. (He was up in the balcony with the broken floorboards.) Ross became the official audio technician for the Pops, and we soon had our own wireless microphones, mixer, and other recording equipment. Ross often came to rehearsals to acquaint us with how to use the emcee microphones. He became our first (and only) non-singing member.

Saturday Morning Rehearsals

With all this activity, we had to build a repertoire to be flexible enough to perform for any audience. My home was near our rehearsal site, and I had a piano. I sent out an invitation. Every Saturday morning from 9:00 to noon, my home was open for anyone to come and rehearse our music. I put a coffeepot on the stove at 9:00, and someone usually brought donuts. I never scheduled what songs we would work on. Open house: any part, any time, whatever music was needed by whoever showed up. My first question of the morning was, what do you want to work on? Some couldn't come till 10:00 a.m., and some left at 10:30 a.m. We rehearsed the songs they needed. Sometimes we had eight and sometimes four. This rehearsal was for anyone who wanted to sing and learn. This continued for many weeks. We were constantly learning music and it felt good—building friends and music.

27

Developing the "Wow!" Performance

WE HAD ALL OUR building blocks together, and the chorus was running smoothly. We were comfortable with each other. Friendships developed, and our social lives with each other became full. Julianne or Caren hosted our New Year's Eve parties. Darrel and I hosted an outdoor picnic in September at our home. Barry and Lisa had an open house around her pool, and Marji had many impromptu gatherings throughout the year. The teams were together and functioning.

And the opportunities to sing just kept getting better and better. We added two more barbershop chapter shows and several retirement villages to our performances.

We were asked to sing at a golf club's end-of-season banquet, after the guests' dinner meal was over. The room was crowded, but we fit tightly into a corner, and the audience was quite close to us. The crowd was having a wonderful time. They loved us and sometimes sang along with us as we performed. Some dinner guests decided to join us and danced around the tables as we sang. We had to laugh because they were having such a good time—but we almost lost it when they decided that dancing *on* the tables was much more fun than dancing *around* the tables. We didn't mind. It was fun, and they were having such a good time with our music. All of us survived the evening with many fond memories.

♮

Someone from Longwood Gardens had seen us perform and invited us to sing for them at Christmastime. This was a big deal. Longwood Gardens is an American botanical garden in nearby Kennett Square, Pennsylvania. It is over a thousand acres of flowers, woodlands, and meadows. They have fountains, open-air theaters, ballrooms, and a conservatory for performing groups. Our December performance was two half hours scheduled at 7:30 and 8:30 p.m. We used the conservatory's risers and sound system and sang among the poinsettias and wrapped gift boxes that lined the stage. We sang eight songs (a little short of a half hour), which gave us time to visit the audience before the room was cleared, cleaned, and restocked for the next show. The workers liked that. This became an every-other-year invitation.

One Christmas season, a young woman in a wheelchair listened to the performance from the back of the conservatory. Her cousin, her mother, and her aunt had brought her, and, after the first half-hour performance, they brought her up to me to say hello. She was part of my family, related to me by marriage. She had a radiant glow to her face. Her family all smiled through their tears, from the performance, from our mini reunion, and from the illness my cousin faced. There seemed to be an aura around the group. I saw that they were bathed in a strange pink-white light. We hugged without talking. I returned to my chorus for the second performance, and they took her home.

♮

The American Pharmaceutical Association planned a convention in Philadelphia to celebrate their 150th anniversary. They came to us with an unusual request. They wanted only fifteen minutes of song, divided into three five-minute segments. And they wanted music from specific decades that spanned their 150-year history: 1850 to 1900, 1900 to 1950, and 1950 to 2000. This would take some planning. Dan, Tom, and I sat around a table and looked at our repertoire. We found only six songs that would fit into the 1900 to 2000 segments. We had nothing for the 1850-to-1900 time span. But we accepted the gig. There was plenty of time to find and learn three songs from the last half of the nineteenth century.

Dan searched the internet and made a list of music titles from that era. We only needed five minutes for the first part of our fifteen-minute performance and this list looked good. Dan suggested we contact Jay Giallombardo to arrange a medley for us. Jay was the baritone of the Grandma's Boys who won the Barbershop Harmony international quartet contest in 1979. His magnificent arrangement of "The Star-Spangled Banner" and "O Canada," sung together as the finale, was a highlight of their Canadian Conference. We were there.

Jay agreed to help us. We sent him copies of the music and said, "Put them in any order that musically works. We don't care." Within a few short weeks we received a package of sheet music that Jay had labeled "19th Century Popular Songs Medley." Between each of the songs he had added either a two-measure musical segue, a key change, or just a quiet pause or two. This became the glue that made it easy to move from one song to the other, an easy transition between the eight songs.

1 "Row, Row, Row your Boat"
2 "Pop! Goes the Weasel"
3 "Shoo, Fly, Don't Bother Me!"
4 "Listen to the Mocking Bird"
5 "Beautiful Dreamer"
6 "Oh, Dem Golden Slippers"
7 "Ten Little Injuns"
8 "Oh! Susannah"

Six minutes of fun to sing and listen to, thanks to Jay's arrangement.The staging was taught to us by a friend of the Pops who worked with the Mask and Wig Club from the University of Pennsylvania. His idea was to treat the medley as a series of nineteenth century tintype pictures. We were to stand perfectly still for each song. During the segue to the next song, we would change to a different picture pose.

The chorus needed no encouragement. Each song was given the Pops treatment. They took to this idea with all the creativity they had. The next rehearsals were filled with all kinds of props; each evening brought something new. We had black high hats, large bonnets, fancy umbrellas, lace handkerchiefs, and many large fake mustaches for the men. The chorus made me laugh. The staging made the music come alive. We produced eight staged pictures for the medley. "Pop! Goes the Weasel" popped the chorus.

One tenor tipped his top hat each time he sang an echo of the word *valley*. It went like this: "I'm dreaming now of the valley

Pops goes the weasel.

(*valley*), of the valley (*valley*), of the valley (*valley*)" And a very low bass added the Jolly Green Giant. "I'm dreaming now of the valley, *Ho, ho, ho!*" The favorite song of the medley, especially at the retirement villages, was Stephen Foster's "Beautiful Dreamer." We were happy we had included it.

♮

Pops was only three years old when we got an invitation to sing at Carnegie Hall. How did this come about? It had been years since Janellen Farmer had worked with the Valley Forge Chorus to improve their vocal sound, but she had become a friend during that time. She was still a friend, and my husband and I often attended her performances at local theaters and teahouses. She had attended several of our A Cappella Pops concerts. She said that she was producing her own show at the Weill Recital Hall at Carnegie Hall on March 2, 2003, a celebration for St. Patrick's Day.

"Would you be interested in coming to New York City and performing for about thirty minutes on the second half of my show? I can't pay you, but you'll be singing at Carnegie Hall."

"Yes, yes, yes!"

Excitement ran high for this gig. At the request of Janellen, we learned one Irish song, "Galway Bay," which would open our part of the performance. We planned our performance to the very last applause, writing emcee spots and introductions. All forty-four of our members were making travel plans and telling friends and families about our trip to NYC.

Kaboom! The stage at the Weill Recital Hall was not big enough to hold our entire chorus. Had we been able to bring our boxes we probably would have fit, but the local unions would have had to put our boxes onto the stage, at a tremendous cost to us. We could only have twenty-four singers on stage. We had to cut people.

Tom told me *I* had to do it. I spent hours going over names. A few members self-selected themselves out of the trip, saving me a little heartache, but most did not. It was the worst thing I've ever gone through. I had to select only twenty-four people out of forty-four to perform at Carnegie Hall. And I loved them all. It was like someone saying, "OK, the boat capsized. You've got three kids. Which two are you going to save?" That was exactly how I felt. It was horrible. I hated it. All my singers are good. We had chosen them to sing with the Pops because they were that good, and now we had to pick just twenty-four of our members, and not necessarily even twenty-four of the best singers, but twenty-four that I felt would blend the best. It was the ultimate stress.

First I decided just what we needed from our performers. All the voices had to blend. Each person had to be secure in their

Rehearsal at Weill Hall. (courtesy A Cappella Pops)

notes and their stage presence. I couldn't have any "deer in the headlights" on stage. The mix of parts had to produce the best sound. We had to have voices that would carry to the back of the auditorium because there were no mics. We also needed an ensemble sound. That is no individual styling, no wide vibratos, and no prima donnas.

Finally, I announced my selection. I had not chosen many of my top soloists for the performance at Carnegie Hall. And no matter how well I may have handled it, I still had hurt feelings. I could have told every single solitary person why I did or did not choose them. But no one asked—so I never told. Do you trust the people in charge to have the best interest of the chorus, or do you feel there is favoritism? I suppose there was a bit of both of those feelings within my chorus during that time.

The Sunday of the performance was here. We arrived at the stage door at our appointed time. Janellen welcomed us. We checked out our stage positions and did a bit of vocalizing, staging movements, and trying out the emcee spots. It was awesome standing on that stage. We could feel the grandeur of being at Carnegie Hall. Our final warm-up was among the rafters, water fountains, boxes, and curtains in a backstage area. As we ran through our performance songs and I listened to the sound of my chosen twenty-four chorus members, I knew I had done a good job. It was magnificent. The sound was full of beautiful chords, lots of energy and joy—the true sound of A Cappella Pops. As much as I hated the job, I felt good about the results. It was a near-perfect sound.

As we entered the stage, we were able to see the audience. There, right in the middle of the auditorium, were members of the chorus. They had come to Carnegie Hall to hear their chorus, A Cappella Pops, perform on stage. We sang to them. We could see them from the stage during the performance. They smiled and applauded and loved us. We had given a ticket to the concert to Mary Ellen David, our costume consultant, and she was there, too. The audience was mostly Pops and friends of Janellen. There were many empty seats and from the stage we missed the applause and cheers that we had become accustomed to. The dream of singing to a full house at Carnegie Hall had not materialized.

There was a little feeling a disappointment, but also pride in what we had done. When we returned home, Tom Halley sent us all an email.

SUBJECT: The question of benefit...

Many times, as a performer, I have prepared for a show, and I anticipate that it will be wonderful—a large, big-name theater that boasts an electric audience that gives great accolades, big publicity, etc. But the experience when we get there is disappointing. I'm left feeling let down. The benefit? Hmmm.

I've had other times when I expected little—going to a small-town show with little publicity, and really no info, but the event turns out to be magical—a great jazzed audience, standing ovation, laughter, fun, connecting with the audience, the works. I walk off stage, stand in the wings and shake my head, and say "go figure." The performance was solid, the audience was perfect, the lighting/sound/stage/mood all lined up and there was MAGIC.

The benefit? It's obvious in this case.

Sometimes it pays off and you get to experience the thrill of one of those magical moments. But sometimes the benefit is that you LEARN how to be a better performer, you get the experience, and you find out what you are made of.

You can ask "Why did we go to all that trouble?" now. That's ok. That is natural.

When we headed down this road toward that dream, CARNEGIE HALL, many months ago, the vision was:

A Cappella Pops (all of us) singing to a packed house, on the main stage, and the New York critics rave, and the audience is electric, and we are respected and we "move up."

Life changed along the way, didn't it?

Jan nailed the benefit on the head in her email. We got the most out of the event we could hope for under the circumstances. But the customer didn't sell that many seats, and so, much of what we as performers hoped for was a little flat. If there were 300 more people in the seats that gave reviews similar to the private ones I heard afterwards, we would have claimed a major victory and FELT more successful.

But trust me; there will be good things that will happen behind the scenes, based on what we did on Sunday. We did our job—what they asked us to do. We rolled with a barrage of punches.

Pops adjusted, and we put an excellent package on the stage. Leaders rose up within Pops. Whoa. That was a major move in the right direction.

Did you personally benefit from it? I can't answer that question. Only you can.

I know I did.

Many of us placed a little brick down on the Pops Road to Excellence.

The road is continuing.

Onward!!

And this is what has happened. After our performance, Janellen invited the Pops to a little restaurant, Trattoria Dell'Arte, across the street from the hall. It was a time to be introduced to her many friends and family. This was New York City. Many who were in attendance were singers and songwriters. We met Byron Summers and Norman Rae, a music and lyrics team of songwriters. They had just written a Christmas song, "Merry Christmas Wishes," which received the NYC first-place award for the newest Christmas song of 2002.

At home, in Janellen's living room, she had a CD of Byron singing and playing this song. I loved it. I wondered if Byron would give it to A Cappella Pops to sing. I asked for his phone number and gave him a call. Of course, we could sing it, but could we have it arranged for an a cappella group? Oops! At that time, we didn't know anyone who would be able to arrange this for us. Byron started a search. He asked his NYC contacts and came up with the name of an arranger living in Washington, D.C. This is how we were introduced to Steven Bishop. As a favor to Byron, he arranged "Merry Christmas Wishes" for the Pops, and we learned it for the following Christmas season.

One of our favorite Christmas performances was in the conservatory at Longwood Gardens. At the next Christmas concert, Byron and Norman Rae, the lyricist, joined us for the initial performance of "Merry Christmas Wishes." We introduced them from the stage, just like we had seen on television. We were so proud.

Byron and Norman asked us to make a recording of the song, and they came to the studio to make sure it was what they wanted. They made suggestions and we followed them. We were working with two New York City professional musicians and we knew it. Their idea was to present this song to the TV programs in New York (such as the *Today Show*) and hopefully have them bring us to New York to perform it for their show. It never worked out for them, and I know we were all disappointed. However, we continued to sing it on our Christmas performances and we even put a portion of the song on our Christmas CD. Marji and I traveled to New York to attend the opening of Byron and Norman's new musical *Tusks.*

Steven Bishop arranged two new songs for us. They were some of the most beautiful and most challenging songs we would learn. Several months later we received an invitation to perform at the opening of the new Comcast Center in downtown Philadelphia. It was a referral from Jim Dell'Orefice, the pianist who accompanied Janellen Farmer at Carnegie Hall. He owns the company Specialty Entertainment.

Tom Halley was right. Look what happened.

The Comcast Center performance has its own story. It was the day they welcomed the world to the brand new Comcast Center in the middle of downtown Philadelphia. We were part of the entertainment provided to those who came to see this new building. The lobby was huge, the ceiling was three stories high, and the lobby floor was large enough that one could drive on it with a truck. With all the marble, slate, and glass, our sound bounced off the walls. They put us on an open three-level staircase at the side of the huge reception area.

We had to position ourselves on the staircase so that we could hear each other. This took several tries, but we had help. The center had its own sound system and personnel. And we had brought with us our own sound man to help us. Sean climbed all over the staircase, adjusting the stand-up mics, and the Comcast people were alongside adjusting knobs. They finally found a way to make it all work. The chorus stood on the landing between the two staircases, up one level from the floor, around the corner and on up to the second level. They could all hear each other and see the people milling around the lobby. Perfect. But where was the director? There was no place for me except on the floor of the lobby about twenty feet from the staircase. I could see the chorus and they could see me, but that's all we had. They were nestled around the second-level landing. Thank goodness the sound system was excellent.

Funny what you remember from a performance: this little kid on his tricycle riding around the lobby floor. His favorite trail was between the staircase and the director. This was a perfect roadway without any obstruction. He could go as fast as he wanted, and he did. While we were singing, he would buzz down his trail between us and head to the center of the lobby, only to come at us again.

And we sang. And we laughed. And then he was gone.

28

This is Theater!

A VISITING BASS WASN'T SURE he wanted to sing with us. He was a trained classical and chamber music singer. He took one look at our rehearsal for an upcoming performance and said, with amazement, "This is theater!" He joined us then. (Singing with the Pops brought out his funny side, and he became a real showman. I had him tagged for *Brush Up Your Shakespeare*.) In May, 2019, I met a well-known judge in SAI, and she said to me that she remembered that when she heard Valley Forge sing, she felt like we were singing our story. She said that we were the first Sweet Adelines chorus who were storytellers. I like to direct that way—as a storyteller with a theatrical flair—and the Pops responded. Tom and I both liked storytelling, and this worked well with the Pops. We were able to push the boundaries of our performances.

When Pops was new, Pam's first job was to become our emcee chair. She was a natural with the command of the stage. On the days she wasn't singing with the Pops, she was performing in a play with one of the little theater groups she belonged to in our area. We talked together about what kind of conversation we wanted to do during our performances. We also talked about what we wanted *not* to do. (My pet peeve is the emcee who says, "and the *next* song . . ." It should be obvious there's a *next* song, just as it should be obvious when the performance is wrapping up. I want our emcees to be more creative.) Pam and I worked closely to refine our performances. We asked questions of our marketing team. Who was coming to this performance? What was the age group of the audience? Will there be young folks? Are we singing during the dinner?

This was no small challenge. We had to learn what kind of songs each audience liked, and we tried to adapt our lineup to fit our audience. As an example, when singing for a retirement village, most of our audience will be well up in years. The songs that they will enjoy the most are ones that are most familiar and that are usually upbeat. They don't want to hear us show off with a crazy arrangement of a popular song. We saved those songs for the younger crowds. At a performance in Maryland, we were asked to sing before the dinner, during drinks and appetizers. The room was so big that their sound system did not work for the entire room. Because of this, we chose to present a parade-style performance—just music, not too much talking. Maryland is famous for the crabs that the Chesapeake Bay produces. Our audience had crab claws as their appetizer. All we heard during our performance was the banging of wooden hammers as the crab claws were cracked open. There was nothing we could do about that. The front tables were very attentive to our music, so we sang for them. They liked us. No one else could hear us.

We wanted to create an event with our gigs, rather than just put on a concert. Pam and I used the flow chart from "Planning Your Standing Ovation." With suggestions for the music selections, Pam worked to weave the emcees and the staging together to make a smooth and enjoyable experience for the audience. The emcees were positioned where they were needed. Often, she had ideas and suggestions for a change. It was nice working with someone who understood drama and wasn't afraid to try something new and different. We developed the style of staging while singing.

Our newest song was "Zoot Suit Riot," arranged for us by Brian Beck. Cindy Hansen, who was well known in the barbershop world, was hired as a performance coach. She opened our eyes to the possibilities available to us because we had no risers to keep us contained. She also choreographed "Zoot Suit Riot" in such a way that each individual member was a star on the stage and was encouraged to perform any way they wanted as long as it followed her guidelines for the staging.

This took a lot of time, practice, and some attitude changes for all of us to buy into this concept. If you didn't move while singing, you were noticed by the audience. Everyone *had* to do some movement. It was the only song we ever sang with that much freedom of movement, and it was a welcome challenge to place it into our performance lineups. We soon discovered that not too many of our retirees liked that song. It was not familiar to them, and our performance had way too much to look at. Younger audiences loved it.

Our new ballad "Can You Feel the Love Tonight?" was arranged with two soloists singing to each other. Instead of having both soloists leave the chorus to come to center stage, we put them on two of our sixteen-inch-high boxes and positioned them in the middle of the chorus just to the left of center stage. Then, by moving the rest of the chorus a step away from them, on the floor or smaller boxes, we were able to spotlight them while they sang. I stepped to the far right so that the audience didn't have to look through me to see them. It worked.

For soft ballads we sometimes turned a box on its side to make a seat for two people. Some sat on the floor. At one performance, a female singer sat on the lap of a guy while they sang. It really looked cute. Most of these ideas came from the Popsters themselves. If it didn't look right, we would fix it before it went onto the stage.

Solos from the middle.

We had guidelines for these moves. We were to look at the audience ninety percent of the time, and the rest of the time at each other. Except for love ballads that are really emotional. Then it was necessary to look at the director (me) one hundred percent of the time, because sometimes the song was so beautiful that I got emotional and slightly changed the timing. Oops! Watch the director.

From my Connecticut friend Katie came a YouTube recording of a chorus of young people from Germany. They had divided themselves on the risers, boys on the left and girls on the right. The girls told the boys to "Hit the Road, Jack." During one verse, the boys actually walked off the stage in protest. "You guys ought to do this," Katie said.

The director's name and contact information was right there on the screen. All it took was to send him a letter. "May I use your arrangement of "Hit the Road, Jack" for my thirty-five-voice mixed a cappella group called A Cappella Pops?"

And the answer came back from Germany. "Of course." And he sent the music, too. We worked on the song. It was so different from anything we had done previously. Nothing was very musical in the presentation. Rules were broken. The second line's, "Don't you" became "don'tchew." Those of the chorus who had been enjoying our musicality were now asked to forget how to sing proper English. They asked me if I really wanted them to sing *chew* instead of *you* and I swallowed hard but I had to say yes. Although, I was afraid (just a little) that I'd have to re-teach them the proper way later.

We tried several different ways to stage this song, but everything seemed to take away from the fun. We finally decided to do as the German chorus had done and separate the men and the women. We moved to the music by stepping side to side to the rhythm. This worked. In the middle of the song the women had a rap telling the men not to come back. This is when the men became angry at the women and stormed off the stage begging the women not to be mean and saying they'll have to pack up and leave. And they left the stage. The women said good riddance. The women continued to softly rap for a few minutes till the men returned to the stage singing their rejoinder, with the women getting in one last dig. They never did make up, and they ended the song with their backs to each other. When the audience began to laugh and applaud, the women turned to the men with a big hug.

Rehearsals were fun as we put this song together, and we laughed all the time. We had to throw out some of the motions that were suggested. We weren't *that* mad at each other. The women crossed their arms in front of the men and scowled at them. They all chose something different to do at every rehearsal.

It was fun to watch. I loved the fun nature of the Pops. I didn't direct this song. I would have been in their way.

At a rehearsal before one of our performances, the emcees for this song created the final touch. They asked that before they spoke, as the chorus chose sides, the men look off into the distance pretending they were together drinking beer and watching a ball game on TV. The men made the appropriate ball game comments. The women paid no attention to them. Then the emcees spoke. Walking up to one of the men, she said, "Honey, will you light the barbecue for me?"

He, watching the game, replied, "Later, sweetie. Me and the guys are watching the game."

"But I need the grill warm before dinner."

"Heat up some TV dinners!"

Hit the Road

"Light up the grill, or it will be the last warm thing you'll get tonight."

After a pause, the man continued, "How is that different from any other night?" He turned back to watch the ball game.

And as she turned to go back to the chorus who were now rapping the first line of the song, you could hear her mumble, "Mother told me not to marry him."

And the song began. At rehearsal the chorus couldn't stop laughing. We added it to the performance.

♮

We kept striving to make our music tell a story. We were rehearsing the song "Stand by Me." On TV, I heard a group who sang it as a soft, warm love song, and I loved it. Their arrangement started out with a rhythm dum-dum-dum sung by the basses. It sounded like they were whispering in their lover's ear by singing a soft d with lots of warm air. To mimic this, our basses had to sing that sound. First, we had to design the "soft d." Yep, we did it. We kept the air flowing while singing a d and made sure we put sound on the m (and thought about singing into our lover's ear). This was not easy, but our basses did it, and the sound was there for our soloist, Joan. It was a different, unusual interpretation. And it was beautiful.

We decided we needed a patriotic number to add to our repertoire and sometimes use as our finale. I went again to the music publisher J. W. Pepper and found a beautiful Kirby Shaw arrangement of "America, the Beautiful." It sounded like it was made just for us. At home, on my own piano, I played through the music again and again, trying to get a feel for the arranger's intended interpretation and how to prepare it for A Cappella Pops. I kept seeing tired, hungry refugee families on a ship coming into Ellis Island after a night on the sea. The morning mist was on the water, the sea gulls were squawking, and even the air smelled different. The passengers realized they were landing in America and ran to the railing of the ship to see their new land. We wanted to tell this story.

As the chorus learned the music, we created the staging. We wrote an announcement of the arrival of the ship at Ellis Island. A friend of the chorus who had a foreign accent made the welcoming recording. Ross created the sound of seagulls and faraway ship whistles as our backup sound. It was our finale and we played it after our emcee said goodbye to our audience.

"Ladies and gentlemen. The ship will be docking at Ellis Island in fifteen minutes. Please prepare for disembarking by collecting all your personal belongings. You will be leaving the ship on the port side. Please have all your paperwork ready for review at Immigration once you've left the ship. Please form a queue on the left side of the terminal. On behalf of the captain and the crew, we wish you Godspeed in your new home in America."

If possible, when performing, we would ask to have the stage lights lowered, because it was night and the travelers were tired. They would restore the lights as we sang.

The Pops members created the picture of tired refugees. During the recorded announcement, everyone had their heads lowered to appear to the audience that they were sleeping or just weary. Some of the women would rest their heads on a man's shoulders. A man would put his arm around his "wife." One woman held a pretend little baby. Several singers sat down on one of our stage boxes. Everyone was different, and it looked better every time we rehearsed it. Quietly, but with determination, we began to sing the four-measure introduction, very slowly and very softly.

"America, America, God shed His grace on thee."

We thought of everything we had left behind. All we had going forward was faith that what we were doing was right.

"Oh, beautiful for spacious skies, for amber waves of grain."

It was early morning, and all was quiet when the ship approached Ellis Island. Out of this early morning haze, some of us saw land. We raised our heads and touched our neighbors to wake them.

"For purple mountain majesties, above the fruited plain."

We smiled to each other and pointed to the land. As the ship got closer and the sky became brighter, we raised our faces to see the Statue of Liberty. Our voices were excited. We were all smiles.

"America! America!! America!!!"

With the first *America*, one of the front-row men grabbed the hand of his "wife" and ran four or five steps forward to the edge of the stage to better see the statue. The second *America* brought another group to the edge of the ship to see the statue, and the third *America* brought one very tall man from the middle of the chorus down to the front row. We sang with great joy as we arrived in the United States of America.

"America, America, God shed His grace on thee. And crown thy good with brotherhood from sea to shining sea."

By this time the whole chorus had seen the statue, and many stood by the ship's railing, stage front facing the audience, smiling and laughing and singing with all their power. America! America! America! America! Three times increasing the volume, and then a small hold, and the fourth was as a reprise. Accepting the applause was a thrilling experience. The audience was usually on their feet. What remains in our memories is the picture of the older couples still sitting in their chairs, holding hands, with tears streaming down their faces.

29

Montreal

IT WAS 2002 AND we had just been invited to perform at the Barbershop Harmony Society's convention in Montreal, Canada, July 2003. Every year BHS sponsored a World Harmony Jamboree and invited a variety of performers from all over the world to sing in their Friday afternoon show. This jamboree had been part of the BHS convention for almost fifteen years. Joan Darrah was the director, with the assistance of Don Farrell, and both were members of A Cappella Pops. They nominated A Cappella Pops to be included in the concert, even though we were not a barbershop chorus. The World Harmony Council approved.

This meant a weekend trip for the Pops, our first long-distance trip together. We were to sing three songs for a convention audience of 3,500 people. We were also included in an evening singing for the Mixed Harmony Showcase, held the evening before the concert. We had a year to get ready.

It was several days later, on the radio, that Andrea Bocelli and Sarah Brightman caught my heart with their just released duet of "Time to Say Goodbye." My mind raced. How I would love for Pops to sing that duet! And why not on stage in Montreal? I thought of inviting Debbie Connelly and husband, Joe, to be our soloists. They were a well-known barbershop couple living in Florida. Debbie is a music teacher and can sing opera as well as barbershop. Both were winners of their international quartet contests. Joe has one of the best barbershop lead voices, but he wasn't Andrea Bocelli. Would they be coming to Montreal? Could they do it?

At the BHS convention in 2002, the year before our performance, I looked for Debbie and found her in the auditorium. There was an empty seat next to her and I sat down. I wondered if she would like the idea of singing with us.

"Will you be in Montreal?"

"Yes."

"My chorus, A Cappella Pops, has been invited to sing in the World Harmony Jamboree next year. We want to sing 'Time to Say Goodbye.' Would you and Joe be our soloists? It is opera...Can Joe do it?"

"Joe can do anything!"

The next steps were to get permission to have the song arranged, find an arranger, teach the chorus the music, and send the performance to Debbie and Joe for them to put their solo voices into the Pops sound. Whew! The recorded song was on the new CD of *Time to Say Goodbye*, but we also needed the sheet music, which was not yet in stores. On the CD was the name of the owner of the copyright. I called the company. Did they have the sheet music with the words and chording so that I could give it to an arranger? Somehow, I was put in touch with the right person and, after explaining what I wanted, she said, "The sheet music hasn't been printed yet, but there are a few copies hanging around the office. Could we send you one within the next few days?"

"Yes, thank you."

In the mail came one of the first printed copies of "Time to Say Goodbye." Next we needed an arranger, and the one who could arrange anything was, once again, Brian Beck. I really don't think he needed the CD and the printed music that I sent him.

Within three weeks, he sent the most beautiful arrangement of a most beautiful song.

Introducing the song to our chorus was the next step. From the very beginning it was clear that the two solo voices for the Montreal convention were going to be Deb and Joe Connelly. We had to learn and perform the song this next year in order to be ready for Montreal. The soprano solo voice from our chorus was no problem. Deb Brooks was the perfect soprano with a beautiful operatic voice. The male soloist was not so obvious.

My husband was also a barbershop singer but not a member of Pops. His vocal range was first tenor, and he had an operatic sound. He was taking voice lessons at the time, so I knew he could be taught the Italian, but he was not an experienced soloist. This was a tricky decision for me, deciding whether to put my husband in the chorus as a soloist, but it was also going to be only temporary. As a rehearsal and performance understudy, he was available to work with us at any time; and so he learned, polished, and performed with us to be ready for the Montreal stage. (He went back to barbershop after this performance.)

On the original recording, the double bass has a beautiful sound that creates the rhythm. Hmmmm...How to get that into our performance? We have a friend in Baltimore who has one of the lowest bass voices we've ever heard. He could make that sound, but asking him to put together the sound of the double bass, join us in Montreal, and stand on the side of the stage with a microphone during our performance was the next challenge. Luckily for us, Mike Kelly said yes to all of that. Several months before the performance we sent him our rendition of "Time to Say Goodbye," and he put in the *bum, bum* sound of the double bass. Beautiful. The chorus sang with a full rich tone, filling their bodies with as much resonance as they could.

We sent the finished product to Florida along with the copy of the Italian words. The Connellys acknowledged that they had received the package and said, "See you in Montreal."

Soon, it was convention time. We would travel by bus, vans, cars, and airplanes, staying in motels and country inns. Some of us drove in caravans, using our personal walkie-talkies to travel across the Canadian border. Montreal, here we come!

Along with the Jamboree on Friday afternoon, there was a concert on Thursday night, after the evening quarter-finals quartet contest, for mixed-voice groups (men and women singing together). It was called the Mixed Harmony Showcase. We were invited, so we arrived at the ballroom at 11:00 p.m. to wait for our moment on stage. We waited. And waited. We were scheduled to perform last, and that became 1:00 a.m. Many of the audience had stayed to listen to us. We were something new and different. People had heard about us and were curious as to how we sounded. We sang a shortened version of our planned performance. It was late and we had to sing the next day. Fortunately, that was an afternoon concert with plenty of time to rest before our pre-performance rehearsal.

The next day, we were assigned a special room at our hotel and were able to rehearse on one of the sets of risers used for the chorus contest. When Brian Beck stopped in to see us, we sang his arrangement of "Zoot Suit Riot," our first song. We were getting ready to sing on a concert stage with an audience of 3,500 people. There was more to do than just sing the music. The majority of members had never sung on a stage that big or in a convention center with that many seats. Lights would be shining down on us from all angles. Tom and I prepared the chorus. Between the two of us, we tried to talk about everything they might encounter.

We practiced walking on to the stage—long strides, head level, arms relaxed, smile on the face. We wanted to take command of the stage. We wanted to look confident, so we practiced it. "When you are on the stage, before you are announced, look out. Find the exit signs, find the lights, find the levels of seats. Look at the audience, be familiar with the concert hall, make friends with the audience and the venue."

We were ready. We stopped for lunch and then to get dressed for the show. Next would be our first (and only) rehearsal with Debbie and Joe Connelly. They met us in the waiting room just before we were to go on stage. They radiated professionalism and they looked stunning. We could feel the confidence and excitement that they brought to the moment. Standing with their backs to us, as they would on stage, we began to sing "Time to Say Goodbye," and it was breathtaking. At the end of the song no one spoke. Joe and Debbie turned around to face us. They had this huge wide-eyed happy look on their faces. That was the best unspoken compliment we'd ever had.

And then we were on! The stage was ours! 3,500 people were waiting for us. It felt good.

Song # 1—"Zoot Suit Riot"   It was a wild arrangement (thank you, Brian Beck) with us doing some really crazy staging (thank you, Cindy Hansen). We sang "Zoot Suit Riot" as though we were accompanied by a jazz piano, drums, and a rhythm guitar. The audience gave us great applause, but we knew we still hadn't connected with them. I think they were expecting something a bit more conservative. They weren't sure how to react—it was our first song, and it was really different.

We only had three songs to win over this audience, and we wanted them to see and hear the best of us. We chose a beautiful ballad for our second song.

Song #2—Billy Joel's "Lullaby"   Pam, our chorus emcee, told the story of Billy Joel and this song he wrote to his daughter. The chorus moved to new places on our platform boxes, touching

Montreal Zoot Suit Riot

shoulders, sitting on the edge of the box. It was a picture that made you think of tucking your little girl in bed for the night. We sang with tenderness and love, as though we really were Billie Joel talking to his daughter.

At a pause in the music, when I could hear the sound of our preceding chord bouncing around the convention hall, I held still, with my arms raised, until the reverberation began to fade. Then we continued our song. When we ended "Lullaby," there was a moment of complete silence from the audience and then an audible sigh. And then thunderous applause. Some of our chorus members had tears running down their cheeks.

And then for our final song... We positioned ourselves to look and sound like an opera house. If we could have changed into long beautiful gowns and tuxedos, we would have. But we couldn't, so we had to *look* like that's what we were wearing.

Song #3—"Time to Say Goodbye"   Pam stepped forward and introduced our soloists. Debbie and Joe entered the stage from the side curtain, Mike took his place with his handheld mic and the audience grew quiet as we started our final song. We sang as though we were a full orchestra with our soloists resounding, just like in an opera house.

The last chord bounced around the walls. The audience was momentarily still. And then they were on their feet, clapping, cheering, and shouting. We took our bows, the chorus, Debbie, Joe, and Mike. We were numb with excitement. The audience had given us a standing ovation. They seemed to love our performance.

We had given them the sound of A Cappella Pops. We didn't know how they would accept a non-barbershop group. It was an indescribable moment. Over the applause we could hear the show emcee say, "Try to pick the bones out of that one!" That's a phrase I had never heard before. It meant try to find something wrong with what you have just heard. I dare you.

"Time To Say Goodbye" with Debbie and Joe Connolly.

Whee!

Back to reality. Our stomachs were empty. About fifteen of us
decided to go out together for dinner. We walked into an Italian
restaurant, and it was packed. Pat (his real name is Pasquale),
our six foot two bass with black curly hair, went to the maître
d' and said, "I'm here with some of my friends, and I wonder if
you could get us a table for fifteen." In five minutes, they had put
together a table for us. From that moment on, Pasquale's nickname was "the don."

One of our fondest memories of our trip to Montreal happened
on the ride home. We had a caravan of cars, two of which had
walkie-talkies with them. And yes, they sang every song they
could think of, taking turns starting any song and then making
up the harmonies between the two cars as they drove along. The
border guards must have wondered about us.

This was our first big gig outside of our hometown area. The
professionalism, confidence, and excitement of our trip were
apparent as we moved through the three days. The talent and the
stage presence of the competing quartets and choruses were very
apparent. Those of us with barbershop experience were renewed
once again. We loved bringing something different and new to our
world. And it was obvious that we were excellent singers. It was
an outstanding experience. One comment from a Pops member to
me was, "You were just glowing. I've never sung with anyone like
this before. This is so cool. It was such a different experience for
me. A total departure. This is where we belong."

Don Gooding was one of the guests attending the convention.
He and his business partner Deke had earlier helped me figure
out what sort of music Pops should perform. After seeing us perform on the Thursday night show, he made this comment in his
newsletter: "We had a glimpse of the future when we saw A Cap-

pella Pops perform. A Cappella Pops is leading the way into new territory. The biggest thing you notice about them, as they sing their hearts out, is they are all having a huge amount of fun."

Little did we know that Don and Deke were thinking of a whole new idea for A-Cappella.com. They knew that when kids leave school, sometimes there is no place for them to get together and sing their kind of music. Don's vision was to develop new choruses throughout the United States, using a cappella arrangements and producing CDs. It would be an exciting new business venture for him. It was a new, unique, and workable idea. Tom and I talked at length with Deke about the kids who had no place to sing when they left school. Having choruses like A Cappella Pops for the young folks to join would be a solution. It would be like community choruses singing contemporary jazz. The fall edition of Don's newsletter, *Mainely A Cappella*, included a write-up of who, how, and what this new student-oriented chorus would be like. And Pops was the example he used to describe it. Many emails flew around the country with ideas for directors to start this kind of chorus. Then back came the emails as to how to organize them, what kind of members to recruit, what kind of music, how to teach the music, how to choose a director—on and on—all before any chorus was started. These directors never would have believed that we started A Cappella Pops with just three rules:

1 Learn your music.
2 Come to rehearsals.
3 Pay your dues.

Unfortunately, the mixed-chorus idea never got off the ground. Timing is everything, and this idea needed a few more years before it matured. It also needed a leader who "burned." From the newsletter article:

Contemporary A Cappella: Coming Soon to a Community Chorus Near You!

OK, so maybe we're being a little optimistic on the timetable, but we recently had a glimpse of the future when we saw A Cappella Pops (Malvern, Pennsylvania) perform at the SPEBSQSA International Convention in Montreal back in July [2003].

As a background, American adults who participate in group singing generally choose from among a few options: church choirs (about 250,000 nationally), classically oriented community choruses (about 7,000 in the U.S.), and barbershop choruses (about 1,200 in the U.S. and Canada). Perhaps 200 ensembles in the collegiate style (eight to fifteen singers) dot the landscape in organic but unorganized clusters (MAC's three office employees sing in one, Acappellago). Plus, there are at least 1,000 smaller groups (under eight singers) scattered about. However, nothing is available on a large scale that allows the growing population of college and high school students singing contemporary a cappella to continue as adults.

Enter A Cappella Pops, formed in 2000 by Jan Muck (music director) and Tom Halley. Jan had a vision for 15 years previously of directing a mixed chorus that would be "different." Originally conceived as a 200-person mixed barbershop chorus (reflecting her background), in time the idea evolved to embrace jazz, gospel and popular music and to stay away from pure barbershop—in part because the Philadelphia area is already well-served by barbershop chapters. Her vision was to have a performance chorus, singing songs the public wants to hear, and performing them in a way that the public likes to look at.

As it stands now, the chorus has about fifty auditioned members, ages twenty-two to sixty-five, with the mean age in the forties, and 55% women (although the goal is 60% men). There are about thirty-five songs in the repertoire, unlike community choruses that typically learn new music for each concert and then stop performing it. About a third of the arrangements were commissioned, including "Zoot Suit Riot," "Satin Doll," and "Good Vibrations," and the rest are commercially available, such as Billy Joel's "Lullaby," "Blue Moon," and several King's Singers arrangements, among others.

A Cappella Pops tries to avoid risers, instead choosing to stand on boxes they've made for themselves. They add a bit of movement for visual interest but stay away from the complex choreography embraced by top barbershop choruses and show choirs. Their incredibly tight singing is the only hint that half of the singers have a barbershop background—the founders talk about using the barbershop singing "craft" but not singing in the barbershop style. They've also embraced the idea of using coaches for improving the sound and mapping out the modest choreography.

This is common practice in the barbershop world but very rare among community choruses. Jan Muck's philosophy is that a music director can do 70%–80% themselves, but outsiders can help produce the final nuances necessary for a world class "full entertainment package."

The biggest thing you notice about the singers, as they sing their hearts out, is they are all having a huge amount of fun. It's very much a reflection of Jan Muck's philosophy to "sing and have fun." Over three years the group has developed a tremendous camaraderie as they've worked very hard to improve their sound and their performance. And some of them have formed smaller ensembles (e.g., an all-female group) to perform pieces that give a variety to longer shows....

A Cappella Pops is leading the way into some new territory. If you know someone who should be heading in that direction—it might even be you!—we'd like to encourage you to help this emerging phenomenon. Contemporary a cappella community choruses are an idea whose time has come.

♮

Every good idea doesn't always take off right away. Establishing mixed-voice a cappella choruses throughout the United States was not easy. When Dan joined A Cappella Pops, his talents were growing with our music. He was assisting me as our director. He sang in a mixed-voice quartet as well as several barbershop quartets. He attended the BHS's Directors College and several of Deke Sharon's Director Seminars. He became the director of the Chorus of the Brandywine in 2008 while still singing with the Pops.

Dan and Eileen moved to Seattle in 2014 where he joined the Northwest Sound barbershop chapter in Bellevue. And in 2019, because of Dan's A Cappella Pops experience, he was instrumental in the creation of a mixed-voice barbershop chorus within the Bellevue Chapter. After nineteen years, the time had finally come for the mixed-voice show chorus.

30

Happy Together

WE HAD LEARNED HOW to sing as an ensemble—how to move and breathe and think together. We had developed a personality and a sound that was unique to Pops. It was time for us to make a CD. Our audiences were asking for it. And so we began our journey. We had several members who had recording experience, and Tom put together a team to guide us through to the finished product.

The first step was selecting our music and deciding on the number of songs to record. Twelve was the magic number, and we chose four groups of three songs to take to the recording studio for each session. This was the director's job, my job. Who better to decide which songs would need the most work to make them ready to record? We made the list, knowing that it might have to be changed.

Selecting the right studio was a huge key to a recording success. A heavy-handed studio staff can create tension, which can flare tempers. A non-participative staff can leave you hanging and destroy the kind of artistic energy that is needed. We considered several studios and selected Milkboy Studio in Ardmore, Pennsylvania. (They later became MilkBoy the Studio, in Philadelphia.) The staff and company owners had the perfect touch for our group, and they took a personal interest in our project. We decided to record on the same night as our rehearsals so that all our members could attend the sessions.

Recording on the weekends would have been nice, but just not practical.

Taking three songs at a time, we dissected the songs, cleaned up the details, and made sure each singer knew every word, note, tuning, and nuance of the music. As much as we thought we knew the music, we found that many of the Popsters had learned incorrect notes, misinterpreted tempos, and even wrong words. Since Pops normally rehearses only two hours per week, it was an intense work schedule to get ready for each recording session. The studio is not the place to *prepare* to record. Following each studio session, we started on the next three songs on the list.

We needed at least one good take at the first session to assure the chorus members that we really could cut a record. We wanted that early success, so we started with a song the Popsters loved to sing, and that they sang well. "Happy Together" was our choice. (In reality, we love singing anything together.) The recording sounded great, and it gave us all the confidence we needed to prepare for the rest of the sessions ahead of us. It became the title track.

Tom and I had to make decisions quickly. The chorus was patient as we reviewed the recordings with the studio engineer and listened and discussed each song. We took home sample mixes after the sessions, to listen to in the car and to live with them for a while. We then decided what was needed for the next session. Each session in the studio was about three hours. It was a small recording studio, and it quickly became hot and stuffy. By the end of the evening, the members were drained and ready to go home. They were also excited, because during the sessions there were moments of magic, and we all knew it was going to be a good CD. At the end of each recording day, some of us were hungry. Marji had found a nearby restaurant that served food till ten and we ended our day with a drink and a sandwich.

We recorded "Time to Say Goodbye" and wanted Mike Kelly's bass rhythm to be part of this song. We digitally sent the final cut to Chesapeake Star Records in Maryland; Mike recorded his work there and then sent it back for the final mixing.

We had to re-record one of the songs of the "19th Century Popular Songs Medley" because the melody line was not audible above all the other parts. I worried that we might have a different sound than the other seven songs, and we would have to record all of the medley one more time. Didn't happen! There was no difference in the sound of the new recorded song. Whew!

We decided the order of songs to be put on the CD, the length of the pauses between the songs, and the volume levels. We continued on to the job of the cover design and royalties, a thankless task which is almost a full-time job. The end result was not only

A Cappella Pops
...Nothin' but Cheer!

a product in a jewel case, but a reminder of a journey, a focused effort on the part of A Cappella Pops and our supporting team that ended in a recording that will forever be in our CD collection. It was a snapshot of where we were in 2005.

Milkboy Studio was with us for many years. They were also the recording studio that Pops used for Byron Summers's original Christmas song, "Merry Christmas Wishes." (I made copies of the CD and sent them as Christmas cards to several of my friends.) A few short years later we created our own Christmas CD, *Nothin' but Cheer*. For this taping we used the new barn building at the St. Peter's Church in the Great Valley. We had performed for the church several times and knew that the sound would be acoustically correct for our songs. Milkboy brought their equipment to the church and recorded our CD for us. We had more room there, but we recorded in July, during a heat wave. Fortunately, the church's air conditioner was in good working order to keep us cool, but it made noise as it cycled. We had to turn it off, let it cool down till the clicking stopped, and then, after we finished the taping, turn it back on to cool again before we began the next song. But we got it done. Word must have gotten out, for the church has continued to offer their barn to other groups who want to record their music.

We had our CDs for sale at each performance, and we continued to order more copies. They made excellent memories, Christmas presents, hostess gifts, and thank you cards.

31

Touching the Big Time

BECAUSE THE POPS WAS so different and new (and so good), we attracted many musical professionals who were curious as to how we sounded, how we looked, and how we performed. Each of these people was exciting to us. Each gave us another direction to investigate, another opportunity to ask ourselves, "Can we do this?" Each gave us more reason to laugh and to love. And to plan.

A friend of one of our members was a talent agent who invited us to present a bid to perform for the opening of the inaugural season of The Village Theater at Cherry Hill. In Michigan. This new Theater of the Performing Arts planned to offer "an extensive variety of art forms to the community: dance, visual arts, drama, comedy, vocal and instrumental music, and much more." We were part of the "much more." For us, this meant a plane ride to Detroit, overnight accommodations, food, and an hour-and-a-half performance. They accepted our bid, and with the help of the agent we made the travel arrangements. Because the trip was funded by the arts center, every one of our members was on stage. Tom and I were relieved we didn't have to pick who could go and who would stay behind.

We planned the lineup of songs and rehearsed the stage movement and speaking parts. This is when we found the talent hidden within one of the Popsters—a tiny five-foot-one alto who had had a ton of stage experience singing all over the country with a successful barbershop quartet. Renee helped make our staging look professional. She moved people around on the boxes, made a soloist (Tom) walk across the stage while carrying a mic, and made him sing at the same time. She reminded members to "put on a happy face." We worked hard to prepare our performance. We were ready when it was time to travel. We packed our suitcases and then counted the number of boxes that we would need for the stage. We put these boxes into cardboard boxes, taped them shut, and divided them among the Popsters who had luggage allowances.

We arrived at the Village Theater on Saturday for our scheduled sound and lighting check. This theater was brand new,

A Capella Pops
November 20, 2004
8:00 p.m.

Cappella Pops is a high quality auditioned group of singers who are committed to erforming exciting and unique a cappella arrangements of progressive music - mixing the ounds and styles of jazz, folk, Broadway and Gospel. We perform often, in our own roduced shows, and as paid performers or guests on other shows and festivals. This is a horus like none other in the Philadelphia area.

The Music

he music is contemporary and exciting. The arrangements blend men's and women's oices to produce a unique and wonderful sound that is a joy to be a part of and listen to. lany of our songs are our own commissioned arrangements by some of the top vocal rrangers in the country.

Unique Characteristics

- Multileveled staging of individual singers / groups of singers, not riser steps
- Minimal choreography - emphasis on excellent musical performance
- Multi-part, modern and custom musical arrangements
- Possible combined performances with instruments and orchestras
- Solo and special ensemble opportunities

Affiliation

We are an independent singing organization and currently have no plans to join any musical organization.

Musical Director

The director of music is Jan Muck, internationally known as cappella chorus director and coach.

The Village Theater.

smelled of fresh lumber and paint, and was absolutely beautiful. We were astounded. We were among the first musicians to be invited there to perform, and we were humbled by the honor. The stage extended right up to the audience, which allowed us to do what we do best—sing directly to the people.

I remember walking down the long walkway from the front of the auditorium to our dressing rooms and hearing the sighs and aahs coming from the Pops as we found the dressing rooms full of bright lights and mirrors. For thirty-five men and women who love to sing and laugh, we were strangely quiet.

After a few short hours of rehearsal, we had dinner, dressed, and went back to the theater for the show. It was wonderful working with a professional stage crew who took good care of us. Everything ran smoothly. The audience responded warmly to our music. As we performed, we looked directly at the audience and they laughed and clapped with us. It was a good night. And then we went home again the very next day. This performance was a bonding time for us. We all realized what we had within our group. We were now on the same level as professional entertainers who have an agent. Our behavior had to be professional. I think we all walked a little taller.

A few weeks later the same agent offered us a gig in Hawaii, but we could only take a small number of singers. Tom and I didn't even consider it. We had vowed never again to take a gig if we had to choose who would go. But this was a compliment for our performance in Canton, Michigan, and we would treasure the invitation.

The White House, December 11, 2005

One evening after his work, Ken sat at a local bar having a short drink before he went home. Sitting next to him he recognized his congressional representative, and so he struck up a conversation. Ken mentioned that he sang with an a cappella group called A Cappella Pops and asked the representative how we could sing for the president. The representative told Ken about the Christmas concerts held every year at the White House and then handed Ken the name of the person to contact. Ken followed up with a phone call. He was asked for a CD of our Christmas music. Then we waited. And waited.

And then we received our invitation, and the wheels began to spin. The time given us to perform for the White House was a Friday afternoon. We had to know which Popsters would be able to make it. Some couldn't leave work, but with the members who could go, we had the right blend of voices—whew! We would have had to cancel if we didn't have the sound. Then we had to send the social security number of each member of the group to the White House security team.

It was about a three-hour trip, and we rented a van to take us there. As we arrived at the White House, the van was motioned to stop over special boards in the driveway to the parking area. We left the van and headed for a back door where security checked our social security numbers against their list before we were allowed to enter. Meanwhile, dogs came out and sniffed around the entire van before security allowed it into the parking area. When the dogs were through sniffing and the guards were satisfied, the van entered the special parking place for visitors.

We had our own attendant to take us around and show us the entire downstairs of the White House and then into a little passageway as they led us to where we were going to stand and sing. We noticed many other musicians performing in doorways and corners as we walked around the White House. It wasn't all singers; there were violinists, a pianist with a flutist, and just about any other combinations you could put together. Most of the

At the White House.

performers were from the Washington, D.C., area. I believe we had traveled the furthest. There was no talk among the performers—just a polite nod as we passed through. Everyone had their place and time, and the White House guides monitored all this. We sang on the steps that you often see on TV when the president and the first lady descend into the large waiting room where the guests are standing, waiting for their arrival.

It was Christmastime and the White House was beautifully decorated. The swarms of people entering the front door, where we were singing, would glance over at us and immediately turn to look at the other rooms and the decorations. It was definitely not a "concert of Christmas music," but rather a background of Christmas music for everyone to enjoy as they toured the White House. When our time was over, we were taken to a large room with refreshments for all the musicians. There were also guests there from other countries and, of course, we sang for them, too. Many had never heard a cappella music before and asked us questions that we gladly answered. We spread out and talked with as many visitors as we could. It was thrilling to be there, talking and singing with people from other countries.

It was still early in the day, too early to start back home, so we left the White House and found a restaurant that could accommodate us. Now picture this—twenty men and women, all dressed in their Christmas finery, noisily walking into a bar in the middle of the afternoon and taking it over. It was before the cocktail hour so there were still plenty of seats at the bar and at the tables. We weren't intentionally noisy, we were just happy, like we had just taken off our "be quiet" manners. We teased the bartenders and sang and just had a wonderful time with the servers. We didn't stay long, just enough for a sandwich and a beer, and then we were back in the van to go home to Pennsylvania. Several weeks later we received from the White House a large Christmas card with a picture of the White House and a thank you for participating in the Holiday Celebration. I had it framed.

World Café Live, May 6, 2006

The Pops members seemed to be always on the lookout for unique places for us to sing. One of our newer members, Tom Emmi, was developing a radio program called Studio Jams. His studio was on the campus of the University of Pennsylvania at 30th and Walnut Streets. The art deco building was a former factory that housed UPenn's radio station, WXPN. Tom's idea was to bring jazz musicians into his studio to jam with other people. They would choose songs and then spend a couple hours just playing with the music, sometimes each taking a turn for a solo spot. Tom recorded it for his program on WXPN. Oftentimes when jazz musicians passed through Philadelphia on their way to a gig in Atlantic City, Tom invited them to join the group at his studio. This was great to listen to and was educational to all who wanted to learn how to jam. At the time, the building was being renovated to become the World Café Live—a multi-level music hall for casual dining and a listening space with music and food.

When the World Café Live was almost completed and began to look for performing groups, Tom Emmi asked if we were interested. Oh, yeah! He introduced Tom Halley and me to the manager and we were on our way. It was our job to plan the program and tell everyone we knew to come eat and listen to the Pops at the World Café Live.

Their stage was not deep, but it was wide. It wasn't meant to hold an orchestra with a two-hundred-voice choir standing behind them on risers. We didn't need our boxes. The Café suggested using their long and wide levels (normally used to elevate drummers, for example). This opened a whole new concept of staging for us—a challenge we happily accepted. We actually thought of putting a tall ladder at the end of one of the levels, with a platform for a singing member. We only thought about it, we didn't make it happen. The most fascinating thing about this gig was the professionalism of the stagehands as they checked the sound and the lighting. We felt like we'd made it to the big time.

This was the only performance where I played a part. During our newest song, a medley of jitterbug music, Rick, one of our talented basses, came down to the front of the stage where I stood, and invited me to jitterbug with him—which I did. Most of our audience was our friends and neighbors. They enjoyed the music and the meal.

Tom Emmi went on to achieve success with the Studio Jam. He became so busy that it was necessary for him to leave the Pops. We were sorry to see him go, but he kept in touch, and he invited Renee and me to be a part of the audience during his recording sessions.

JoJo's Dream Cart

In August, 2007, my husband was at an airport waiting for his flight home to Philly. Sitting next to him, waiting to fly to her home in Maine, was an attractive young woman. He began a conversation (of course). Her name was JoJo LaRiccia, and she was the producer of a Maine TV program for kids aged five to ten. It was "a new, interactive, motivational TV show for kids to

JoJo.

believe in themselves and in their dreams." It was called *JoJo's Dream Cart.*

JoJo was putting together a segment on healthy eating. The theme song, which she had written, was about how to love fruits and vegetables. Darrel told her about my chorus, A Cappella Pops. When she heard about Pops, she thought that it would be a great idea for us to sing her healthy song on her TV show. She asked for contact information. She called and told us about her song. Her plan was to have it arranged in four-part a cappella harmony, send it to us to learn, and when we were ready, she would come to our rehearsal to film us as we sang her song. After talking with her, it was easy to agree to do this.

So there we were—forty grown men and women learning to sing a little ditty about fruits and vegetables. JoJo traveled from Maine for one rehearsal evening to film us. Special thanks that evening go to John Yaschur from our neighboring state of Delaware for lending a hand. It was fun watching JoJo and John set the mics and the lighting. When JoJo was satisfied with the sound, we began the recording. She filmed our faces as we sang her song. But we couldn't look at JoJo—we had to look at our TV audience. And we sang about fruits and vegetables as though they were the best thing in the world, as, of course, JoJo said they were. Not having Maine's TV programs, we never knew if they used our segment. But it was something really different for us. And, as always, a heck of a lot of fun. No, we didn't include the song in our programs. Maybe we should have. It would have been a great story to share with our audiences.

Kimmel Center

"I think I can get you a half-hour gig at the Kimmel Center. Would that be OK?" Oh, yeah! A new Kimmel Center for the Performing Arts was being built in downtown Philadelphia. A friend, Jay, worked there with the sound and music department. In the magnificent lobby, right outside the entrance to the recital hall and tucked alongside the bar and the staircase to the second floor, was a wonderful space for visiting musical groups to perform. There were tables for the customers who wanted to have a drink and eat a snack while waiting for the doors to open for their event. Some people just meandered around looking at the beauty of the enormous Kimmel Center Lobby. It was here Jay wanted us to sing. We were scheduled for a half hour on a Sunday afternoon and arrived several hours early for Jay to position us on their risers and set up their sound system.

As I stood in front of the chorus, I was fascinated while listening and watching Jay work. There in the corner of the lobby, he asked us to sing different songs as he moved the mics to create our best sound. I could hear what he was doing.

After the performance, we had time to become good friends with Jay. He talked to us about the need for a group to perform all over Philadelphia during the Fourth of July celebrations. We were interested because this was something we would have loved to do. He had the contacts but not a performing group to fill the schedule.

Here was a chance for someone to professionally coach us and to be an agent to schedule our performances. Working with Jay would move us a step ahead of where we were at this time—way beyond our knowledge and experience. We talked to him about taking us on as a client. However, at this time our patriotic repertoire consisted of "America" and "The Star-Spangled Banner." We would need at least six more songs, memorized and staged, to complete a thirty-minute performance. Also, if we were to sing all over Philly for a week, we wanted more than an eight-song repertoire.

Increasing our repertoire would not be a problem if singing was all we did, but all of us had day jobs. We didn't want to learn six new songs that we would sing only for one week a year. (We did learn a "George M. Cohan Medley" and choreographed it; after the holiday it didn't stay in our repertoire.) But we still wanted to know more about having Jay as our manager. We invited him to come to us on a Saturday afternoon for a four-hour coaching session. He wanted to see just what we could do, and we wanted to see what he could do for us.

We asked him to take three of our songs and connect them with sound and staging and turn it into a three-song presentation. He chose one of our fun songs and turned us into a trolley car, complete with windshield wipers and wheels. We moved all over the "stage" (our rehearsal hall) singing and acting—and laughing! It was a Broadway stage show. As a musician, I heard all the musicality of the chorus hit rock bottom. This didn't bother me because, from experience, I knew that once the staging was learned, the good singing would return. But some of my group just didn't want to be windshield wipers. After the session, we sat together for a question-and-answer recap. It went like this:

"What do you envision this group to be like if you worked with us for five years?"

Jay's answer: "I would like to travel all over the United States with you and your style of music. I would want to rehearse at least one full Saturday a month and maybe a few extra times a week during the month."

All of this sounded exciting, and we all agreed that if we didn't have full-time jobs, we would love to make our living singing with Pops all over the world. How close we came to this dream! It just wasn't going to happen. But it would have been wonderful. We had to be satisfied with putting our CD, *Happy Together*, in the Kimmel Center Gift Shop.

Shorty's Death

Shorty was in Jordan during the first few years of Pops, building an entertainment complex. His background was movies
and performances. It was such a gift for the Pops to be friends
with him. I asked him one day if—when the entertainment complex was finished—the Pops could sing in their theater. Shorty
said, "Absolutely, but you would have to fund your own travel
expenses."

So while he was finishing the complex, I let that thought rest,
thinking there must be a way. Then in 2004, just before the complex was completed, Shorty ran off the road in his car. He didn't
survive. It changed the lives of many, many people. The Jordani-
ans finished the complex without him.

I had been anticipating Shorty's return to our world. He
would have enjoyed taking a major part in guiding the Pops into
the entertainment world—into the wow factor. Later, Jean, his
widow, said to me, "You know, you are part of our family." I will
treasure that comment.

A Visiting Professor

In 2007 my barbershop friend from North Carolina, Debra Shapiro, told me she was now a professor at the Robert H. Smith
School of Business at the University of Maryland. To me, she was
just a good singing buddy who said she wanted to visit one of my
A Cappella Pops rehearsals. Our rehearsal was normal for us—
hard work and lots of fun. As always, we sang several songs just
for Debra. We took her with us when we went out later for some
refreshment and a bit more song. She spent the night at our home.
And then she said, "How would like to come down to the University of Maryland and talk to my class about how you started the

Pops? You are doing, at your rehearsal, just what I'm teaching my business students to do to run a successful business."

"You've got to be kidding!" I said. Being loquacious was not in my character. I gave up being a trial showmanship judge in the SAI organization because I couldn't find the words to justify my score (which, by the way, was always accurate). Neither Valley Forge nor the Pops encouraged me to talk on stage. An emcee did a much better job than I ever could.

Debra responded "Not at all. I'll ask you questions, you'll answer them, and then I will ask the class how this relates to what I've been teaching them."

"For instance?"

"Well, how do you find—and accept—singers for Pops?"

"Oh! That's easy. I could answer that."

And so the plan began. Debra designed the class. We had the A Cappella Pops CD and several performance pictures that we could put up on the video screen. She checked with the university for their approval, and then sent it all to me to see if I could do it. By August 2007, we had our lesson plans approved and we were ready for our class. I took the train from Philadelphia to New Carrollton, Maryland, to present two classes to Debra's graduate students at the University of Maryland. The classes were titled, "A Live Case Example of Getting Teams Humming: The Creation of the A Cappella Pops Jazz Chorus."

I was a visiting professor!

The classes worked so well that we repeated them the following year. Watching Debra weave my story around her lesson plan was brilliant. After our second year of teaching, we started feeling that this class should be available for all business students. We wondered if the Robert H. Smith School of Business might be interested in sponsoring the class at other schools around the country. You know, Have Class, Will Travel.

When the school gently turned us down, I said, "Well, let's write a book." We thought about it. We were a team. The right brain (me) would provide the stories and the left brain (Debra) would convert it to a textbook. We tried, but I couldn't make it work. I couldn't write as a teacher. I make music with my hands—not with words—and I couldn't find a way to put any good words down on paper. No book for Debra and me. Not then.

Years later, at a Main Line School writing class, Vivian introduced me to the fun of memoir writing....

32

The Master Class

EVEN THOUGH I WAS no longer a front-line director of a
Sweet Adelines chorus, as an active member of the Sweet
Adelines International Music Faculty, I was still able to attend
education seminars and competitions. One weekend in July in
Greenville, South Carolina, 800 Sweet Adelines members gath-
ered at the Bob Jones University to attend our IES.

That year, the International organization introduced a new
program to any small chorus (under thirty) that wanted help
improving their contest performance scores. If the chorus wished
to participate in the program, they would be paired with an international faculty member who would donate one free coaching session.

It was my job as the newly appointed mentor of a small chorus to establish a relationship with my assignment, the City of
the Hills Chorus in Oneonta, New York, and their director, Flora
Beth. We met for the first time that weekend at IES and set a
date for our coaching session. Oneonta was only a four-hour drive
from my home in Pennsylvania, and so we decided that I come
on Friday and stay for the weekend. This way, I could spend free
time with the chorus members, and they could get to know me. I
stayed with Flora Beth.

Our first coaching session couldn't have been better. This
chorus was fun, active, and full of good singers, just the kind
of people I like to work with. They had scored at the C level for

about eight years and were tired of it. You couldn't ask for better motivation.

When you are first introduced to a new chorus that you are about to coach, it is always best to ask them to sing four or five of their favorite songs for you. If you stand next to the director as she directs her chorus, you are watched. Every expression that comes over your face is picked up by the chorus. You must love them. They will do anything for you if they know you are not going to embarrass them. You need to free them to make mistakes when trying new things.

As I listened to them sing, I heard recurring musical techniques that could be improved upon. These "mistakes" were in all the songs. There's no need to work on singing correct notes even if there are wrong notes in all their songs. You don't need to waste their time and yours teaching the right notes. Instead, we concentrated on two or three singing techniques that I knew they could master. When they felt they understood and were comfortable with these changes, we added them to their favorite songs, the ones they had sung for me at the beginning of the coaching session. No matter what song they sang, they sounded better. (Oddly enough, the bad notes began to disappear, too.) This gave them great joy and a lot of laughs. We all hoped it would mean higher scores in the next year's competition. And it did. Their scores improved, and I was invited back.

Each time I visited them I would challenge them with a new technique, always one that I thought they could master and that would also raise their performance score. They kept building on these sessions. (And no more wrong notes.) They were hard workers, and Flora Beth, the director, was a good taskmaster for following up with what I was teaching. They really didn't think of winning a contest, they just wanted to keep getting better. For five years we were a good combination—chorus and coach—and their contest scores kept going up.

These were the same years when A Cappella Pops was developing into a strong performance ensemble. We were traveling to faraway places and performing at high-level venues. It came time to suggest that the City of the Hills Chorus might like to invite the A Cappella Pops to come to Oneonta to be guests in their September show. This was a big step for both choruses. City of the Hills Chorus had never had out-of-town guest performers in their shows, and the Pops had never taken an eight-hour round trip in one day for an afternoon show. Our plan was to take a morning bus ride, perform on the show Saturday (at about 4:00 p.m.), enjoy a potluck supper with the two choruses around 6:00 p.m., and then be on our way home, arriving back very late at night. We polled the chorus for availability, made sure we had the right singers to create a good balance of sound, and then we accepted the gig. We had almost a year to prepare. We would sing a forty-five-minute performance package on their show.

Flora Beth wrote me about an opportunity for Pops while we would be visiting with them in Oneonta. She mentioned to the chair of the Hartwick College music department (located in Oneonta) that we were coming in September as guests on their show. She gave him the Pops website address. His name was Jirka, and he was in Prague at the time, working with a choir festival. A few weeks later he asked Flora Beth if we might be interested in presenting a workshop at the college to be held from noon to 1:30 p.m., just before our 4:00 p.m. performance. This workshop was for his students and perhaps any of the general public who wanted to attend. To us, this meant leaving our homes at an early hour that would make it an even longer day.

Jirka also asked if we would be interested in performing the following July at the choral festival in Prague. Our website showed our versatility with singing and staging, and he wanted us to present this in Prague. Whoa, so much to think about! Unfortunately, we had to turn down the Prague trip. Grants for travel were not easy to find. But we were excited to put together a master class for Hartwick College. We had the talent in our chorus to do this, both teachers and lecturers. They just needed to create a *music class* and then teach us how to teach it to others. Something new to do. My concern was whether or not we could design and implement this project and still have enough stamina left to put our best performance on their stage—the reason we had been hired.

I wanted to do this master class. It was new, different, and we would be creating an exciting event. I knew this was a decision for our Pops leadership team. Planning this hour-and-a-half class was going to take a lot of non-music time from many of us. The chorus had to be supportive of this. We prepared a presentation for our next scheduled leadership team meeting. When we realized most of the work would be in the planning, and that the chorus only had to follow a script, it was easy to vote to go ahead with the master class.

We immediately had our committee volunteers:

1 An organized person to plan our meetings and establish a timeline, which included several run-throughs for the chorus: Caren

2 A teacher who would coordinate the script writing: Janet K.

3 A theater person to plan the stage movement and enhance our presentation skills: Renee

4 The music director to help choose the type of music to best explain the *why* of this group: me

We confirmed with Flora Beth and Jirka that we would do the master class.

Now we had to write it. We made a phone call to Jirka (he was home from Prague). "What do you want for this class?" A Cappella Pops always asked the person or group who hired us what they would like to see. Our repertoire was varied, and we never wanted to inadvertently disappoint someone when it was so easy to please them.

Jirka answered, "Whatever you want to do for us."

In other words, we were to design it the way we wanted it. We liked that. We knew we were a different kind of chorus, so we decided our first plan was to analyze what we were and why, and then write that down. From there, we had to figure out how to demonstrate it and then how to teach it. Sounded like a good idea. Let's go.

What and who are we? We chose five characteristics.

♪ We know our personality and stayed within it. We don't create something new. Our music encourages the audience to express a variety of emotions as they enjoy listening and watching.

♪ We are each individually one hundred percent responsible for the quality of the performance, vocally and visually.

♪ We change the way we stand on stage to match the message and emotions of the story.

♪ Individuals are encouraged to move freely to express the emotion of the song.

♪ Each individual is free to choose their own costume and staging within the guidelines of the chosen theme.

The challenge was to keep all of this individual input—both on and off stage—while still presenting to our audience a visual unit and accurate vocal blend and harmony. We divided our plan into teaching subjects.

1. Intro

Explain what we plan to present to the class. Open with an explanation of who we are, what we are going to do, and how we plan to end with all of us singing together.

2. Sound

How we vary song styles with vocal styling. The director does not usually direct in the traditional beat patterns; the word phrases and sounds are more important. Demonstrate this.

3. Staging

Show the use of proper movement to enhance the emotion of the song. Demonstrate the correct and incorrect style using both an uptune and a ballad.

4. Examples

Use individuals in the chorus as examples. Explain the use and positioning of soloists and the responsibility of the other members during solos. Show how to move with the music while keeping the focus on the soloists.

5. Transitions

Show how to smoothly move from song to song without disrupting the flow of the performance. Describe various methods—emcee, music segues, putting on costumes, and so forth. For example, show the clip-clop of the high heels of an announcer between two beautiful ballads. Even with the transitions, we are asking for a total visual performance that enhances the sound of the chorus and that constantly focuses the audience.

6. Finale

To wrap up the class and cement what we are teaching, sing "Lullaby" by Billy Joel. "Lullaby" is an example of how to create an emotional performance. Invite the students to join us on the stage to sing this final song together.

It was Labor Day and the college kids had started classes. It was then that Jirka said we should send him the music and an MP3 of "Lullaby" for his music students to learn. Our show was in only two weeks. We had forgotten how quickly young minds learn new things. The room for our master class at the college was called the Music Circle. We set up our boxes in the middle of the floor, and the audience was on seats circled around us on an incline.

At noon the students arrived. As they took their seats, we were close enough to say hello and ask their names. This is what we liked to do. As we started the class, we suggested that they open their minds and *not* do what they normally do. This was a workshop and we wanted them to think outside their traditional box. We sang bits and pieces of thirteen songs to help demonstrate what we were teaching. It also showed the spectrum of music that we were able to sing. It was exciting for us to present this class, and the students enjoyed the newness of our presentation. They were responsive and asked questions.

In no time at all, the hour and a half was almost over. It was time to sing together for the finale. We brought the entire student body onto the stage and had them sit or stand any place they wanted. We mixed them with our team. We put our arms around them, touched them, some of us sat down on our boxes and pulled them to sit next to us. Everyone chose where they wanted to stand or sit and with whom. Some of the kids tried to find someone singing their part, and they would stand with them. Then we sang, together. Oh, my goodness! I don't know who was more impressed, those who were singing or me who was directing. We all noticed that one student in particular thought it was so beautiful she started to cry. Can anything be more wonderful? That's exactly what this workshop was all about.

We had a couple hours to rest before our 4:00 concert. City of the Hills opened their show with an hour of their songs. A fifteen-minute intermission followed, and then Pops performed for their forty-five-minute show. The venue was a large church, and the sound was great. Their friends and family filled the church. Following the performance, we had a potluck supper waiting for us in the parish hall. And both choruses enjoyed eating and chatting with each other. Very quickly it was time to load the bus and be on our way.

Shortly after arriving home we received a note from Flora Beth saying how much they loved having us as their guest performers and how many compliments they received from the audience. And about the Pops in particular. Their members especially enjoyed socializing with us during dinner. The best comment was that in the beginning they weren't sure they could do all the work that was necessary to put on this big a show, and then they got it all done successfully. And they wanted to learn to do some fancy staging like we do.

For a while after we returned, we thought about marketing our master class to the colleges and universities in the Philadelphia area. It sounded like a good idea. We had heard that there were seventy schools in the area that we could contact. We had a Pops member volunteer to look into this idea. It must not have been something the Pops wanted to do because the enthusiasm just disappeared. I think we were so busy that even I forgot about it. Oh, well. Onward!

33

Dr. James Jordan

DR. JAMES JORDAN WAS associate professor of conducting at Westminster Choir College of Rider University and the conductor of the Westminster Chapel Choir. He was invited to be the visiting professor for our Sweet Adelines IES in San Antonio, Texas, in August 2006. His many classes were all concept oriented. I was captivated by his style.

He said, "Intonation is a window to the soul."

This handout[1] is from his lecture. I devoured his ideas.

1 The quality of singing is not rooted in technique.
2 Human nature—to flock and to be individual. Choirs fill this need.
3 Part of rehearsal is dumping responsibility on the chorus and taking none yourself.
4 Find a place in your life when you've been "____" [fill in with an emotion, for example, happy] and go there.
5 Music making is being aware. I envy perfect sound.
6 You have to protect your singer's ego when their voice doesn't work.
7 Every conducting motion comes from an embrace.
8 Start from a calm—music comes from quiet.
9 When you conduct—touch the sound.
10 Put your smile on first and sing under it.

---

1   Used by permission, Dr. James Jordan.

11 Concentrate on vowels and on the breath singing—not pitch.

12 Pitch errors are born simultaneously with the attacks.

Dr. Jordan completely affected my style of directing. Sitting in his classroom, I understood each of his twelve statements, and with each statement I began to evaluate my perceived ability. It gave me the confidence that I was on the right track as a director. But it was number seven that stopped me cold: "Every conducting motion comes from an embrace."

Never in all my directing classes had I heard this before. This is the way I interpreted his statement.

Conduct from an embrace. Hold your hands and arms as though someone whom you haven't seen for a while comes walking toward you. You lift both your arms to embrace them. Your arms are apart and just under shoulder high. The palms of your hands are facing each other—perpendicular to the floor, thumbs facing straight up, reaching forward. And the first thing you say is Hi, with a slight motion of your arms and maybe a little nod. This is the beginning of an embrace. For the chorus, it is the beginning of a sound.

This tilts the ictus[2] from being parallel to the floor to being a vertical straight line. I now had many more commands at my disposal. This was perfect for the type of chorus I was directing (A Cappella Pops) and the type of music we produced. I needed to direct them with the same finesse and emotion that I wanted from them. And that's how they wanted to sing, with feelings and creativity. Directing this way was how to make it happen.

I immediately started experimenting with directing from this embrace. Starting and stopping the chorus was now done by mov-

---

2   The term *ictus* is used in conducting to denote the specific point in a visible pattern of beat points that articulates the pulse of the music to the ensemble.

ing either one or two hands toward the center of my body. Short, fast-moving phrases worked better directed by a quick motion in front of my body toward the center. No more heavy downbeats. This gave me many different ways to create the sound that I wanted to hear. I realized that it was so much easier to communicate with my hands than with my words. I could direct this way throughout the entire song.

♮

Several years before I met Dr. Jordan, Pops was coached by the director of the local barbershop men's chorus (Mainliners). As usual, I watched his hands and listened to what my chorus was producing. I remember when I realized that, although he was keeping the timing of the music, he wasn't directing the rhythm at all. He was directing the sound. I found this beautiful to watch and thrilling to listen to. I began to teach myself to do this— keeping the timing precise but directing the sound. At the time, this was new for me, and the Pops were responding to it very well. Of course they were. Most singers know how to count. They didn't need me to beat the rhythm.

When you conduct—touch the sound. When I saw this in Dr. Jordan's notes, I realized that this is what I had learned several years ago by watching the Mainliners' director when he coached my chorus. I memorized the motions the director was using, and then I taught myself to use them to direct the sound of the Pops. Now I knew why it worked.

I internalized numbers seven and nine. *Every conducting motion comes from an embrace* and *When you conduct—touch the sound.* The new me. I went home determined to incorporate the embrace into my Pops rehearsals. Our music and style were perfect for this kind of directing.

During one rehearsal, the love ballad that we were singing was soft and schmaltzy, but the Pops were singing with a very heavy beat. I wanted a softer approach. I decided to experiment!

Fists

I asked the chorus to repeat the intro for me, and I turned my hands to face each other (in an embrace) and started the song. Yes, smooth and lovely. Then I said to the chorus, "One more time," and returned to the normal downward motion. Bam! Heavy. I felt my face create a Cheshire Cat grin.

Breaking a directing habit takes a long time (I was still trying to remember what Greg Lyne taught me years ago). Now, whenever the Pops didn't respond to my direction, I remembered to try the embrace. Almost always they gave me the sound that I wanted. And it was so much easier. My hands could be soft and loving, or I could make a fist and get a stronger sound. It was so much fun to direct this way, and it allowed me to be so much more creative. I could create something on stage that I had never done at rehearsal—just by using my hands and face—and the Pops returned exactly what I wanted them to sound like. It was a slow process to change a forty-year directing habit, but the rewards were worth it. It felt like I was a pottery artist molding a beautiful masterpiece with my hands.

34

Goodbye, Tom

WHEN I APPROACHED TOM with the concept of a new chorus, the first thing he liked about it was that this chorus was something new and different, something that had never been done before. The exciting thing for the two of us was watching it develop. Tom and I built a relationship that was unlike anything either of us had ever experienced. We talked to each other. We were both passionate about what we were doing. Together we found the best way to handle all situations. We were straightforward and didn't need to worry about offending each other.

He trusted me with the music, and I trusted him with the chorus management. Developing Pops was a huge undertaking and required a ton of effort. Each person in our new chorus had a recommendation for how we should grow this musical group.

Tom

We looked at each suggestion and asked this question, "Is this the flavor of Pops?" Tom once told me that I was not afraid to say no and that I generally wasn't afraid to let people down— gently. That helped develop the core of what we wanted for the Pops.

Tom and I talked about the vision of how Pops should look, and then we kept it in mind at all times. Whenever any negative things would come along, if it didn't have an impact on the big picture, we didn't let it cloud our vision. We knew exactly where we wanted to go. Tom's motto was "Protect the product." How did he protect the product? Never put onstage anything that was crap (his word). If it wasn't ready, it didn't happen. No practicing on paying customers. The song made the cut, or it was held until it was ready. What wouldn't make the cut? Wrong notes, wrong words, singers being out of sync, and so on. Crap also included members who were not ready to perform: they weren't sure of the words or staging, or their faces looked scared or frozen. They would simply have to wait till they looked and acted the same as everyone else on stage. It could take six months of rehearsal to be able to perform a ten-song performance. Tom believed it was best not to encourage new people to perform with the chorus before they were ready.

Here's an example: We had introduced a new song that included a solo part. After just a few rehearsals our soloist stumbled over the words. Quietly, without anyone hearing it, Tom suggested to the soloist that having a solo with the Pops chorus was an honor, and you don't let the chorus down by not knowing your part. He was right. Tom had always enjoyed building a dream, trying his hand at something he hadn't done before. He knew he was good for our start-up and that it might be only for three to five years before things were set up and running smoothly. I knew him well enough to know that about him. He constantly pursued new interests, challenging himself with something he'd never done before, blazing new trails.

Knowing this didn't make it easier when, after five years, he announced he was leaving us.

♮

A Cappella Pops was humming. Our fast train was speeding along. All major decisions had been made—name, costumes, finances, marketing, recruiting, music choices, and contacts for major performances. Our membership was growing. Tom was losing interest. We were becoming more corporate. We had actually had a goal-setting meeting, just like running a business.

Tom was a happy, positive thinker. He was always having fun with us. He was our tenor soloist when we sang "Yesterday," a beautiful Beatles song with an arrangement sung by the King's Singers. We were preparing for an upcoming performance, and it was time to rehearse Tom's solo. The music started with a beautiful four-measure intro. Tom began to sing. "Yis-terrr-deyee." This was the worst hillbilly twang you ever heard. The chorus broke up. Half the chorus continued singing the beautiful arrangement (to keep us on pitch), and the other half sang using Tom's hillbilly accent. Three and a half minutes of this, and then it took much longer to settle down and finish the rehearsal; it was such a funny time.

Tom also had a warm emotional side to him. He loved the solo sung by Renee Walsh, "When I Look in Your Eyes," from the *Doctor Dolittle* movie. Renee told us that she thought of her grandfather each time she sang it. The chorus sang a beautiful orchestration to support her. She stood center stage with a hand-held mic. I stepped away from her and stood closer to the chorus, off to the side, so I could see her and pick up any slight variations in her interpretation as she sang to her grandfather. Each performance was slightly different. I had to follow her timing and the chorus had to follow me while they listened to her. All the Popsters put their voices and their hearts into Renee's song. This happened every time we sang it. You could almost touch the love. This was Tom's favorite song.

And now he wanted to move on. It was time and he knew it. This was traumatic for me. Our relationship was so tight and so unique. He was always there when I needed him—to guide and support me. He was my buffer. I could confide in him. No one could see into the future as Tom did. When he was gone, I felt untethered. No one else completely understood our mission for Pops. The chorus knew that Tom needed to leave, and they could sense that I felt untethered. But we still had wonderful songs to sing and new places to perform. The friendships that we had developed were strong. It was no time at all before we pulled ourselves together. Tom was gone, but we could still sing, perform, love, and have one heck of a lot of fun.

And I healed.

35

Sean, My Grandson

MOST OF US CAN imagine how it must feel to have our child or grandchild join us in our work or hobby. It's hard to hide your pride. Music is no different, especially in my world of choruses and quartets. It was the summer of 2000, the year A Cappella Pops was born, when our grandson Sean moved from Miami to Philadelphia to attend Drexel University. He stayed with us until his freshman dorm was available. With him came an enormous amount of experience performing as a tenor for his high school. During his school years, he was accepted into the Honor Choir of the University of Miami and attended a weekend retreat with Moses Hogan, a pianist, conductor, and arranger of international renown. He traveled to Europe for a three-week concert tour with the National Collegiate Choral Association. I invited Sean to our Pops rehearsals.

He was singing tenor with us, and during the rehearsal of one of our songs, he stopped the chorus cold and said, "That tenor part is wrong. It doesn't make sense. The chord structure is wrong. It should be one note higher."

Whoa!

There was quiet at the rehearsal. I know the chorus wondered, "How is she going to handle this? It's her grandson. What is she going to do?"

I wondered myself what I was going to do. My feeling was to stay cool. He's just a kid. And so I said, "We'll look at it later."

And later that night after rehearsal, we sat at my piano and played the chord. He explained to me, again and again, why he was right. And, finally, I heard what he was saying.

I sent an email to the chorus. "The kid was right."

We changed the note.

He tells the story this way:

I was visiting my grandmother's chorus, singing tenor with a bunch of people I'd never met before. We were doing this song a couple of times, and I was thinking, "This note...It doesn't fit. This is not the right note. It's gotta be one note higher." So I said it. Loud!

I didn't have the political finesse that comes with experience. I'm sure I sounded a little arrogant. At best, I sounded just socially ignorant.

Yep.

While at Drexel University, Sean auditioned to join an a cappella group called Eight to the Bar. Soon he became their music director and arranger. We invited the guys to perform with us on our next A Cappella Jam at the Colonial Theatre. He made friends with the chorus. I heard that he and Mark, one of our basses, were putting together a medley of songs for Pops to sing: "Jitterbug," "Heat Wave," and "Build Me Up Buttercup." It was two generations ahead of what we had been singing. The chorus and Mark loved it when we added some motions. Depending on the age of our audience, we often used the medley as our finale.

For a couple more years, while Sean was still in Philly, we enjoyed the excitement and talents that he shared with us. We brought back "Satin Doll" and had a sextet sing it. Sean created staging for it. (The chorus never learned it well enough to put it in our performances.) Our Christmas song "Zat You, Santa Claus?" (recorded by Louis Armstrong) was too straight and choppy. Sean didn't like it. So he took on the whole chorus, phrase by phrase, and zapped the tempo. He didn't write anything down. He said he "stored the tempo in their bodies." I guess he did because we never sang it any other way after that. He came with us to the Comcast Center (where we performed on the staircase) and to Maryland (where we shared the performance with the crab claws.) He helped place the mics.

One day Lisa handed me a recording of three songs. "Which one do you like the best?" she asked. I chose "Superman (It's Not Easy)" performed by Five for Fighting.

"Thank you," she said. "I'm going to ask Sean to arrange it for us." He did, and it became one of my personal favorites. In his arrangement, each phrase is sung by a different part. I had trouble phrasing it into a story, so we made it a solo. That worked. Wolf was our tenor soloist for this song. He created the story this way: As the chorus sang the intro, Wolf came on stage dragging a folding chair, with his jacket draped over his shoulder. Spinning the chair around, he straddled the seat and told the audience his story.

"It's not easy being me."

He walked the stage as he sang to the audience, pausing to sing a duet with the altos on the front row. He made the story come alive. "Superman (It's Not Easy)" was scheduled as one of our songs for our performance for St. Peter's Church. Wolf, our soloist, was unable to be there. I knew Sean was free that Sunday afternoon and I asked him if he would sing it for us. He said yes. So he sat in the audience and when it was time, he was introduced and he stepped up to sing his song. I loved it.

Marilyn was our chairman for our holiday show at the Colonial Theatre, *Nothin' but Cheer*. She asked Sean to be our stage manager. The first act for this show was a gathering at a home.

Sean Santa on a bike.

We had a fake fireplace and Christmas decorations on stage. We partied and sang on stage as we waited for Santa to arrive.

"I saw Santa on a bicycle. He had a flat tire."

"Santa's bicycle hit a fire hydrant and bent the front wheel."

"I saw a truck that ran into Santa's bicycle."

At the end of the first act, Santa finally arrived. He came down the aisle of our auditorium on a broken-down bicycle. It was Sean with his Santa Claus outfit and beard completely skewed.

Then came intermission and a guest performer as we changed into our black and shiny gold Christmas outfits for a twenty-minute parade of Christmas songs. It was quite a show. Soon Sean was on his way to California to be a rock star.

36

Flash Mob

OUR FLASH MOB PERFORMANCES began with a young woman about to be married. After attending a Pops performance, she asked us to be a surprise addition to her wedding service. The plan was to serenade the couple after the wedding ceremony as they turned to walk down the aisle together. The bride came to our rehearsal to make plans for a wedding on June 5, at The Church of St. Francis Xavier in Manhattan. She wanted us to sit in the church, scattered among their family and friends, and then stand up and sing "Happy Together" to the newly married couple before the recessional. The bride, the priest, and the organist were the only ones who knew about this. When we had all these details worked out, the bride said goodbye to us with a "See you in New York."

This was our plan: In the music arrangement of "Happy Together," the introduction starts with the bass section singing *bm, bm, bm*. The melody line moves from one section to another. This made it easy to plan our surprise. When it was our time to sing, we would have one bass stand up, interrupt the service, and start singing. As each part is added, they would stand to sing. Soon the whole chorus would be standing and singing to the couple.

This took some planning, and Renee was perfect for this. She gave each of us numbers and, on our sheet music, marked when to stand and when to sit. Our rehearsal room was big enough to practice this, so we set the chairs up as the body of the church. We were placed around the room to give us the best sound and the best way to hear each other so we could stay together and in tune (my job). We practiced many times. Soon we had memorized when to stand and when to sit. We knew this was going to be a great wedding.

It was quite a trip to New York City. The morning of the wedding, we climbed into the hired bus. Most of our members lived in and around the Philadelphia area, so it was more convenient for some members to have the bus make several pickup stops on our way up to New York. We dressed in our finest summer wedding outfits. The men carried their ties. It was a hot June day. The air-conditioning broke, and the driver lost his way. As we approached New York City, we started to warm up our voices and sang several songs including our wedding song, "Happy Together."

We drove around Lower Manhattan looking for our church. We finally saw it, and the driver parked the bus around the corner from the church. The men put on their ties. All of us, dressed in our best wedding clothes, pretended we were guests and meandered by twos and threes into the church. Just in case, the bride told us something about the two of them. Depending on which side of the church we sat, we all had our stories as to how we knew the bride or groom.

The wedding was beautiful, and the church was cool after the heat of the bus.

"And I now pronounce you husband and wife." They kissed and turned around to face their friends.

"Dm, dm, dm, dm, dm," sang the basses. The tenors joined in with the first line. Soon the whole chorus was standing and singing to the bride and groom. The cameraman was buzzing away.

The guests were looking around, smiling, laughing. We enjoyed being the surprise. We heard the church echo our sound like a fully miked performance. As we finished, the congregation gave us a round of applause, and then the organist started the recessional. We scurried out immediately behind the bride and groom because the bride wanted us to sing outside the church while the two of them went back in for their pictures.

So we huddled at the side of the beautiful stone steps and sang all the love songs we had in our repertoire. The stones acted as a sounding board for our songs and we sang into the sound coming back to us. Not only did the guests from the church stop to hear us, but the people walking along both sides of the street stopped to listen. Neighbors hung out of their windows to listen to us. When the bride and groom came running out of the church and into the waiting limousine, the bride turned around and gave us a thumbs-up, along with her biggest, happiest grin. Then it was into the hot van and back home we went. (P.S. The van company reduced our rate.)

Several months later, the flash mob video appeared on You-Tube under "Love Actually Inspired Wedding" (check it out).

When we were first planning this trip, one Popster said, "I'm not going all the way to New York City to sing one song." There is always one. The Pops is a volunteer group, so that was OK. We left him home. I wondered if he was ever sorry he missed this event.

And so it began...

Brandywine Valley Talent

It's funny how things happen. Pam and Ken Taylor were having dinner with some friends, and they mentioned how much they were enjoying singing with the Pops.

And Ken said, "Pops is looking for other opportunities to sing."

And his friend said, "Well, I know the gentleman that runs BVT [Brandywine Valley Talent], and you should talk to him to see what they can do."

So Ken did. This talent agency represented bands and string quartets for weddings and corporate receptions. Marketing an a cappella group was really out of their comfort zone. Ken showed them the YouTube video of the wedding in New York City. They asked if we would be interested in doing a flash mob performance for five showcase events they were having during the next couple of months. They added our YouTube performance to their own website.

At showcases, clients are invited to a hotel ballroom to hear several musical groups perform ten-minute presentations. The clients would then, hopefully, hire one of these groups for their upcoming event. Stages complete with light and sound equipment were set up along three walls. The foyer had wine and light fare for the clients. As the event began and the doors were opened, the guests (including us) entered and sat at round tables in the center of the room. The Pops would sit at separate tables, ready to pop up and start singing—just like a flash mob. We were to have no more than fourteen Pops perform for the showcase. The tables were reserved for Brandywine's clients.

We had five dates to divide among our many singers. Out came the spreadsheet with all singers listed by parts. One column was for availability and another for attendance. All of our members responded with their availability and then we chose our groups for each event (again, my job). How did we choose? Well, we looked to see if we had enough of each part to produce a good blend of voices. Our stage experience was invaluable because we had to be flexible with any unexpected change. We reminded the Pops to immediately connect with the audience (we only had one chance). We tried to give all members the opportunity to perform on at least one of these scheduled showcases.

We kept good records about who performed when. We had a disgruntled tenor who felt he wanted to be asked for more than one showcase performance. Months later we found the telltale spreadsheet and it said alongside his name: Y (yes) for the first gig, and a big N for the other four. I think that meant not available. He had forgotten. Even with records I couldn't win. Sometimes we would sneak an extra Popster on stage for a showcase because we needed the sound.

This is how it worked. After the second group had performed their ten-minute segment, the emcee of the night introduced A Cappella Pops. We started to sing from our seats and stood up to move through the tables. We knew, at a certain time, we had to reach a designated space along the side of the room. We wound around the tables and sang to our tablemates and guests as we passed. Sometimes, we were late to our spot because, as we passed by the tables, the audience would talk to us and shake our hands. We arrived at our space, finished performing our one song ("Happy Together"), accepted the laughter and the applause and left the ballroom. This is why being experienced was so valuable. We had to be comfortable to deal with the unexpected. Most of us then retired to the hotel bar for some food, drink, and camaraderie. We did not sing there.

Did this work? Not the way we thought it might. But...

A man at the showcase had asked his fiancée to hire us for their wedding reception. For eight months she told him she was looking for us with no luck. But she secretly asked us to be at their wedding reception. It was a crowded room with everyone eating and drinking. We had a hard time finding our way to be together so we could sing for them. We hid behind the other guests until they showed up as husband and wife. We made it. We found each other. We started singing as soon as the groom looked our way. He turned to his new wife and said,

"You found them!" Of course, we all heard it and loved being his surprise.

And then it started...

The word was out: A Cappella Pops does great wedding flash mobs.

♮

One of the most exciting times was when the bride came to our rehearsal and told us what she wanted. She was not shy. "Your song is too long. My guests are going to want to get out of the church to go and drink." We skipped the second verse. "It doesn't start out fast enough!" We cut the intro and went straight to the body of the song. "OK. Let me hear it!" We sang our revised version. "Great," she said. And it *was* great. It was perfect for her wedding. Short and sweet.

The wedding flash mobs were a wonderful way to share our talents. We always invited the client to come to our rehearsal. We wanted them to hear us and help us find what would be the best way to incorporate the flash mob into their day. Each wedding was different. Sometimes the bride didn't know, sometimes the groom didn't know, and sometimes neither the bride nor the groom knew—but their parents did.

At one of our weddings, it was all arranged by both sets of parents without the knowledge of the couple. After pronouncing them husband and wife, the minister requested the couple come up and turn around to face their guests. Then he said to the guests, "I'd like you all to sit down for a moment." And everybody sat down. At that time, our first voice started to sing the verse of "Happy Together." We added voices until the whole chorus was standing and singing. You could feel the excitement in the room. Soon the bride and groom stood up and started dancing to our music. The guests were thrilled and applauded the bride and groom at the end of the song. This is what A Cappella Pops is all about—being flexible enough to please each audience.

We learned something as we performed for our wedding parties. We thought, because our fee was for just one song, that we should at least offer them something for the reception. When they accepted, and we sang, it didn't work out well. The guests wanted to talk, drink, and start to party. Maybe we could sing one song, but by the second song the bar was three deep and people were busy saying hello to their friends. No one wanted to hear us. We learned to sing one song and silently steal away, with no announcement. This is a good example of learning from your audience. As good as we were, and as much fun as we shared with our audience, we learned when it was time to go.

37

The Pops New Zealand Story

Early March 2007

THE CHRISTCHURCH CHORUS, IN New Zealand, was growing in talent and numbers. Their director, Virginia (Virge) Humphrey-Taylor, was a dynamo as she developed this chorus and traveled around New Zealand coaching and training the new members. I spent two weeks with them in March of 2007. Virge invited me to coach the chorus and several of their quartets—and to see the beautiful town of Christchurch. The idea of a concert tour for the Pops began to form. Several Sweet Adelines choruses had already toured New Zealand. "Why not A Cappella Pops?" I thought. Pops was a small chorus of men and women singing contemporary music—something I thought would be new and different for the many SAI Chapters in New Zealand. Who was better to help answer that question than Virge?

"Would it be possible to have A Cappella Pops do a concert tour in your country?"

"Sure," said Virge. "Contact Kate Veeder. Here's her email address and phone number. She's in the States right now."

It was that easy. With Kate's contact information in hand, I returned home to present the idea of a New Zealand concert tour to the Pops. They acted positive and excited. They wanted more information. I contacted Kate. She and her husband, Joe, would plan our entire trip for us—concerts, tours, travel, food, and lodging. She wanted to work with one contact from our chorus, and she suggested that we choose March 2009 for the trip. She would send us the approximate cost per person.

Could anything be better? It was time for us to get serious. Our Popster Owen volunteered to be the contact for the trip. We took a count as to how many would go. There were lots of yes votes, some maybes, and many nos. But we had enough yeses to make a good sounding chorus, so we began to put the plan together. We invited family members and a few guests to join us. Owen contacted Kate. The following fall, at our Sweet Adelines International Convention, Kate and I met for the first time. She was easy to find among the eight thousand attendees—I just looked for the New Zealand flag draped over the balcony of the convention center. Then I asked all the Kiwis for Kate.

Our chorus treasurer set up a bank account for those who wanted to save a weekly amount by making a deposit at each rehearsal. People changed their minds. Some decided they were able to go, some had to drop out. Wives, husbands, and friends joined us for the trip. We actually had a new person join the chorus so that he could sing tenor with us and bring his wife to New Zealand. There were no grants for travel expenses. This was a serious decision. Each person was responsible for the funding of all travel and incidentals.

Owen and Kate planned the trip while I took care of the music and the (mental) health of the members. I remembered that when the Valley Forge Chorus went to Russia, some who stayed behind felt left out. We tried hard to not have this happen with Pops. We used a New Zealand email list, rather than chapter announcements, for special rehearsals held on Saturdays. We tried to be inclusive but not overbearing.

Costumes for our performances were an easy choice. We used our own black, gray, and silver outfits. This way, everyone brought several outfits of their own clothes for the concerts. Kate scheduled four concerts: Auckland, Hamilton, Wellington, and Christchurch.

We didn't want to use risers, but we were stumped as to how to transport our performance boxes all over New Zealand. We thought of putting them in individual shipping containers as freight, but the cost was huge and would be inconvenient traveling through their countryside. Then one day, to our surprise, our New Zealand hosts from Hamilton suggested they make boxes for us. They asked how many of each size we needed and what were our requirements: strong, lightweight, and collapsible so that they would stack in the undercarriage of our travel bus. And when the concert tour was over, the Hamilton Men's Chorus would have a new set of levels to create another style of staging for their own concerts. You can imagine how relieved we were to have such a wonderful solution.

♮

We learned one new song especially for the trip. It was "Heart to Heart," written by Malcolm McNeill and recorded by Dame Kiri Te Kanawa and Malcolm McNeill on their CD *Heart to Heart*. It is the song I had heard in 1994 in New Zealand when I was staying with Marilyn and Jan while coaching the Sweet Adelines choruses in Auckland. To get permission to sing this original song, I googled "Malcolm McNeill" and up popped "jazz singer—contact me." I did and he gave his permission to arrange and perform his song. Dan suggested we ask Jay Giallombardo to arrange this song for us. As soon as we learned it, we immediately put it into our performance repertoire so that all members sang it, not just those going to New Zealand. Several years later, when Dan and

Eileen married and all the Pops were invited to the wedding, they asked us to sing it as they danced their first waltz together as husband and wife.

Christchurch, New Zealand, is the hometown of Malcolm McNeill. The Christchurch Chorus invited him and his Jazz Combo to perform with us on their show. Malcolm asked if Pops would be willing to sing a medley of show tunes with them. He would arrange the music and send it to us in plenty of time to learn it for the show. We agreed. So now A Cappella Pops was going to be singing show music with a bass, drums, guitar, and what else? We didn't know.

We needed to learn this music at home, outside of our weekly chorus rehearsals, because not all members were going to New Zealand. This wasn't the best thing to happen. We did take some time during rehearsals to acquaint ourselves with the music, but in no way did we have it memorized in time. (Many members took this music with them to New Zealand. We didn't even take it out of the suitcases until we arrived in Christchurch.)

Departure date was about three months away, and we scheduled several special Saturday rehearsals for just the New Zealand group. We certainly didn't need notes and words, but we did need to blend our sound. We needed to get used to the sound of those around us, and to learn to relate to the personalities of those near us. Who better to work with us than our own Renee Walsh? She was an international quartet finalist and had years of experience on the stage but couldn't join us in New Zealand. The rehearsals were intense. I would direct and she would pull beauty out of their voices and fun out of their stage presence. I would fix any parts of the music that I thought could be better. It also gave us a chance to review Malcolm's Gershwin medley. It became a bonding time for those of us going to New Zealand.

Early March 2009

This was the longest plane ride most of us had ever taken. We arrived in Auckland at 6:30 a.m. and we were excited. Those who deplaned first waited in the terminal and took pictures of others as they came through the walkway from the airplane. Together we found our luggage and headed to customs. We were looking forward to meeting Kate and Joe Veeder, our guides and soon to be our very best friends. We all had to wait for Julianne—she didn't make it through customs. The security dogs had sniffed something in her luggage.

"Come with me," said the customs official, and they took her and her luggage to a small private room. Kate had reminded us

Deplaning in New Zealand. Let it begin.

not to bring produce into New Zealand. Julianne had brought along an orange and a banana to eat on the long ride across the ocean. The orange had been delicious, but the banana stayed in her luggage—forgotten—until customs found it. Julianne's only comment as she joined us was, "I just paid two hundred dollars for the most expensive banana I never ate."

Kate and Joe counted heads as we boarded our bus. It was too early to check into our rooms, so we took a short scenic tour of Auckland. It was then that we were reminded that our pickup time for our first performance was 3:00 p.m. for our 5:00 p.m. show that afternoon. Comments from inside the bus were everything from "I'm staying up" to "Not me. Get me to a bed." When we arrived at our hotel, the Parnell Inn, there was a light buffet

With Kate and Joe.

Eric, our coach driver.

waiting for us. After most of us had had our quick afternoon nap, we heard a distress call from Pam's husband, Ken. Pam decided to shower and wash her hair, but the converter she brought for her hair dryer didn't work. The SOS went out. Ken found a replacement, Pam dried her hair, and we were all ready by 3:00. We sang our first concert as the guest performers on the Greater Auckland Chorus's Sweet Adelines show. Dinner following the show was provided by the Greater Auckland Chorus at their rehearsal hall. What a welcome this was for us from the States, to spend time with our host chapter. We were treated to our first taste of smoked marlin. The next morning Kate and Joe introduced us to Eric. He was our bus driver for our entire trip. We were on our way to Hamilton.

At each of the cities where we performed, we were taken care of by the members of the host chorus. Often they would provide a potluck supper for us. Most of the time they didn't dine with us but just brought trays of food and set them out on a long table. No standard American diet. We had fruits and vegetables and casseroles, very little fried food and no pizza. The food franchise business had yet to invade New Zealand.

Hamilton

I think we made friends with the entire town when we arrived in Hamilton. We immediately were introduced to Colin and Barbara Smith, friends of the Veeders, and they joined our tour group. Colin, a Hamilton barbershopper, was superb with backstage traffic patterns, lighting, sound, and all manner of show production. Barbara was the director of the Waikato Rivertones Chorus of Hamilton. They had won the top mid-size chorus award when last they competed. Barbara was of enormous help to Kate with putting together our self-catering breakfasts and picnic lunches all the way through our trip.

Colin had invited every musical group in the town of Hamilton to come to the show. The six-hundred-seat auditorium was packed with singers. The cushioned seats were arranged in a semicircle around the stage. There was carpeting on the floor. There was a balcony at the back. Even the lights were soft. This was a beautifully warm and friendly place to sing. The Waikato Rivertones Chorus and the Hamilton Riverblenders men's barbershop chorus produced this show. The women opened the show. They were followed by the men's group. We were fortunate to be able to sit up in the balcony and listen and watch the two choruses perform. Many of the Popsters had never heard nor seen barbershop choruses, and this was awesome for them. We had been told that in New Zealand they applaud both with their hands and with their feet. They stomp on the floor. The Pops watched from the balcony and were having a good time using their feet as well as their hands to applaud the choruses.

The intermission was over, and it was time to switch places with the choruses. They made their way to the balcony so they could see us, and we went backstage and found our new boxes that they had made for us, which were now on the stage. We loved them and thanked the men for making them. As we waited to go on, the emcee requested that we were not to leave the stage at the end of our performance. Not knowing why, we entered, took our places, and made eye contact with the audience. What a beautiful theater. We looked for people we had met. We sang to them. They cheered and stamped their feet. They gave us a standing ovation and then asked us to sing an encore. We hadn't prepared one. Someone told us that Kiwis don't ask for encores. We kept saying, "We don't have one." There was a very slight hesitation as we finished. No one moved. It felt as if someone was saying to all of us, "We don't want this to end." We didn't move from the stage, and they didn't sit down. Everyone was waiting. The stage manager must have felt it, too, for he quickly stepped up to the mic and said to the audience, "Let us sing 'Pokarekare Ana' to them." "Pokarekare Ana" is a Maori love song that they sing in times of deep emotion, times when their hearts are so full of love and joy that they have to sing. We listened with our hearts as six hundred Kiwi voices sang to twenty-seven men and women who have come halfway around the world to sing for them. There was one row of seats that went around the top row of the auditorium. The folks up there had entwined their arms and were swaying to the music.

Deb, one of our altos, said it best. "I cried like a baby on stage. Some lady came up to me after the performance—found me in the crowd—and said, 'I just wanted to give you a hug.'" She wasn't the only one who cried. Every one of us had tears in our eyes, men and women.

Barbara and Colin were officially added to our team as stage managers for our tour. The next day they left for Wellington, our next concert venue, while Kate, Joe, and Eric took us to Rotorua to see—and smell—the hot springs. Onward to the Rotorua Village where we watched a Maori cultural show. Our men were

The Maori village.

invited to come on stage and dance with the Maori men. They did—with bare feet, no shirts, and lots of tongues. They mimicked the dance steps and the body movements of the men dancers. They stuck out their tongues. They really did. The Pops women cheered and laughed and laughed at their men up on stage.

We toured the Rotorua Village with a wonderful Maori woman as our tour guide. She called us her family.

"Come over here, my family, and see the steaming water. You are my family, you know. Come have some corn on the cob cooked for you in the hot steam."

As she showed us her village, we asked her questions about her people. We were drawn together as she shared her Maori background and upbringing. And then it was time for us to leave.

"I call you my family because I want you to come back. You sing? Sing a song for me, my family."

We were about to board our bus, but we stopped and, circling around her, sang "Alleluia," by Larry Gatlin of the Gatlin Brothers. The words of the song made tears roll down her cheeks. As we boarded the bus for Taupo, we left pieces of our hearts with the guide in the Maori Village. We visited the Huka Falls and then stopped at the Taupo bungee jumping tower. As Eric opened the door of the bus, we rushed out to watch people who were waiting for their turn to go up the ladder. We didn't want to miss the jump (or push, depending on how scared you were). The platform was 154 feet up. You stood there with your ankles tied together and fastened to a long rope. Then you dove headfirst into the air.

That's bungee jumping.

The jumpers had finished and were on their way to their next stop. It was our turn. Four gutsy Pops women climbed up the ladder, allowed the attendants to strap their ankles to the rope and, one by one, willingly jumped off the platform, diving headfirst toward the river. When the rope stopped bouncing them up and

The rope.

down, the men in the boat who were beneath them untied them and brought them to the shore. They waited for each other at the water's edge and came back up the trail—hugging, singing, and laughing. Lisa went back up the platform. She had forgotten to ask for a video of her jump, so she did it again. None of the Pops thought this was unusual. Taking risks, being courageous, and having fun seemed to be something we accepted because that's who we were. It's what we did every time we accepted a new challenge. Like flying halfway around the world to sing for people we had yet to meet.

It was back on the bus as we headed to Wellington for our third performance. The bus became home to us as we traveled this beautiful land. We saw mountains and sheep, rivers and sheep, and farms and sheep. Eric was becoming family.

Our city tour guide that day was a member of the Wellington City Chorus, and our dinner before the show was provided by the

The bungee jumpers' triumphant return from the river.

chorus members. We sang that night with the Wellington Chorus in Lower Hutt Hall.

At 6:30 a.m. the next day we left the hotel for the Inter Island Ferry Terminal. It was a three-hour ferry ride to the South Island. Kate and Joe had decided to bring our bus with us on the ferry, but we had to leave Eric. It was his mandatory free weekend. We would meet him in two days on the South Island. Our first stop with our new driver was at the Alan Scott's Vineyard in Renwick. As we found our way to the outside patio, I heard someone say, "Jan?" Seated at a table, having lunch, were my neighbors from home who were vacationing in New Zealand. Not only did they know me, but the wife also recognized the husband of one of our Popsters, a fellow teacher. There is a lesson here someplace. We settled ourselves on the patio under their outdoor canopy, talking, laughing, and sipping wine. We were together and it was catch-up time with each other.

The Marlborough Sounds men's barbershop chorus was close by in Blenheim, and Kate had planned an afternoon concert with them. They tried to make it work, but the timing was just too close. It wasn't easy to find an audience who could quickly come to a concert in the middle of the day. When our lunch was over, the patio door opened, and the Marlborough Sounds men's chorus came in to join us. We cheered a welcome for them. It was so nice of them to come to sing for us. Then we sang for them. Soon, four young men came into the winery and waited at the side of the room as we sang. They were casually dressed, and they came to sing for us. A few of the Pops who were from the barbershop world recognized them as the Musical Island Boys from Wellington, New Zealand. They had won the Men's International Collegiate Barbershop Contest in 2006 and were preparing to compete in the international quartet contest that coming July. (They would win the quartet championship in 2014.)

With the Musical Island Boys.

We sat down at our tables and the Musical Island Boys sang for us. Oh, my goodness! What clarity, what emotion! What a special treat! Their final song was "Once Upon a Time," and when they finished, I hoped that no one else wanted to sing. Their sound bounced off the walls. We had to be quiet so that sound wouldn't be disturbed. It was amazing.

At Lake Tekapo our lodging was a motel right along the shoreline. Each of our rooms faced the water, with chairs outside our door so we could sit and enjoy the view. That night, we all went into the town for an early dinner. Most of the restaurants couldn't handle forty people without notice so we split up into four or five groups, depending on our food preference and a restaurant that served it. Eric gave us the time to return to the bus to go back to the motel.

My special memory of this beautiful lake was the quiet solitude. That evening after dinner no one was outside, and I slipped out the front door to look at the lake and listen to the water and

The evening meal.

the birds. It was so still. No one was on the beach, and I could see
the water and the sunset and feel the breeze. It was time to take
a deep breath and enjoy this land. And there was Wolf, our tenor,
strolling down the beach, kicking a bit of sand out of the way as
he walked. He was all alone, obviously enjoying the moment. He
was holding something to his mouth. I watched as he came closer
to me. He was our trumpet player. Back home, in his spare time,
he and one of his friends played gigs at the local taverns and at
private parties. He needed to keep his lip in shape. He couldn't go
two weeks without playing so he had brought his mouthpiece with
him and was walking the lakeside in silence, by himself, making
sounds through his mouthpiece. I stood still and watched him for
a long time, then silently slipped back into my motel room.

♮

We went for a scenic drive to Mt. Cook and visited the Sir Edmund Hillary Alpine Center. It was here that we had the one and only picture taken of the entire group, with Mt. Cook in the background. Next we traveled from Mt. Cook to Queenstown, almost a four-hour drive. We took a trip across Lake Wakatipu in a coal-fired historic steamship and had dinner at the Walter Peak High Country Farm. After dinner we saw a real sheep shearing and then watched the working dogs bring the sheep in from the pasture. It was time to return to the hotel.

We waited by the water for our ship to return for us. The daylight hours were getting short and the way back across the lake was long. The night was clear, and the stars were bright. I'm sure all of us had heard, before we came to New Zealand, that the water in the sink in the Southern Hemisphere supposedly

All together on Mt. Cook.

went down the drain in a counterclockwise motion, opposite from the Northern Hemisphere. But we hadn't realized that the moon and all the constellations were going to be upside down. We found the Southern Cross in the sky, and it wasn't long before we were singing the Crosby, Stills and Nash "Southern Cross" song. It was here that many of us found out that the stars of the flag of New Zealand were of the Southern Cross. It was midnight when we returned to the hotel. Early the next day we were on our way to Te Anau and the Milford Sound.

On our way back to Christchurch at the end of our four-day vacation we were able to spend a full day in Queenstown. This seemed like a city that was made for all outdoor sports enthusiasts. There were stores all over the town from which to choose your equipment. The feeling in this city was outdoor sports and high energy. So much to do, so much fun to have in Queenstown. When we left Queenstown for Christchurch, one of our altos, Caren, stayed behind. She needed to return to work and was scheduled to fly from Queenstown to Auckland and then to home that evening.

She tells this story:

It was quite a wait for my flight. I was having lunch all alone sitting by a window. Up in the sky was a tandem paraglide. I watched for a while, and then thought "Hey, I have a couple hours before my flight, why not?"

I decided to do it. There was plenty of time to catch my plane.

You paraglide by running as fast as you can off the edge of the mountain to fly "like a bird over the sights of Queenstown," according to the brochure. None of us witnessed her flight. No one was there to cheer her when she landed. That makes four Pops bungee jumpers and one tandem paraglider.

We had left at 9:30 am for our seven-hour drive to Christchurch. Some of us rested and drifted off to sleep. But the group sitting right behind Eric, our long-suffering bus driver, decided to see how many commercials they could sing. When they couldn't remember any more, they started on theme songs from TV shows: *Father Knows Best*; *My Three Sons*; *The Flintstones*; *The Jetsons*; *Car 54, Where are You?* This was all with harmony and strange pickup sounds of instruments.

Finally, they exhausted their memories as the bus arrived in Christchurch. We were welcomed with a special performance by the 120-member Christchurch Chorus (CCC). They sang to us, and then we were divided into small groups, ones or twos, and invited into their homes to have dinner with their families. We met their husbands, wives, and children. After dinner, we were able to visit awhile before it was time to leave. When we arrived back at our hotel in the evening it sounded like the *Can You Top This* TV shows, as we were all eager to share stories of our wonderful host families.

♮

Kate and Joe had scheduled two days to see Christchurch before our evening performance. We also had to find time to rehearse for our final concert. We hadn't sung for a week and we were rusty. That night Kate and Joe had scheduled the first rehearsal with Malcolm McNeill. We had learned our music. Now we had to put it together with the jazz group. It was weird singing with instruments, but after two or three run-throughs we felt like seasoned performers. Their drummer commented to us that they had tried this many times with other groups. They were pleasantly surprised that this time it worked. Someone had brought a white

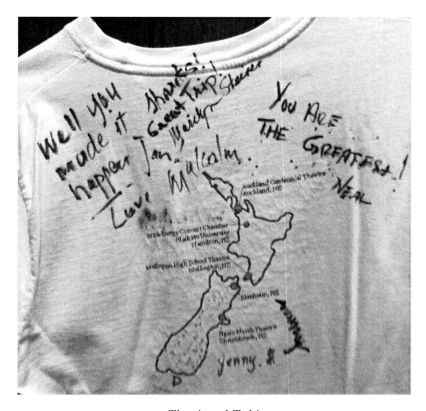

The signed T-shirt.

T-shirt for me, and everyone signed the back of it (I still have it). We sang "Heart to Heart" for him. It was a wild and joyful time together.

The next morning, the last day in New Zealand, we went to our theater for a quick lighting check. Then Angela Blank, one of the CCC members, took us on a guided tour of the city. Among the many places we visited were the Canterbury Cathedral, the Arts Center, Botanic Gardens, and the Antarctic Center. We also went punting down the Avon River in Christchurch. A punt is a small, flat-bottomed boat propelled by a guide (a punter) dressed

Punting.

in Edwardian clothing. We sat in soft, comfortable, cushioned seats as the punter propelled us through the city and past the trailing willows and leafy banks of the Botanic Gardens.

Back to our hotel for another rehearsal and a quick dinner, which was set up for us by the chorus. CCC opened the show. Most of us had neither heard nor seen 120 women singing barbershop music. They were good!

Malcolm McNeill and his jazz musicians were next, then the Pops sang our performance package for the last time in New Zealand. As our finale, we introduced Malcolm's song, "Heart to Heart." We told the audience all about how we heard the song and had wanted to sing it for Malcolm McNeill here in New Zealand. Malcolm was standing backstage watching us as we started to sing his song. Wolf saw him standing there, and you can imagine his surprise (and mine, too) when Wolf bolted from the chorus, ran over to him, and pulled him up onto our boxes to stand right in the middle of the Pops. With Wolf's arm around Malcolm's shoulder, he sang the rest of the song with us. How thrilling it was to see so much emotion on stage. It was exactly the right thing for Wolf to do but who could have predicted it? Thanks, Wolf. What a variety of music was put on that stage that night. The mayor of Christchurch and his wife came up on stage and welcomed us to New Zealand. Pictures were taken. It was a good show.

The next day Eric drove us to the airport. We were heading back to the United States. Here we were at the end of our tour. Every day had drawn us closer to each other and to the New Zealand people. We had spent two weeks with Kate, Joe, and Eric. We said goodbye to our friends. We said goodbye to our fellow Pops travelers. We were going home with a trunk full of memories.

Several weeks later the Pops received an email from Malcolm McNeill:

Thank you for what you brought into my life—you wouldn't have known the richness of what you and your group gave me. Good, isn't it, how music allows for the things we really need to come into our life at precisely the right time. The gift you all brought me—the connection I felt—you would not have known how wonderfully it filled a space in my life that I needed—JUST NOW!

Thank you. So very much. I loved the way you did "Heart to Heart." I may have written it, but it seems to have come from someone who knew much more about life than me.

And to me, personally:

You are one sharp lady, Jan. That you know how to shape the phrase—it's a rare art these days—and so when one

With Malcolm.

comes across it in others it's a bit like finding a Zen master gardener who knows how to remove every third pine needle from the branch, but then leave one or two just for aesthetic reasons (or just to confuse the English). Good taste—but not drawing attention!

Good, isn't it? That you are a persistent person, that something in your psyche leads you to where you should go. You do a wonderful thing for the members of the A Cappella Pops, not least of which is the way you step out of the way when they are rolling. Now, *that's* the gift. You shape the phrase, as the writer intended, and you know clearly how that should be and then you step back. So clear where your heart is—in the music.

By the way, loved your leather outfit. Swanky and hip. Let's do more. I'm Travelin' Light.

And thoughts from Kate:

The Pops was an incredible close-knit group of singers who had such a passion for their craft and executed their performances brilliantly. So classy and so much thought put into the program. A Cappella Pops was unique and something completely different for us to experience in New Zealand. We had never had a mixed a cappella group perform in New Zealand before you came to our shores. Professionalism is what A Cappella Pops was all about—from start to finish. And they so embraced our Kiwi way of life! The travel itinerary... The Pops loved the coach driver, and they sang, sang, and sang throughout New Zealand. You departed with the love of so many of us who were blessed to spend two weeks with you as you toured my beautiful homeland. I am like the others who helped with the trip—our hearts are so full of memories.

And more thoughts from Kate, a few years after our trip: There was not a single thing or song you did that we did not like. We loved the beauty of your presentation. We loved how informal it was, with the use of those boxes, which now are housed at Waikato Rivertones Chorus! Nothing was confusing. We were hungry for any/all a cappella music, and we loved the way Pops embraced all of us. It was like being together as a large family.

Little did we know that in a few years, on February 22, 2011, almost all of Christchurch as we remembered it would be destroyed by a huge earthquake. We had been inside many of the buildings in this city, and every picture in the news was a familiar sight to us. Members of the Christchurch Chorus would lose their homes. A Cappella Pops had brought back names and email addresses of our friends in New Zealand and we were able to contact them. Fortunately, all were well.

38

Memories of Music

Misty

THE CHORUS TELLS THE story this way: We were standing in a circle in no special order during one of our rehearsals when we decided to sing "Misty." This eight-part song was given to us by special permission of Val Hicks, the arranger. It had become one of our favorites. As we started to sing, we closed our eyes to listen only to each other—hearing the beautiful sound and putting together our parts—not by being directed, but just by the feel of the music. We sang with the give and take of the parts around us. We blended our voices. We responded vocally to the emotion we were producing. The chorus started to rock left and right with the tempo of the song. The music ended and we quietly opened our eyes. We will never forget it.

Didn't My Lord Deliver Daniel

We had been looking for a gospel song for months and I finally found one: A spiritual arranged by Donald McCullough titled "Didn't My Lord Deliver Daniel?" This arrangement was crazy. The arranger had written some high Hallelujahs at the end of the song. I loved it. It rocked. I asked two of my strong sopranos, Deb B. and Eileen, to sing it with all the gusto they could give.

♫ *397*

Each of them had a nice vibrato that they usually kept in check for our a cappella style singing, but I asked them to let it rip for the tag.

They stood on the center back row, one on each side of Dan, our bass. Every time we rehearsed it, Dan would stagger down from the back row with his hands on his ears and look at me, pleading, with crossed eyes. Both women laughed a bit at Dan's discomfort. It was just what the music called for—and they loved teasing Dan.

Embraceable You

We performed at the Merion Cricket Club, in Philadelphia, for about three hundred people. We were to sing three songs in the cocktail lounge and then move on into the ballroom for a twenty-minute formal performance. It was so crowded in the lounge that we could hardly separate the guests from our chorus. Sometimes guests would walk among us just to get to the bar.

Our first song was "Orange Colored Sky," a peppy song with a solo by Deb and a catchy rhythm background. Someone found a working microphone and we immediately put it to good use. We gave it to Deb so at least she would be heard. We had planned to sing "Embraceable You" as our second song. It is a beautiful love ballad arranged by Kirby Shaw. His arrangements always made Pops sound good, and we loved singing his music. But we knew we were in trouble at this performance. No one was listening, we could hardly hear ourselves sing, and only a few people could even see us. Time to change plans. I raised my arms, started "Embraceable You," and said to the chorus, "Follow me." We turned toward a young couple that was standing in front of us. Imagine seeing twenty-five singers heading straight for you.

The chorus knew immediately what we were going to do. They circled the couple and continued singing. The couple smiled, put their arms around each other, and hugged as we sang. We held them captive for a little while and soon found another couple to serenade. We walked around, serenading couples, until we had finished the song and found ourselves outside the lounge and in the ballroom where we would complete our gig.

The most beautiful thing about this experience was the ability to say "follow me" to the chorus and watch them take control of the presentation and make it memorable. We were A Cappella Pops and this is what we did. It was a proud moment for me.

We were invited to stay for dessert. It was a warm summer evening, and while I stayed in the ballroom, most of the chorus went up to the rooftop lounge to look at the stars. Some guests were also there enjoying the night air.

"Who are you?" they asked.

"We sing and just performed in the ballroom."

"Would you sing for us?"

The warm summer air, the stars, the moonlight, and the quiet rooftop all said, "Embraceable You!" And so, without a director and from their hearts, they sang. And when it was time to go home, and they saw me in the ballroom, they could only say, "We sang 'Embraceable You' for the people on the roof." And I knew that they had just experienced a special moment of love and joy.

Mary, Did You Know?

We had an SSAA arrangement of "Mary, Did You Know?" for the women of Pops. Laurie recorded all four learning tracks, and the two of us worked together to make the interpretation right. The women Popsters loved the song; it was beautiful. Every Christmas Pat and Marie's aunts and sisters would attend our Christmas performances and cry as we sang about Mary. And as they arrived at the venue for our performance, they would wave to us with their handkerchiefs to tell us they were prepared to cry for "Mary, Did You Know?" And they always did.

39

Caring

ONE OF THE MAGICAL things that happened with the Pops was that most of us became good friends with each other. We generally liked each other, but it went further than that. We cared. Sometimes we spent an evening together doing an impromptu serenade at someone's home, or we went to concerts together. We attended each other's activities and presentations. We partied together. Sometimes we even spent our vacations together.

We were never out of each other's minds so when rare opportunities presented themselves, we were there. We brought food when there was sickness, provided taxi service when it was needed, and attended funeral services of members' relatives.

Many couples joined us just so they could sing together: Janet and Dale, Pam and Ken, Deb and Owen, Connie and Bob, and Marie and Pat. Sometimes we were lucky enough to join in the happiness of those who found someone in the Pops to spend the rest of their lives with, like: Dan and Eileen, Dan S. and Laurie, and Sebastian and Lisa.

Smile, Dammit!

Lisa and Sebastian tell a great story. Both of them worked at the company where we rehearsed. Sebastian was from Germany. He was very tall, nice looking, and he had a good voice. But he never smiled. I had to do something. I knew the audience's eyes would find him and watch him instead of listening to our music. When he first joined, Lisa stood near him as we rehearsed. I took her aside and said, "Lisa, I can't put him on the stage with no smile. Both of you work at the same company. Can you take him aside and teach him how to smile when he sings?"

They didn't know each other well—then—but they soon became a couple. Lisa did her job extremely well, and Sebastian liked it.

Martin Committee Trumpet

When my husband was a little boy, his father bought him his own trumpet. He paid $100 for it. Darrel learned to play on this trumpet all through high school and later in the ROTC marching band. After, it stayed in its case, unused, for years. One year, as a Christmas present, we had it cleaned and reconditioned. It was then that Darrel learned it was a 1948 Martin Committee trumpet—the one almost all jazz players preferred. One day we were in the company of Roger Blackburn, our barbershop buddy and a trumpet player in the Philadelphia Orchestra. We mentioned to Roger that we had this Martin Committee trumpet. Of course, he knew all about it. Much later, we got a call from Roger asking us if we would like to come to the Mann Music Center to attend a morning rehearsal of the Philadelphia Orchestra, and, oh yes, bring your trumpet. Contemporary jazz trumpeter Chris Botti was the star performer that night. We were excited for the opportunity and couldn't pass up the chance to invite Wolf to join us. Wolf, a tenor with Pops, has a degree in French horn and trumpet from the Curtis Institute of Music in Philly. Most weekends you'll find Wolf playing a gig somewhere in the Philadelphia area.

The Mann Music Center is a huge open-air theater. Most of the audience sits under a covered roof. There is plenty of room for hundreds more to sit on the grassy slopes behind the seats. We sat in the empty seats close to the stage as we listened to the orchestra's rehearsal. At the first break, Roger motioned us to bring our trumpet and come to the stage. We were introduced to Chris and handed him the trumpet. He immediately took it, looked it all over, replaced the mouthpiece with his own and began to play. After a few notes he stopped and motioned to his piano player to accompany him. Then he turned to face the empty seats and played a song to the audience that wasn't there. It was thrilling for Wolf, Darrel, and me just to be there. The rest of the orchestra paid us no attention. We three were truly awed to stand on a big concert stage right next to a virtuoso as he played Darrel's childhood trumpet. When he finished, Chris graciously thanked us and commented about the great Martin trumpet. Some pictures were taken, and then he was gone.

Chris with Darrel's Trumpet (photo by Roger Blackburn)

Don and the Danube

Don and Joan were charter members of Pops. They were the reason the Pops sang at the World Harmony Jamboree in Montreal, Indianapolis, and Philadelphia. Joan was one of our soloists, and Don, besides being an active singer, was our constant fun-loving tenor. He was not shy about mooning the chorus members when the opportunity presented itself. And somehow, the opportunity kept presenting itself...

Don and Joan had been together for many years, and when they decided to marry, the whole chapter joined them by the lake for their ceremony. Sadly, many years later, Don was diagnosed with ALS. One of the items on Don's bucket list was a cruise down the Danube. We planned a surprise party to raise money to help them take their trip. We invited all the Pops, Don's family, the people who worked with him, plus friends from the ALS Society. There was food, singing, and music by Wolf and Company. We sat

The wedding.

Don in a chair in the center of the room, and the Pops accompanied Joan as she sang her solo, "Stand by Me," to Don.

It was obvious that all of this was a surprise to Don, which made it all that much more fun. Pops raised enough money for Don and Joan to fly to Germany and take their trip down the Danube. When Don was not able to sing with us anymore, the men from the chorus made sure someone fetched him to come (in a wheelchair) to our performances. When it was time for him to leave us, several Pops members spent the day with Joan and were with her when he passed. He was carried to the funeral limousine by a beloved Popster.

Pokarekare Ana

Ross (our sound man) became ill with a sudden and fatal disease. Several Popsters gathered at his hospital bedside to say goodbye. Ross's brother and sister-in-law and the hospital nurses stood in the doorway, listening, as the Pops serenaded Ross with the Maori love song "Pokarekare Ana." Ross's eyes were teary.

40

A Cappella Pops Incorporated

TOM SUGGESTED WE HAVE a music committee. I said no. I should have asked, "What will they do?" I should have asked, "How should I work with them?" But I didn't. And Tom said yes, and the committee was formed. It seemed like a good idea. Tom was the Pops manager. He selected past and present barbershop members who had experience being on music teams. It sounded good. To be honest, I didn't pay much attention to them. I still chose the music A Cappella Pops sang. I didn't have any guidance to give the new committee. I didn't think I needed them. And it showed.

By this time, Janet K. had joined the performance team and added her style to our shows. She and Pam were doing a great job with the performance lineup and emcees. One time the music committee offered a different lineup for an upcoming performance, and Pam and I didn't use it. I should have shown the committee the "How to Plan Your Standing Ovation" flowchart so they could plan a better lineup, but Pam was doing such a fine job that I never thought to give the job to the music committee. Their lineup missed the standing ovation finale, and we were getting used to having one at the end of our performances.

We were planning our CD when the committee suggested a plan for choosing the order for us to rehearse and record our twelve songs. It was nice of them to do that, but musically I knew I wouldn't have time to perfect the songs in the order they had chosen to record them. It would have been better if I had explained this to them. It felt as if unrest was developing in the chorus. So when Pat Shea joined the Pops, I begged her to fill the vacant position of music chair. There was method to my madness. I knew Pat would be a good conduit between me and the music committee. It was still a happy time, full of good music, good singing, and good friends. We performed ten to fifteen times each year—a New Year's Eve First Night Festival in New Jersey, a performance at Longwood Gardens, many benefit performances such as the Tourette Syndrome Benefit, and our annual senior living communities Christmas shows. And our parties...always our parties. We really enjoyed singing together.

The Pops had established a leadership committee to meet once a month in a private room before a rehearsal. I was invited to join. I said no. They said yes. I lost. It was OK being a part of the leadership team when they discussed musical subjects, but when it was time for the financial report, I wanted to run away. I didn't want to sit in on non-musical topics. I had a chorus in the other room ready to sing, and I wanted to be with them. I wanted to focus on the music.

Some of the Pops, especially those on the leadership commit-tee, wanted to develop the governance of the Pops, rather than let-ting things grow organically in a musical direction. They tended to work in the corporate world and had responsible positions in their jobs. They wanted to contribute their expertise to making A Cappella Pops more organized. "Let's have a goal-setting session," they announced. So they brought in an outside corporate planner to lead this project. Half of our rehearsal time was used to iden-tify the structure of the Pops management—finance, marketing, music, and so forth. After much discussion and using sticky notes to gather everyone's input, the planner chose several areas for our group to focus on to improve our organization.

The last area on the list was called the wow factor. My heart sank. Did this mean it was not my job to look for more wow performances anymore? Did it mean that the chorus would take over this responsibility? Would they appoint a committee to plan this part of our performances? I assumed that's exactly what they wanted, so I backed off (I may have misunderstood this). Did they only want me to wave my arms? I had no idea what the chorus was going to do with this goal-setting information. I lost a little of my burn.

I was aware that the whole session that evening was strangely similar to the lesson plans I had formulated for my classes in goal setting that I had taught for the Sweet Adelines. I realized that there was a whole part of my life that the Pops knew nothing about—like when I became DMA for Region 19 of the Sweet Adelines. I had divided my Regional responsibilities into five categories to describe the job I had to do. I selected the chairs and helped them plan their work. Then I let them do it.

I had experience organizing a chorus, but no one knew that, so no one asked me about the pros and cons. Having a leadership team was a good idea. Including the whole chorus in the goal-setting session about organization was not. But we did lack a musical goal, which may have made room for the business-oriented goals. During my years with Valley Forge, I noticed that if we did not have a strong musical goal to focus on after a contest, the chorus grew restless. Big egos with big ideas emerged. More disagreements turned into arguments. We learned to have something planned for when we came home from a competition—a big performance, a self-produced show. Even a big open house party. Anything to focus our attention on a musical goal for the future.

A Cappella Pops had just returned from New Zealand but didn't have a musical goal lined up. Instead, the Pops started creating committees for this and committees for that, and there were even more announcements at rehearsals. This was not the way most of us wanted to go. I overheard comments like, "I don't like it. That's my day job. I just want to sing." Personality conflicts developed. People were not coming together musically like they used to. More of my burn faded.

Then the leadership committee thought it would be a good idea if they had a plan to find a new director if anything ever happened to me. The chair of the committee took me out to lunch and asked me to describe what another director would need to be. I wish they hadn't told me. While my brain told me that this planning ahead was a good idea, my heart didn't handle it well. I still did my job and still directed the chorus—but there was a difference within me. I felt like I was driving the family car instead of my Jaguar sport.

I was leaning on Pat Shea for someone to talk to. She had this sense about her that music was the draw and not the structure of the chorus. She understood Pops. She also had been a director of a Sweet Adelines chorus in her early years. Pat was a piano teacher and had perfect pitch. And she was a personal friend. I loved working with her. I felt a kinship with her, a little like when Tom and I worked together. One Saturday the leadership team planned a retreat. By my choice, I didn't go, but Pat did.

During the retreat, Dan Meyers talked about making the learning tapes for the chorus and putting the results on our member website. A steering committee was in the process of putting together the master class to market to colleges in the area. (I thought that idea had been forgotten. Pat Shea must have revived it. She had been busy.) Peggy reported that she was hard at work making sure our written music was up to date. Pat and Dan talked about new songs we had planned to add to our repertoire.

In addition, the leadership committee talked about the quality of the singing of our Pops chorus. They didn't like it when some members missed a couple of rehearsals and then showed up to sing in a performance—a common problem with most performing choruses. They felt this lack of practicing was affecting our sound, so they planned a way to keep this from happening. Their solution was to assign the section leaders the responsibility of deciding whether or not a member who had missed rehearsals should sing in the performance. In other words, it was the section leaders who told the members not to sing.

We had a section practice planned for the rehearsal after the retreat. Pat was with the sopranos, and she told them about the new ruling. They didn't like it. They felt strongly about it, and they were not quiet about it, to put it mildly. They felt that it was the director's responsibility to refuse a person the right to sing on a performance. Pat agreed. And I agreed with Pat. We were a volunteer group that had always policed ourselves. We always encouraged personal responsibility. People who didn't know their music would normally not sign up for the performance, and I liked it that way. I wasn't afraid to tell someone that they couldn't sing or that they needed to change something in order to be a true Popster. It was my job, but only when necessary.

After rehearsal, Pat Shea said to the leadership team, "This won't work." After all the hard work the preceding Saturday, this was not a welcome statement. The rebuff of her comment started right after the rehearsal, continued on the elevator to the exit floor, on into the hallway, through the front door, across the parking lot, and into the front seat of Pat's car. The next day Pat resigned from the chorus. She felt that the way the leadership team wanted to achieve the goals for Pops was not compatible with her feelings, and that the leadership team was going in a direction that she didn't believe in. I lost my buddy. And I realized I wasn't having fun anymore either. I missed working on fun, unique, and crazy ideas.

Here are a couple of them that I thought of, but never initiated:

1 How about a jazz duet with the chorus and a flute? We'd need to find the right music, but we could make it work.

2 My daughter had just married a drummer, and I envisioned having part of "Sing, Sing, Sing" (Benny Goodman) arranged for the chorus. My son-in-law could play the drums while we sang.

3 One year when soprano Janet W. re-auditioned, she held two puppets in her hands. They sang to each other. I thought, "Let's get her song arranged and we'll put her and her puppets in our performances." The song was "Popular" from *Wicked*.

4 Rick had sung a duet in Mimi's *Bits of Broadway*. I wanted to get "Brush Up Your Shakespeare" arranged for Pops. Don H. would have made a perfect partner for that duet. They could dance and sing. (I found out later that Don H. had performed this with another partner in a choral group he had sung with. Darn. Another missed opportunity.)

5 Linda had a deep bass voice. One day she mentioned that her neighbor played the jazz piano. They would entertain at parties. She would scat (like Ella Fitzgerald) as he played. I wondered if we could have one of our basses sing a duet with Linda, maybe even with chorus accompaniment.

But the performance I really regret not putting together formed in my mind one spring when Wolf took his trumpet to New Orleans. He went to Jackson Square and joined the street musicians. He hung out on Royal Street and became part of their music. Maybe we could do that. Maybe some of the musicians would start to play their instruments as we sang. My plan was for the chorus to fly to New Orleans on a Thursday night, sing on the streets and tour the city, perform with the local BHS barbershop chorus for a Saturday night show, sing a little Sunday morning, and fly home Sunday afternoon. The chorus members would lose only one day of work or vacation, and we would see NOLA, sing on the street, help a BHS chorus earn some extra money and have a wow time. It never happened.

Any one of those ideas would take a lot of work to make happen. I didn't think I had the drive to do them all alone. I was afraid to suggest any of them because they were a little too far out, and my chorus was losing its uniqueness, maturing from a Jaguar to a sensible family sedan. I couldn't make anything happen in Pops. I needed something to excite me.

Pat left, and I missed her support. Soon the corporate structure began to show up at rehearsals. We lost several good members. Their most common complaint was, "It's not fun anymore. I really don't care who is going to chair the next meeting." Soon the chorus asked the board to address this situation. "How do we get the fire back?" they wanted to know.

Marji had the leadership meeting at her house. This was important, because she had set up her home for a small party with snacks and a wine table. She wanted to help us bond—it was going to be a tough meeting. Almost everyone spoke about how they were feeling and gave their opinions. It was a good gathering of concerned Popsters. I did not talk but listened to the conversations. At the end Rick turned to me and asked, "How do you feel about this?"

I paused before I answered him, because I had begun to realize that there was an obvious solution to the problem. So I took a deep breath and I said it. "I think you need a new director."

Dead silence. Finally Marji said, "Well, I think it's time for some wine." And we followed Marji's lead, stopped the discussion, and enjoyed the wine and the friendship.

Out came the succession plan from the files. It had been on the shelf for almost two years. The leadership team gave the chorus a questionnaire to remind them of things they would be looking for in a new director—musical skills, rehearsal preparation, variety of music styles, ability to teach music, and awareness of our culture. "Musical Director Wanted" ads were placed in the most prestigious magazines and newsletters that potential music directors would read. The Pops received many responses. Some were recent college graduates with no experience. Others were members of choruses who had never directed before. One lived in Italy. The team chose four and separately invited them to visit the chorus on our Wednesday rehearsal night. It was important to see us rehearse and to hear and watch us perform. We wanted them to see our personality, our trademark.

The team took each candidate to dinner before the rehearsal. I wanted to be involved in picking my successor, to meet the candidates on a personal level before they directed the chorus. They didn't think it was appropriate, so I didn't join them. As each prospective director came to visit, I felt it was important to be ourselves, so I held regular rehearsals. We would rehearse music, perform a variety of songs for our guests, and share ourselves and our love for our music. We worked hard and had many laughs. We left time for questions. This was for the prospective directors to see us and decide if they would like to be a candidate.

We invited two to return to conduct a short rehearsal. We sent them a recording of three songs from our current repertoire and asked them to choose one to direct the chorus. We also asked them to teach a one-page piece of music of their choice. During these rehearsal auditions, I did not voice an opinion or ask a question. It wasn't as hard as I thought it would be. I knew the chorus would be watching my every emotion. I was aware that a slight smile, sigh, or even a twinkle in my eye, might influence the vote. Through the years they had come to read my face for approval, displeasure, and all the other emotions that show when people sing for you. I felt that the chorus should decide for themselves who they wanted to direct them. I kept very still.

I felt the final two were strong candidates. Either one would have made a fine director for A Cappella Pops. There was much discussion among the members during the final days before voting. How fortunate they were to have two candidates who really wanted to be the director of A Cappella Pops. The vote was taken, and the new director chosen was Pat Montenegro. I thought he would be perfect for the job. What did they do with me? I was given the title of Director Emeritus and asked to stay with the chorus as they made the transition.

We were heading into the Christmas season with seventeen songs to refresh or learn for our nine performances, including one flash mob wedding and one performance that was only half Christmas songs. That's a lot for any new director to learn. Pat M., the new director, asked if I would mind directing some of the Christmas songs and we would share the performances. It was a hectic time, but together Pat and I learned to work it out. I liked him. He made it clear to me that I was a valuable asset to the chorus, and he wanted me around. One of my jobs was to help with four new songs for the Christmas season. We needed some extra rehearsals. I directed them.

Our last performance of the year was with the Chesapeake Brass Band at the World Café Live at the Queen, in Wilmington, Delaware. The band performed, we sang, and then we sang with them. Our new director arranged music for us to sing as the brass band played selections of Christmas songs. How proud we were to sing his arrangements. This was a dinner theater, and the Pops had reserved a large table for us to have dinner together after the performance. Pat and I shared the stage. He asked me to direct the last few songs. The theater was filled with friends of the Pops and friends of the band. Friends whom I hadn't seen for quite a while were in the audience. My family was there, too.

As I was about to direct the last song, Pam, our emcee, stepped out from the chorus and began to talk to the audience. I had no idea what she was doing or when I was supposed to begin the last song. So I stepped to the side and waited for her cue to continue. She shared with the audience that I was retiring. She talked about the Pops under my direction. Everyone on stage knew what she was doing, and they watched me squirm with the praise and love she shared with the audience. Then Pat M. brought out a bouquet of flowers for me.

After the performance we milled around with the audience, hugging old friends and loving and laughing. I noticed the chorus was seated and having dinner. I was busy catching up with old friends and spending time with my family. I suddenly became hungry and asked if my husband and I could join their table. They responded with a funny laugh and a "Sure!" They gave us seats at

"The Street of Dreams"

the head of the table. How clueless I was. This was a retirement celebration. For me.

For the last few months, the chorus had been planning a gift for me. They had contacted my family and all our former members and invited them to the concert. In addition, they had commissioned a painting of a street scene with the names and places where we had been together. It was packed full of memories. They made me read their card aloud, to everyone.

Christmas came and then the New Year. It was time to retire from directing Pops. It was my life and love for twelve years. It was time for Pat M. to be totally in control. He encouraged me to stay in the chorus. He wanted me to be around, and occasionally he would glance at me during rehearsal with a smile on his face. Now I was one of the members, having the time of my life with my new challenges. I had been singing in a director style (all parts loud and out of my range) and ruining my voice. So now I was on a new mission—vocal exercises and learning music. That didn't last long. I quickly realized it was time to step back and just enjoy the music.

Although I loved the responsibility of directing the Pops, it was nice to have passed it on to someone who would open new experiences, new music, and new audiences. I love the stage. I will always have my friends with whom I've lived and laughed for twelve years. I will forever be awed that this group of excellent singers had decided to continue with Pops. I will always be a Popster. I was invited to their parties, attended their performances, and sometimes met them at their watering hole after rehearsal to wine and dine with them, and catch up on all the gossip.

About this time, my grandson Sean came back from California and became a high school physics teacher in Philadelphia. He was singing with the prestigious Mendelssohn Club. We were reminiscing about this time in our lives, he said this about Pops:

You have to understand what Pops was. Pops was an idea. It was an ethos. It was not people. It was a community. People came to sing because they could express themselves. They could build something greater than the whole. Good artists allow the art to develop on its own. "We're off in this direction—let's see where it takes us." It was an experience. If you harness the energy, you rope it into submission. Pops was fragile. This was something they wanted to do. If you tried to direct it as a chorus, you missed the whole thing. You must direct the energy.

My eyes filled with tears. Sean knew what we were doing. He was the only one who noticed my ictus was now perpendicular to the floor. Damn! How did it get so screwed up?

41

Pat Montenegro and Pops

PAT'S COLLEGE DEGREE WAS in jazz piano, and his life was music. He taught at private schools and colleges, directed three choruses, played for church choirs, accompanied soloists, and did anything else he could find that was musical. His wife, Lauren, had a degree in voice, singing opera. He and Lauren had three little girls who loved to run around the baby grand piano in their living room. It was always being played.

Pat enjoyed the culture of the Pops. It was a chance for him to arrange, direct, and express his love for contemporary music. Soon the Pops was singing Pharrell Williams's "Happy." Next

Pat Montenegro

he arranged "Your Song" by Elton John for the chorus to sing at Lauren's upcoming birthday party. Pat was the tenor soloist. There is a story about that day. Susan was flying home from a business meeting, and she planned to go straight from the airport to the party. She spent the time on the plane reviewing the words to "Your Song." Her seatmate, a stranger named David, could hear her trying to learn the words. David's curiosity got the better of him and he asked Susan what this was all about. She explained the chorus and the birthday party for the wife of the director. David loved to sing, and the Pops chorus intrigued him. They exchanged contact information.

That night the chorus accompanied Pat as he sang a love song to his wife. It was a beautiful moment. Several weeks after the birthday party, David came to visit Pops and soon joined them. It wasn't long before Pat asked him to sing the solo for his arrangement of "Sweet Caroline." And several years later the Pops serenaded David's daughter at her bat mitzvah. We wrapped Lauren and Pat in our Pops family life. Every September my husband and I had a picnic for the Pops at our home. That year many old members came back to join us and meet the new director. We have a large deck with woods behind us. Across the street is a horse farm. This was our first picnic with Pat and Lauren. Their three little girls played in the hammock stretched between two trees. They ran down the driveway to feed carrots to the horses in the field. The girls made sure their parents brought them back each year. We loved the cookies that they sold for their school.

Occasionally I bumped into Pat outside of Pops. One Saturday afternoon I attended the final recital of a soprano from Pops who was studying for her master's degree in voice. It was held at a college near her home but many miles from my home. She sang an hour of classical music for her professors and guests. And who was her accompanist at the piano? Pat Montenegro.

We often have dinner with friends at our favorite Italian restaurant in our town. San Nicola Restaurant was sponsoring an opera night. Five soloists sang in their dining rooms on a week-day night for three consecutive weeks, for a total of fifteen soloists. The audience evaluated and voted for their favorite vocalists. On the fourth night of dinners, the top five returned to sing again, and the audience chose a winner. And who surprised us as the accompanist and organizer of this opera night? Pat Montenegro.

My husband was looking for a singing group to join. There was a group called the Masterworks Chorale that fit his interests—a little classical, a little opera, and a little contemporary. They rehearsed at The Church of the Redeemer in Springfield, a town about forty minutes away. The drive was just too far for him to travel each week. This is the town where I had lived and raised my kids. The Redeemer was our church. Who was the director of the Masterworks Chorale? Pat Montenegro.

The Philly CBS TV station invited the Pops to sing Christmas songs on their 6:00 a.m. news program. It was an hour's drive to the station for both the chorus and for Pat. Some Pops weren't sure of the timing (getting up at 4:00 a.m.?), so they met in Philadelphia the day before, had dinner, partied, stayed the night, and were ready to make the next day's early morning call time. Pat met them in the lobby. They sang, and the host of our local station, Jim Donovan, interviewed Pat and asked him about the Pops upcoming Christmas show. Then they sang a few lines of their last song as the TV program faded out. This became an annual event.

♮

Flash mob weddings were still popular, and the Pops were in high demand. One wedding was especially challenging. It was held in a wooded area in the Pocono Mountains about two hours from our homes. There was no music in the meadow where the couple were getting married. Pat had arranged Bruno Mars's "Marry You" for the Pops after he had seen the YouTube video of a couple's lip sync marriage proposal. Now it was the perfect solution to the no-music problem. The Pops were sitting in the audience and when it was time for the wedding, they popped up and moved out to sing. The bridesmaids danced down a grassy slope with their bouquets waving in the air to the sounds of "Marry You." Then the bride followed. She danced, too. It was quite an impressive processional. After they were pronounced man and wife, the Pops sent them on their way with "Happy Together."

One evening after rehearsal we talked with Pat about the wide variety of talents we had in our chorus. We laughed at some of the suggestions (confessions?). Someone mentioned that we ought to have our own talent show. Susan volunteered to organize it. Several months later it showed up on our Pops calendar. On a Saturday night, Pops presented their very own talent show. Just for the fun of it, any member could perform for the rest of the Pops. Susan and her father, Bob, chaired the event. Bob was an accomplished musician. He brought his keyboard and accordion so that he could accompany our members. They emceed and sang duets dressed in their striped vests and straw hats. Wine and finger foods were added to the evening. The audience was Pops members waiting to perform, and they whooped and hollered.

♪ We heard "If I were a Rich Man" from *Fiddler on the Roof*, accompanied by Bob.

♪ We were taught how seniors put hand motions to music using "Dancing Queen."

♪ Our very own college English professor wrote a poem called "A Cat and a Cup of Coffee." It was beat poetry set to music performed by a 1960s-style group with longhaired wigs. Deb kept the beat with her bongo drums.

♪ A couple played a tape and danced the tango.

♪ An all-female group chose a bass from the audience, dragged him to the stage, and sang "It's Raining Men" to him.

♪ A puppet danced on a stick—until it fell off.

♪ There was a stand-up comedian.

♪ There was a couple who sang while playing their guitars.

♪ And the final act was with Dale (our not so shy bass) dressed in drag with long blond pigtails dancing to "I Like My Women a Little on the Trashy Side."

All this because someone mentioned how much hidden talent we had in our chorus.

With Pat as their director Pops kept adding amazing opportunities to sing together. Susan organized a surprise eightieth birthday party for her dad, and Pops surprised him by attending the party and performing a couple of his favorite songs. He was a good groupie. Later the Pops was able to sing their patriotic music during a performance for the Fourth of July Celebration at Independence Hall in Philadelphia. They were invited to travel to the Kent School, in Connecticut, to present a master class for the music department. They arrived just in time to catch the Kent School Boat Club as they returned from an early morning rowing practice. They stopped to watch them put away their racing shells.

But Pat, a full-time musician, was having trouble finding the time to attend the commitments and extra rehearsals of the chorus. In the fall of 2016, Pops hired an assistant director to fill the gap. This was a good thing. In the spring of 2017, Pat missed a couple of rehearsals because he wasn't feeling well. He had the flu. He went to the hospital. He couldn't shake the disease. Nothing made him better. His doctors medevacked him to the University Hospital in Philadelphia. The disease had too strong a grip on his body. Three days later he was gone.

It was difficult. We had spent five years singing with Pat. We all came together to share our tears and our many memories. The chorus clung to each other. We gathered at each other's homes just to be together. He had become part of our family. All of us attended the funeral. But we knew we must go on. The new assistant director was able to step in and keep the chorus together. They had performances through a good and full summer. In the fall, she became their permanent director. It worked well for a while, but in June of 2018, the road got bumpy and she quickly resigned.

It didn't take long for word to get out. I knew right away what had happened. I also knew the Pops had performances, a guest night, and a full Christmas schedule coming up. My heart broke. With a call to Bruce, the COO, I asked, "Is there anything I can do for you?"

"Thanks," he said. And in a couple days I got a call. "Would you direct us until we can find another director?"

It had been four years. I was rusty. But I wanted to do this. They really needed me. In just a few days the Pops was sponsoring a guest night. They had it beautifully planned and were singing three of the songs from our old repertoire. So all I had to do was direct three songs and follow along with anything else they had planned. That was easy. I didn't know they had one more early morning performance on CBS. I was OK with the Christmas music, but not with Jim Donovan interviewing me. I went to Bruce, the COO, and begged off. He said "OK. I'll do it." And he did.

♮

So once again I was directing A Cappella Pops. My responsibility was to prepare the chorus for their upcoming performances and to have them ready to audition potential new directors. Yes, I was rusty. And while the old members smiled as they watched me get back in the groove, the new members tried to figure out just what was going on. We were together for eight months while the Pops looked for their next director. In an email I sent to the chorus, I shared my feelings: "I didn't know I needed you as much as I did. I knew I missed you...but I thought I'd get over it. I'm loving being back at the helm. You need a very good director, and I know you will someday find one. In the meantime...you've got me."

Remember the term *underwear* used to describe basic singing skills? Well, we had a bit of that to do and, of course, my love of the stage told me their performance skills needed a bit of refreshing. The old members, the core group, helped the new Pops members to relax, sing well, and have a good time. I was told that I "reintroduced them to the art of performing." I felt really good about the journey A Cappella Pops and I were on for those eight months. It was good to be directing again. The Christmas concerts were behind us and now they were preparing to audition three of the top candidates for the position of Pops director.

They decided to start each audition with a small performance for the candidate. We had spent extra time during the eight months on the three songs that would be an example of what kind of chorus we were. "A Charlie Brown Christmas" demonstrated our rhythm and diction. "Coventry Carole" was a beautiful ballad that showed our vocal production and emotional style. And the last was "Happy Holidays." I stepped out of the way for this song. The chorus danced and sang and laughed without a director. They actually marched down off their boxes and headed directly to the visiting candidate. This was our style, and we wanted to be sure the candidate knew our personality, one the Pops wanted to keep. For three weeks in a row, they auditioned potential directors, and then they voted. Candidate number three was chosen. February was his starting date. A Cappella Pops was on its way.

♮

At my final rehearsal with my beloved chorus, they said goodbye to me:

> Hope, faith, and love, in that order, you,
> Jan Muck, have blessed A Cappella Pops.
> With invention, inspiration, direction, and
> Wisdom! In each of our 19 years, you have
> Never let us down, understood when it was time
> To step down, and returned to lead us, once again
> Toward a legacy we are proud of!
> "Thank you" seems insufficient for the blessings
> We have received under your watchful eye and
> Guidance. You've taken us around the world
> And into your heart and home and we have
> Followed faithfully, knowing just how fortunate
> We are to have your gift of Pops enhancing our
> Lives.
>
> So it is with grateful hearts we say,
> Merci. Gracias. Danke. Grazie. Tack. Adank!
>
> With love,
>
> A Cappella Pops
> February 2019

I thought it was vacation time for me. And then, on February 3, the phone call came from Valley Forge.

42

Full Circle[3]

February 3: The Call

THE DIRECTOR OF THE Valley Forge Chorus had just resigned. The 2019 Regional Contest was coming up on May 4—just three months away.

The chorus had to make some tough choices:

- Do we want to survive? Yes! We must go forward.
- Do we want to compete? Yes! We want to compete with an interim director.

They also knew that competing on May 4 would be an emotional and exhausting experience for everyone. They were a powerhouse of determination. But it was already February 3. Kat was the Valley Forge Chorus assistant director, and she volunteered to take them to contest. She was a baritone on the front row of the chorus. She knew their songs and how to sing them. She was good. The chorus knew of me—but only as a coach and cheerleader. Ida had retired as an active member, and together we had gone to all Valley Forge's shows and contests. We always found the chorus in the last warm-up room to give them a positive

---

3   A special thanks to all twenty-eight members of the Valley Forge Chorus who shared their love and innermost thoughts while we wrote this: a truly "full circle" chapter.

word of encouragement. We would say, "You've practiced hard. You know your plan. Now just let go and let it fly!"

They needed the right leader. They had two to choose from. They decided to hold auditions. Anne W. was the one chosen to contact me. She called Ida for a little advice. "Would Jan be interested in directing the Valley Forge Chorus in competition on May 4? Do you think she would do it?"

And Ida responded, "Sure. Give her a call. See what she says."

So Anne called me. "What would you think of throwing your résumé into the mix?"

This was a serious phone call. I answered quickly. "Absolutely. Where do I send it?"

   ** You jumped right in and changed your schedule to be available for Valley Forge. We liked that.

A résumé? For the first time in my life, I prepared a résumé, mumbling all the time, "I can't believe I'm doing this." And I had to audition. The last time I auditioned as a director was twenty years ago for the Bryn Mawr Mainliners—and that was unsuccessful. This was all too funny. I called Ida. "Ida, Valley Forge has asked me to be their interim director for the contest. This is a package deal. If they choose me, it's our project. We're in this together, OK?" It was a strong request. And I meant it to be.

We knew how well Valley Forge sang. They had won the contest two years ago singing the two songs they wanted to do for May. They knew what it felt like to do well on stage. They wanted the same this time—a challenge we felt we could meet. "OK!" Ida said. "But I'm out of town until February 26. And I'll need a ride to rehearsals."

"I'll pick you up every week."

   ** We were more comfortable knowing Ida was part of the deal. She was our secret weapon.

Ida and I are a power-packed combination. Ida has a take-no-prisoners attitude when it comes to stage presence and emotional presentation. We had worked together coaching and teaching for many years. We knew what was ahead of us. We knew what we had to do. I wanted her with me, working as a team.

For the audition, Kat would direct the February 5 rehearsal. I would do the same on February 12.

Of the twenty-eight members of Valley Forge, only two had been in the chorus under my direction twenty-seven years before— Leona and Donna. This new Valley Forge was aware that I had a gold medal, but they really didn't know me. I promised myself to just be me—no matter what. We didn't have time for misunderstandings. The week before the audition the video of their ballad from the 2017 contest arrived in my email. The next email was the video of the uptune from the 2018 contest. The message was clear: "These are our two competition songs, and this is how we are currently singing them." They knew we might make some changes, but they were hoping not too many.

I spent the next seven days watching and directing my computer screen. The uptune, "Sweet Georgia Brown," was easy. It was rhythmic and peppy with a great stomp tempo at the right place in the song. The choreography was clever and well synchronized. The ballad, "You'll Never Know," was difficult for me. I remembered hearing Valley Forge win the 2017 contest. I thought at the time that the presentation was outstanding, but as a director, I would have phrased it differently. At the time, I wondered if I could ever understand how they were singing it. They took breaths where I would not have wanted them to breathe. They sang with gusto where I would have sung softly. All this was beautiful but not my style. As I watched the videos, I kept thinking that the beginning and ending of both songs needed a more exciting presentation.

February 12: My Audition

The chorus rehearsal started at 7:00 p.m. For the first half hour, Debbie directed their vocal warm-ups. I was impressed by her talent. Then it was my turn. I directed their two contest songs. I knew I didn't have all their phrasing right. We went over some spots where we had stumbled. They were learning my directing style, and I was trying to remember their phrasing. It was difficult for me—much different from directing the computer screen. Anytime something wasn't smooth, some chorus member would holler, "Watch her hands! Just watch her hands! Everything she wants is in her hands!"

They were trying very hard, and I tried to be my natural self as much as I could while preserving their phrasing. But before they voted I wanted them to know that I intended to change the tempo of the beginning and ending of both songs. This was important to me, as it could be a game changer for the chorus. Other than that I thought everything else would be the same.

" I was scared when I heard you wanted to change the beginning and ending of both songs.

At 9:00 p.m. my audition was over, and I headed back home. The chorus remained at the rehearsal hall to discuss and vote. This chorus was a well-run machine with an obvious mission. They had to decide who would lead them.

" We were told, "If you have a chance to sing under Jan...Do it!"
" We wanted to go a level above where we had been singing. We knew you were an experienced contest director who could lead us there.

♮

The call came the next day. "Welcome to Valley Forge!" The second thing they said to me was "We will send you a list of dates for special rehearsals so you can clear your calendar." Whoa!

February 14: Kat

Kat had been on the front row for my audition. I could sense her feelings. I admired her strength. I felt her support. Her face was always pleasant and attentive. I don't know how she did it.

 ❝ We thought we would have the best of both worlds with Kat on the front row and you as our director.

I called Kat. I wanted her to know how much I respected her and that I was hoping she would remain in the chorus for the contest. It must have been hard for her to sing for me during the audition. She had to be disappointed. I had heard that she was considering leaving the chorus. She lived a couple hours away, and it was a long round-trip drive. She was also the director of another chorus and sang in a quartet. It would be the perfect time to resign. I wanted her to know that my heart ached for her and that I would like it if she would sing with the chorus, but that I'd understand if she couldn't stay. The decision was hers and I respected it. She decided to leave.

February 19: My First Rehearsal

When I walked into the room it felt like it was twenty-seven years ago and I was still Valley Forge's permanent director. I was home. I had just come from eight months directing A Cappella Pops, so I wasn't even rusty. Like riding a bicycle, I guess. You never forget. When I arrived, they asked me if I wanted to do the warm-ups.

I answered honestly. "No. I hate doing warm-ups." Debbie, the very capable member who had warmed up the chorus before my audition, rescued me. She agreed to do them. Not directing the warm-ups was the best decision I could have made for me personally, and it turned out to be one of the smartest for the chorus. I didn't know that Debbie had never directed the warm-ups before. Their previous director had always done them, so this was all new for her. She had a chance to shine. She became a star.

Two other decisions made that night were also well received. The chorus was planning the schedule for the upcoming contest weekend. No, I didn't want a late Friday night rehearsal on May 3: the night before the contest. A good night's sleep is more valuable than one more tired rehearsal at 11:00 p.m. I also asked to end our weekly rehearsals at 10:00 p.m. even though they usually rehearsed until 10:30. I knew I didn't have the stamina to rehearse that late and then drive home, well after 11:00 p.m. Ida and I had both been Sweet Adelines members for many, many years. We knew how grueling that pace could be.

⁀ I was really worried that we would wear you out.

This was a getting-to-know-you rehearsal. I tried to remember names. The chorus was determined to make this work, and that made it fun. They didn't need to tell me this. I could feel it. They giggled when I told them that they were making me realize how committed they were to their competition performance. I knew this was going to take all of what I had to give to them—and it was exciting for me to be in the middle of it.

They surprised me with, "And by the way...We are having a retreat this weekend with Dale Syverson. That's this Friday night, all day Saturday, and Sunday morning. Can you make it?"

I thought, "Well, there goes my weekend. I gotta be there." I rescheduled my time. I also realized that if I hadn't had time, they would have gone ahead without me. Interesting. They were setting the bar very high. And what did they think after our first rehearsal?

" We dove into the deep end with you. We had to do it. We had
no choice. We were ready to go whichever way you went.

February 22–24: The Retreat

Dale's home was in Dallas, Texas. We knew each other through years of competitions and education classes. I had one International gold medal around my neck. She had four. That kinda set the level for the coaching session. I really didn't know if she would agree to the changes I wanted to make to both songs. It was important that she like them. We said hello on Friday night and gave each other a big hug. It was obvious we were excited to be working together. She asked what I wanted, and I told her I wasn't happy with the intro of "Sweet Georgia Brown." It was too long. She listened and agreed. I said a silent amen, then asked, "How do you take away eight measures and still have the music run smoothly?"

Dale had brought along her iPad and an app called forScore. Even with this help we couldn't find which eight measures to delete or how to put the jigsaw puzzle back together. We just couldn't get it right. We were spending too much time on the intro, so we moved on to other things—mostly the tag. This was easier. We just had to learn how to take it home.

The next morning, we were greeted with a few members running into the rehearsal hall shouting, "We got it! We got it!" They had been up till two in the morning, determined to solve the intro problem of their uptune. They showed it to Dale. She put it on her iPad, and we printed it. The chorus tried it, and then cheered when it worked. Nikki had figured it out. And how proud they all were when their two coaches thanked them and added the change into the uptune.

For that Saturday and half of Sunday, we sang through the contest music, fixing the tempos of the beginning and endings of both songs along with anything else Dale and I could hear to enhance the performance. I looked for her approval and guidance, which she freely showered on me. Dale and I were quick to realize that the chorus needed to feel comfortable with me. We needed to transcend the technique and allow the emotion to shine through. That's what makes a good performance. We had to sing together so much that we were one entity—an almost impossible task to achieve in a short time. Normally, when a chorus hires a new director, it takes about three years for the relationship to solidify. We had ten weeks.

Jan and Dale and the Valley Forge women.

I asked for a favor. Could Valley Forge schedule a performance sometime near the middle of April? I felt we both should have a dry run at the contest performance. Sometimes scary things happen when you are competing: you forget the words, you are blinded by the lights, your voice goes away. I didn't know what this chorus would do. And, to be honest, I wanted Valley Forge to have the opportunity to see their director on stage. They needed to trust me. We both needed to know how the other reacted under stress.

> " You jumped in with both feet with Dale, and I thought to myself, "Girl, you'd better get ready for this ride because it's going to go—with or without you. I'm going to ride this roller coaster wherever it goes. I'll see you at the end."

When Dale said goodbye to Valley Forge, we had two solid songs, ready to go. All we had to do was own them. We had made changes to the music of both songs in order to add pizzazz to the presentation. We had to rehearse them to the point of habit. There's no room on stage to think of the technique. And we still had to adjust our stage presence to the new tempos.

February 26: Ida's Return

It was perfect timing. I picked Ida up at home after her three-week visit to Florida, and we headed to rehearsal. The car ride wasn't nearly long enough to tell Ida all the work she had to do. After the warm-up, we reviewed all the musical changes Dale and I had agreed upon. Then we performed our competition songs and turned the rehearsal over to our very own stage presence coach: Ida.

I was having trouble remembering the previous phrasing of the ballad. I felt bad for the chorus. I wanted to sing it my way, but we didn't have time to make unnecessary changes just for me.

** Stop saying I'm sorry when you forget our previous interpretation. Do it your way.

** If you say jump, we say how high! We don't have time to protest!

Changes had to be made in the staging—some because I had changed the tempo, and some because Ida wanted more pizzazz from the chorus: more strength in the fingers, more expression in the faces.

One time the staging had to be changed so much that I worried we didn't have time to relearn all the new moves. I was about to throw it all out, when our choreographer, Donna, rushed to the front of the chorus—on the spot—made the actions fit the new tempo. I smiled to myself and wondered if Donna sensed that I was thinking of tossing out her choreography when she ran to rescue it. And Donna was right. It was easier if we made her choreo work with the new rhythms. There was less change for the chorus to remember.

March 17: Rehearsal Notes

Valley Forge planned a special rehearsal in front of mirrors to work on their visual presentation. They didn't need me, but I could attend if I wanted to. No, I decided. This was their time. The chorus leadership (music and board) had a before-rehearsal meeting with me to address some concerns with how we were singing. They brought up things like, "Tune the chord on *Well.* Elongate the vowel on *tips.* How long is the breath on *Georgia Brown?*" I kept the list with me, and as the chorus became used to my directing, they were able to revert to their customary good-singing talents. Most items they corrected by themselves as their minds were on their music and not on what I was (or was not) doing.

Did they think I was not moving fast enough? Probably. On April 1, they began advertising for a new director to be hired after the contest. (I was their interim director.) They were wasting no time.

April 13: Practice Performance

Transcendence: The power that choral singing has
that other music can only dream of. —Garrison Keillor

The performance Valley Forge scheduled for April was for the Philadelphia Spring Benefit Concert. I was thrilled that our first performance together was not on the contest stage. It was time for Valley Forge to transcend, to move from technique to singing the emotion. This was the performance to put it all together, to see where we were on our journey to the contest stage—both the chorus and me. We both had to know that we were ready to connect to each other and the audience at the same time.

The event was sponsored by the A Cappella Project and held at the William Way Center in downtown Philadelphia. It was the perfect audience for us. When it was our turn, the chorus sang "Paper Moon," then I directed the two contest songs, and then they finished with "Little Mermaid."

They didn't need my direction for their songs. I stood to the side and watched them sing to the audience. They entertained and also maintained their excellent singing techniques. The audience was excited. So was I. Our first performance together was stressful but fun—like a contest should be. We needed to trust each other under stress. Mission accomplished. The pixie dust was working.

   " It was like getting on a ride at an amusement park...
    Whoosh—we're off! We had to pay attention to hang on.

April 27: Friends and Family

On this Sunday afternoon, we invited all our friends and family to our traditional pre-competition Friends and Family show at our rehearsal hall. Valley Forge and their competing quartets were singing their contest music. We all wanted the experience of singing for an audience before we took to the contest stage. In full costumes, we marched onto our risers, and one of the guests announced, "Please close the doors. We are ready for the next contestant. (pause) Contestant Number 18, under the direction of Jan Muck, The Valley Forge Chorus." (Applause)

We sang. I ended up making small changes as I lost myself in the beauty of their singing. They *had* to watch me for those unexpected changes. I couldn't help it. But they always sang right along with the way I directed them. After the performance there were hugs for everyone and then drinks and desserts on a huge table at the end of the room. Our friends and family had seen what we were going to put on the competition stage. And we loved the praise that was showered on us. Now we had to do the same on May 4th.

- ** We had to be on our toes. We had to be ready whichever way it went on stage.
- ** You were the right person at the right time.

May 4: Contest

We were well prepared for this contest. Everyone knew what to do, where to go, and what time to be there. The Valley Forge Chorus took care of me because I didn't know their competition schedule. Someone was always making sure I knew where I had to be. That was necessary but also very nice. I guess they didn't want to lose me. This chorus was an experienced competitor. They were so calm, so ready, and so comfortable. Our final rehearsal was strong. We went over some spots that I felt might need a little refreshing and then sang our two songs. No pressure, no panic. We were prepared.

" If anything strange happened on stage you would handle it! We trusted you.

Finally, it was time to compete. We were announced. We entered the stage.

" It felt amazing on stage.
" It felt like we were a family.
" I hope she doesn't forget and back up and fall off the stage!

With Claire and Stephanie.

We sang. The applause was strong and genuine, and then we left the stage to go to our seats in the auditorium. We had done our best.

We were contestant eighteen out of nineteen competing choruses. We didn't have to wait long for the announcements of the winners. While the judges' scores were being tabulated, the chorus directors were all brought to the stage to receive recognition and applause. One of my proudest memories that night was standing on the stage in a line of twenty chorus directors while the audience clapped their appreciation. On my right was Claire and on my left was Stephanie—both former long-time members of Valley Forge, now successfully directing their own choruses.

The first announcement was the top five small choruses. *Small* means thirty or fewer members. That was us. We placed first. We got our blue ribbon with the gold medal. This gave us a spot on the Saturday Night Show of Champions. The judges announced our score: 637 out of 800 available points. Pretty high. Then they announced the top five medium-size choruses (between thirty and sixty members). Starting with fifth place, we noticed that our score was higher than any of the five medium-size choruses. Oh, my!

　•• The Region was not expecting us to do well since we had just lost a director. We had to prove them wrong.

Now the five top-scoring choruses of the entire contest were announced. We didn't hear our name for the first three announcements. Soon there were only two choruses left—Greater Harrisburg and Valley Forge. We knew we were second, and we whooped and hollered and cried when we finally heard our name called out.

With a huge point score (685), Greater Harrisburg, directed by our very own Claire Domenick, was declared the winner. So proud. We scored so high that we were in the running to be invited as a wild card for either the international small-chorus contest the

A happening.

following year in Louisville (five of the world's top small-chorus winners would be invited) or the big International contest (ten of the highest second-place winners of the world would be added to the contest). We would know in a month or two.

We received both invitations. Valley Forge had to choose which contest to enter. They couldn't compete in both. This was 2019. The competitions would be held in 2020: the year that never was.

But we didn't know a pandemic was coming then. After the Saturday night show following the contest, we all milled around the auditorium getting our winners' hugs. I heard from many old friends who said how great it was to see me back on stage. There were a lot of warm fuzzies. I think it brought back many memories of good times gone by when we were all with struggling new choruses and I was coaching, teaching, and competing all the time. My favorite comments were from those I had coached years ago:

- From a director who is now a top five Regional winner: The best thing you said to me was, "You have A+ music in your head, but your chorus is not singing what you are directing."
- From a quartet champion: "Your coaching session was the best we ever had." They were the first quartet that I ever

Jan and Ida's jello shots.

coached and were pretty new at the time. They never asked me for another session. For years, I thought I had failed them. Who knew?

•• And from another came "Thanks for encouraging me. You made me believe in myself."

Here's how Valley Forge felt about our two-and-a-half-month journey:

•• Valley Forge at this time was like a golden chariot. We were going like the wind and suddenly our chariot was stopped. One wheel got stuck in the mud. Then along comes this small white-haired lady as our director, and we didn't realize she was a combination of Jean Valjean and Ben Hur. But she led us to our exciting finish.

After the weekend, before we went home, Jello shots were served in the hospitality room.

43

Sing the Tag

IN THE EARLY 1960s the schools were integrating, and the Vietnam War had started. Some musicians used music as a vehicle of protest. Drugs were becoming readily available to our children. Some of us mothers were leaving the home to add an extra income to the family, breaking away from the plan our parents followed. Singing in a chorus gave us—men and women both—a haven from the turmoil our world was delivering to us. We left all that, as well as our everyday concerns, outside of the chorus room door. We wanted to enjoy creating beautiful music and to sing all kinds of fun songs. We wanted our time together to be an oasis—three or four hours a week when we could forget ourselves and just enjoy life. This is why there was always a group that met after rehearsal for drinks and food and to laugh and talk.

Many nights I would drive to rehearsals with tears in my eyes, only to know that when I arrived, I would take a deep breath and put on a happy face for the evening. I'm sure there were many others who did the same thing. This kept the outside world away from us. Sometimes, when the world intruded despite our best efforts, I was fortunate enough to find the right song for our chorus. We had patriotic songs for our Veterans Day celebrations. We sang at the courthouse for the swearing-in ceremony for our new citizens. We sang for the injured military at the Valley Forge Veterans Hospital in Phoenixville, Pennsylvania. We put our arms around each other and sang words of comfort in times of emotional stress.

It is important to me to fill my life with all things that are positive. I tried to do the same for those who came to me each week to learn to sing good, happy music with other singers that like to feel happy, too. And these singers, like me, are performers. They share this music and try very hard to touch the soul of the audience.

I have tried to do the same in my book. I hope you laughed. I hope you cried. I hope I touched your soul in some small way.

Acknowledgments

I'D LIKE TO THANK my husband, Darrel, and our entire family for putting up with me while I wrote this book.

I'd like to give a posthumous thank you to Vivian Grey, who tried to show me the art of writing. Without her guidance there would be no book. Thanks go to Linda Baten Johnson for giving me an inside look at what it takes to be a writer. Thanks for writing "What Made Valley Forge Great" and allowing me to include it in this book.

Thanks also go to Don Gooding for supporting the Pops when we were so new and finding our way.

And to Anne Winner, the force behind the chapter "Full Circle." You sent me the Zoom recording, so I didn't have to take notes as we remembered how crazy it was! Thanks!

And thanks to all my friends and colleagues whom I kept asking to reminisce for me. I couldn't have done it without you. You gave me your stories to fill the book with memories.

Thanks to Karen Breidert who was the first and only person to review the entire book before it went to press. (She liked it!)

Thanks to Kathleen (Muff) Allen for her insight into marketing and her many suggestions for a title.

Finally, I'd like to give a special thank you to Val Serdy for her editorial insights; to Dick Margulis, who copyedited the manuscript and designed the book; to Lori Holtzinger, for her superb index; and to Maria Z. Touring, my talented and brilliant daughter-in-law, who created the delightful characters on the cover.

Index

Photos are indicated in *italics*.